COUNTRY on CD

Doug Hall is a Canadian author and broadcaster with extensive credits in a career that is closing on four decades. Prior to entering broadcasting he was, for 7½ years, Senior Press Officer for IBM Canada and a contributor to business and financial sections of many newspapers, trade journals and magazines in both Canada and the United States.

His writing credits include 12 books and he has written numerous scripts for television and radio 'specials'. He has also written and compiled country music documentaries and videos, including *The Real Patsy Cline* and *Thanks Troubadour Thanks – The Ernest Tubb Story*.

For over 30 years he has been a successful radio and television talk show host. He currently hosts the nationally syndicated literary television show *Bestsellers*, which is seen weekly on over 20 stations in Canada and on satellite.

COUNTRY on CD

THE ESSENTIAL GUIDE

DOUG HALL

KYLE CATHIE LIMITED

First published in Great Britain in 1993 by
Kyle Cathie Limited
7/8 Hatherley Street London SW1P 2QT

ISBN 1 85626 113 1

A Cataloguing in Publication record for this title is
available from the British Library

Typeset by DP Photosetting
Printed by Cox & Wyman Ltd

For Gregory
My Son

PREFACE

There is not a published author alive who, at one time or another, is not asked 'Where did you get the idea for your book?'

Truth be told, I had never considered doing a book on country music until one day in October 1992. I received a call from my friend, Bill Hushion, Senior Vice-President of McClelland and Stewart, one of Canada's premier publishing firms, and the man who has the dubious distinction of publishing four of my earlier books. Bill told me that he had just returned from the Frankfurt Book Fair where he had met Kyle Cathie, President of Kyle Cathie Ltd in England. She had told him that she was considering adding to her impressive list of books on CDs and had chosen *Country on CD* as the next one. She was looking for a North American writer and Bill recommended me. The rest, as they say, is history.

Frankly, I jumped at the opportunity as I have been a fan of country music ever since I was a teenager fresh off a farm in Ontario's Ottawa Valley. When I got my first hi-fi (circa 1951) it was state-of-the-art. Twelve vinyl 78s could be stacked at one time, a good half hour (or more) of listening time.

The very first 78 rpm record I ever purchased was Eddy Arnold's 'I'll Hold You In My Heart'; it was followed by 'Bouquet of Roses'. Both cost 75 cents and took three-quarters of my $1 a week allowance. When 'Cattle Call' was added I was in country heaven. Those wonderful 78s were played and replayed until the grooves became furrows and the limited-life vinyls had to be replaced (hopefully they were still in stock). As the years went by many other country music 78s, and albums, were added to my collection only to be joyously replaced with matching CDs when I was fortunate enough to find them.

When playing CDs there is no worry about accidentally

dropping the needle arm and scratching the surface. The tonal quality is excellent. Sometimes I play the old vinyl and then the CD just to hear how far technology has progressed. The difference is astounding.

My country CD library was built one-by-one. At every opportunity I would visit record stores and dig through their CD bins hoping to find a long-lost country treasure. When I stumbled across a CD that matched one of my old albums I was overjoyed.

Many times I was disappointed in what I had purchased because once the shrink-wrap was removed the CD was mine, it could not be returned to the store for credit or exchange. I had no guide in choosing a new CD or adding a new artist to my collection. I had no *Country on CD* to turn to.

It is sincerely hoped that the reader of this book will find the contents a reliable guide to what is being offered on CD and a significant aid in making intelligent decisions on what and what not to buy. The biographies of the artists are just as important as the CD reviews. To know a bit more about the artist than just the sketchy line notes can aid one in making a sound decision.

The subtitle of the book is 'The Essential Guide'. It is most apt. The selection of artists was carefully compiled from the vast list of those who have contributed to the country music mosaic of the past, present and future. Great care had to be taken in choosing which CDs would be reviewed. It would have been so easy just to take the last album and assume it is the artist's best work. In many instances it is. When it isn't an earlier album was chosen. Sometimes, in reviewing an artist's body of work, an early album is combined with the latest one. Some artists, who have survived and are still performing, no longer have a label and have not had a 'hit' song for decades. Some have only had one hit album, but one that was a blockbuster still popular today. More than a few of country music's stars have never had a number one hit, let alone a top ten, but they are loved and respected by their passionately loyal fans. They have a place in the spotlight, even if it isn't dead centre.

It is a fundamental truth that there is no such thing as total objectivity in journalism. Neither is there total objectivity with one's musical selection. Setting aside personal favourites, the majority of which are included in this book, there are the new, exciting artists who are electrifying the country fans. It's the young dynamic artists like Garth Brooks, Clint Black, Patty Loveless and Billy Ray Cyrus who have infused new life into country music and propelled it to the forefront of musical genres. Though some purists turn up their collective noses at the new country sound they should give it a listen. It's exciting music and if it wasn't being played extensively on radio and the albums bought in huge numbers, country music would be as dead as disco.

One remembers the hullabaloo Ernest Tubb created at the Grand Ole Opry when he wanted to have electric guitars backing him up. There were cries of heresy and sacrilege from the establishment. To them Tubb was a young upstart. But he was right and in the hallowed halls of the Ryman Auditorium he changed the sound of country music. Today electric instruments are not even given a passing glance at the Opry. They are the norm not the exception.

Country music has come a long way from just fiddles, guitars, harmonicas, banjos and washtubs with the odd bass or piano. It is the stars of today who will be viewed as the innovators in years to come. Country music survives because of change and innovation.

This book would never have been completed had it not been for a number of people, and organizations, who encouraged, helped and went out of their way in a most remarkable manner.

At the top of the list is my long-suffering family. Joyce my wife, Greg and Mark my sons, Diane my daughter, Barbara and Michelle my daughters-in-law and Gordon my son-in-law. I'm one lucky man to have such a family.

Profound thanks to Charlie Dick, Patsy Cline's husband, a valued friend who proved to be a fount of knowledge. He never hesitated to assist whenever called upon with dates, names, places and footnotes from the past, the present and the future.

Also many thanks to Lloyd Pearson, Nona Lee Hayes and Will Jones who make Nashville's wonderful Ernest Tubb Record Shop a joy to visit.

Special thanks to Ronnie Pugh and Alan Stoker of the Country Music Foundation.

I would be remiss if I didn't give a tip of the hat to Steve Brink at Prism Leisure in the UK; Bill Bannon of Columbia Records, Canada; Dave Watt of MCA Records, Canada; Yumi Kimura of Warner Brothers, Nashville; Ramona E. Simmons and Dotty

Hann of Arista Records, Nashville; Greg McCarn and Jason Heme of RCA Records, Nashville; Rand Hoffman and Kim Fowler of Polygram Records (Country Division), Nashville, and Don Robinson of HMV.

Finally my deep gratitude to the wonderful Kyle Cathie who took a chance on a writer from the colonies.

Editors come in all shapes and sizes and with varying temperaments. When you begin working with one 'from over 'ome', via fax, you are in a total vacuum and don't really know what to expect. What I received from editor Beverley Cousins was one of the most enriching and rewarding collaborations to date when it came to the editing process. Thanks to Beverley's wicked eye for detail, error, reader misunderstanding or total bafflement, she made me go back, rethink, clarify, confirm and correct. If this book reaches, or exceeds, the expectations of everyone who put their faith in it, much credit goes to Beverley whom I've only met electronically but now call friend.

They prodded, they stroked, they suggested and they inspired more than they will ever know. Thank you one and all.

It's been a grand journey. Each stop along the way added yet another thread to my tapestry of *Country on CD*.

Doug Hall
Pickering, Ontario, Canada
September 1993

INTRODUCTION

IT ALL BEGAN WHEN
'THE OLD HEN CRACKLED'

This book is dedicated to the serious lover of country music, who knows the joy of adding a new CD to a cherished collection or of discovering a new artist. It is also dedicated to those who have discovered America's 'true sound' through television or radio and heard enough to whet the appetite. Someone once observed, 'Country music is like salted peanuts. You can't stop at one'.

In 1923, when Fiddlin' John Carson recorded 'The Old Hen Crackled', recording pioneer Ralph Peder, of Okeh Records, thought it was 'pluperfect awful' but the record sold and fans began collecting.

Some visionaries in the music industry foresaw the demise of New York's Tin Pan Alley. In order to survive the musicians turned their sights westward towards Nashville. There was, they felt, a new, lucrative market for the music of the simple, hard-working, below-the-poverty-line hillbillies, farmers and miners who lived in the log cabins and farm houses of Arkansas' Ozarks, the Appalachians of North Carolina, Tennessee's Great Smokies and the coal fields of Kentucky.

By 1925 Americans were singing along with Henry Whitter, as he wailed the mournful 'Lonesome Road Blues', and with Vernon Dalhart, who became a legend, with 'The Prisoner's Song'.

Back in the early 1920s, when National Life, a large US insurance company, was persuaded to invest in a radio station, the company's slogan was 'We Shield Millions'. That slogan became the inspiration for the call letters WSM, probably the most famous set of call letters in North America. WSM has been the only radio home for the 'Grand Ole Opry' since it began as 'The WSM Barn Dance' shortly after the company went on air in 1925.

There is some dispute as to who exactly inaugurated the 'barn dance' programme on Saturday evening, November 28, 1925.

Announcer George Dewey Hay, who called himself 'The Solemn Old Judge', unabashedly took credit for it until the day he died in May 1968. Others argue just as passionately that the credit should go to Dr Humphrey Bate, a country physician from Sumner County, Tennessee. Dr Bate led a hillbilly band called Possum Hunters which played regularly on the programme. He died in 1936. Mrs Alcoyne Bate Beasley, the good doctor's daughter, staunchly defends the contention that it was indeed her father who should be given credit for appearing on the first broadcast and originating what became the Grand Ole Opry. Mrs Beasley claims that the date of the first show was actually around the end of October, about three weeks after the station went on the air. If that were the case Dr Bate preceded George Hay by at least four weeks and would deserve recognition. The Grand Ole Opry officially accepts the Hay version.

How the Grand Ole Opry got its name is equally fascinating. Some call it fact others call it fiction, but the story is still told with great relish. The lead-in programme to 'The WMS Barn Dance' was the 'Music Appreciation Hour' under the direction of Dr Walter Damrosch, an eminent composer and conductor. One night, following Dr Damrosch's closing remarks and sign-off, George Hay, in his introduction to the 'Barn Dance', is supposed to have said, 'For the past hour we have been listening to music largely from grand opera. From now on we will present the "Grand Ole Opry".'

A delicious story, and who cares if it is fact or fiction? The name stuck and has become internationally synonymous with country music.

By the early 1930s country music was gaining a solid foothold as it grabbed the ears and imaginations of entertainment-starved North Americans. It became a Saturday night ritual for families to gather around their battery-operated radios to listen to the static-crackling voices of their musical idols on Nashville's WSM.

Even though country music's appeal was centred in rural America its infectious toe-tapping beat, hand-clapping gospel and love-starved lyrics were spreading out around the United States and seeping over into Canada.

Radio was all important during the Depression years of 'the dirty thirties'. Nickels and dimes were in scarce supply and records became luxury items. Sales were down but in spite of this tracks were still being cut on primitive equipment.

Country music fans could never repay the debt owed to the Grand Ole Opry. A constant stream of tour buses, from the United States, Canada and Mexico, bring wide-eyed fans to the front entrance of the Ryman Auditorium which had its beginning as the Union Gospel Tabernacle. There is almost an evangelical reverence as fans walk back stage to look into the empty dressing rooms and imagine their country music heroes getting ready to go on stage. A magical moment occurs when they stand centre stage. Many close their eyes and, in their imagination, hear the echoes and applause as long-past greats like Hank Williams, Jim Reeves, Marty Robbins and Patsy Cline once again bring a packed auditorium to its feet in a hand-clapping, whistling, foot-stomping ovation.

Up until 1950 Nashville was just called 'the home of country music'. Very few will single out announcer David Cobb for his on-air abilities but he'll go down in history as the one who renamed Nashville 'Music City USA'.

The final stop in Nashville is at one of the many record stores, such as the Ernest Tubb Record Shop, to search through the racks and bins of CDs for a new release or a long-sought special disc that will enhance a cherished country collection.

The 'Singing Cowboy', as personified by Roy Rogers and Gene Autry, also added greatly to the spread of western music through 'B' films, personal appearances, television and records. Western music also owes its popularity, and longevity, to superb groups such as Bob Nolan and The Sons of the Pioneers, and to Spade Cooley who fronted one of the most popular western swing bands of all times. And without the amazing Bill Monroe there would be no bluegrass. This musical giant evolved it, defined it, refined it, still plays it and is the acknowledged architect of this unique brand of American music.

Though Cajun is a corruption of Acadian, and todays Cajuns are descendants of French Canadians who had been disposed of the land they called Acadia (the name given to the provinces of New Brunswick and Nova Scotia in Eastern Canada), the music has it roots in the bayous of Louisiana. Many fine exponents of the Cajun sound began life on a houseboat, like Doug Kershaw who was born near Tiel Ridge, Louisiana.

Recorded music is in its fourth generation, with the fifth on the horizon. It all started with the Edison cylinder. Next came the

78 rpm record. This was followed by the superior 33 rpm record and the compact disc with its unparallelled sound. There is the Digital Compact Cassette (DDC) and the MiniDisc (MD) trying to be the new CD offspring.

Electronic laboratories around the globe are in a headlong race to be the first to perfect the 'flash memory chip' which some predict will be the ultimate storage device. However, until progress shunts the CD into the background, in the same way the CD relegated the 78 and 33 rpm vinyl record into the shadows of time, music lovers can sit back and enjoy the CD's ultimate sound.

The quality of re-mastered recordings reissued on compact disc is remarkable. The superstars of yesterday such as Patsy Cline, Jim Reeves, Ernest Tubb or Marty Robbins originally recorded their songs in studios with recording equipment that is antiquated by today's standards. But, thanks to state-of-the-art technology and superb re-mastering skills, their music is now the equal in sound and quality to the 'hot country' music that superstars like Garth Brooks, Ricky Van Shelton, Diamond Rio or Patty Loveless produce today.

The Compact Disc Digital Audio System offers the finest sound reproduction on what the industry calls small, convenient, sound-carrier units. The CD's superior performance is the direct result of laser-optical scanning with digital playback. It is totally independent of the technology used in making the original records which, in many cases, took place decades earlier. This recording technology is usually identified by a three-letter code on the back cover of the CD holder.

DDD = digital tape recorder used during session recording, mixing, and/or editing and mastering (transcription)

ADD = analogue tape recorder used during session recording, digital tape recorder used during subsequent mixing and/or editing and during mastering (transcription)

AAD = analogue tape recorder used during session recording and subsequent mixing and/or editing, digital tape recorder during mastering (transcription)

In this book, when you see 'circa' beside an artist's birth date it is because, for some reason, the artist is reluctant to make public their age. While it is always interesting to know one must respect their wishes. When it is possible to estimate the year of birth from information gleaned, then 'circa' is used.

Country songs are America's favourite music, and sales for country are growing faster than in any other genre of music, including rock. Country music format radio stations number close to 3000 in the United States and Canada. They're surfacing like mushrooms after rain as more and more rock stations are changing their musical format to country. The country crest which radio programmers link to the wealth of new country artists dominating the playlists took country radio from 9.5 per cent to 10.5 per cent in the last quarter of 1990. According to *Billboard* magazine the country format has never before moved more than two-tenths of a point in all demographic groups and times of day. (A point is a share of hours tuned in a specific market during a given time of day. *Billboard*'s measurement reflects the overall boom in country music radio across North America. The same demographics undoubtedly hold true in countries such as the United Kingdom, Ireland, Australia and New Zealand where country music has exploded.)

J. D. Cannon, music director of Indianapolis' WFMS, which jumped in audience from third to first in its market says 'country's edge is sharper because the music has become song-driven rather than artist-driven. It used to be a basic core of ten to 15 artists that radio kept playing over and over. Now new faces dominate *Billboard*'s top ten.'

There is also an explosion of line dancing nightspots across the continent thanks to Billy Ray Cyrus and his 'Achy Breaky Heart' hit single. The impact of country music was confirmed in May 1993 at the Academy of Country Music Awards show. The nationally televised ceremony, which was watched by millions of viewers across the United States and Canada, was expanded to three hours with 16 performances and drew astounding viewer numbers.

As long as there is a 'hurting' song to be sung or a guitar string to be plucked there will be loyal, dedicated fans of country music.

As long as there are fans, new and exciting CDs will be issued and eagerly purchased. They will be played and replayed and, unlike vinyl, the CD will never lose that unblemished quality of sound which allows the listener to imagine that they are in the recording studio with the artist. This book salutes the country music industry and the dedicated CD collector who revels in the music of the past, the present and the future.

COUNTRY on CD

Alabama

(formed 1979, original members – Randy Yeuell Owen, born
December 13 1949, Teddy Wayne Gentry, born January 22 1952,
Jeffrey Alan Cook, born August 27 1949, Mark Joel Herndon,
born May 11 1955)

It took less than 15 years for three Alabama cousins – Randy
Owen, Teddy Gentry and Jeffrey Cook – to become the bestselling group in country music history.

All three were born in Fort Payne, Alabama, about 60 miles east
of Huntsville and ten miles west of the Georgia border. Even as
children, and before they had begun to sing and play together,
their musical talents shone through. By the early 1970s, when
they were light years ahead of any local musicians or singers of
their age, they formed a group called Wild Country, determined to
break into showbusiness. They knew they were on the first rung
when Canyonland Park hired them to play backup for visiting
stars.

It wasn't until they moved to Myrtle Breach, South Carolina, in
1973 and began recording their own records, however, that they
began to receive serious notice from country music fans, who
found their sound new and refreshing.

Mark Herndon joined the group as drummer in 1979 and
Alabama was created. The following year RCA Records signed the
group to a recording contract. With minor exceptions, each of
their 37 singles has been in the top-ten, beginning with their
debut album, *Tennessee River*, which was released to much praise on
May 16 1980.

The impressive 12-year body of work includes 'Why Lady Why',
'Old Flame', 'Mountain Music', 'Fire in the Night', 'She and I',

'Song of the South', 'Juke Box', and 'I'm in a Hurry' which was released on November 20 1992, twelve years after *Tennessee River*.

An astonishing 15 albums were released between May 1980 (*My Home's in Alabama*) and August 1992 (*American Pride*). Nine racked up sales running from single to quadruple platinum and five were certified gold. All are still selling. Total international sales, for all releases, top an unbelievable 4.5 million. That does not include the 90,000 plus sales for Alabama's *Greatest Hits* video package. Alabama join Kenny Rogers as the most successful pop stars in the history of music.

As was to be expected awards came hand in hand with Alabama's superstar popularity and gargantuan record sales. *Cashbox* started the award list off in 1980 by naming them New Vocal Group of the Year for both albums and singles. Between 1980 and 1993 they have been singled out for nearly 150 awards by the most influential and prestigious industry magazines, music associations and entertainment organizations in the United States. A bulging trophy cabinet houses 15 awards from the Academy of Country Music, nine from the Country Music Association, 26 from *Billboard* magazine and 25 from *Cashbox* magazine, plus numerous others including the 1987 Bob Hope Humanitarian Award for public service work and contributions involving children.

When asked to single out their 'special' award memories all four reply as one: 'Winning both the Academy of Country Music, and the Country Music Association, Entertainer of the Year Award for 1982, 1983 and 1984.' It was an unprecedented achievement in country music.

The musical strengths of each member and the effortless meshing of talents in the studio, and on stage, is outstanding. Owen plays rhythm guitar, Cook is on lead guitar and fiddle and Gentry on bass. Herndon, the licensed pilot, flies both on the drums and in the air.

A major ingredient of Alabama's phenomenal success is a spirited stage presence and a masterful blending of country-pop and soft-rock music. In a capricious business where moments in the spotlight can be fleeting, there is no debate on the importance of their fans: 'I want the fans to enjoy themselves and feel they've gotten their money's worth from our concerts and records,' says

Owen. 'I want them to understand that they are the most important people in our lives.'

★*Greatest Hits* (RCA PCD1-7170)

Unlike some CDs of 'Greatest Hits', this one is right up front. Two of the ten songs are new, identified on the sleeve with an asterisk.

'She and I' is the lead-off song. It is one of the new tracks, recorded on December 30 1985. Herndon grabs immediate attention with a few solid drum licks on the downbeat and there is a nice touch at the end of the song: the familiar fadeout to dead air is standard, but, just when one thinks 'that's it', the beat picks up and the boys come back for the real closing with one more 'she and I'.

'The Fans' is the other 'new' song. It was co-written by Teddy Gentry, Randy Owen and Greg Fowler and is a gentle thank you to the group's fans. It leaves no question about how important they are: 'What keeps the fires burning/Is always you the fans.'

No compilation of Alabama's greatest hits would be complete without the famous songs: the spirited 'Mountain Music' has a Walter Brennan-like spoken intro. It comes in on the tail-end of a wailing harmonica. Images of a mist-shrouded mountain immediately come to mind. Gentry's fiddle work sparkles.

The lineup on this flawless CD includes 'Tennessee River', 'My Home's In Alabama' and 'Love In The First Degree'.

Arnold, Eddy

(born near Henderson, Tennessee, May 15 1918)

The mark of a true music 'legend' is having such a unique, recognizable voice that identification is immediate and no introduction required. This is certainly true of Eddy Arnold. He rose from his father's sharecropping farm to the very pinnacle of popularity in both country and pop music and set the bench mark as a cross-over artist.

Arnold's love for music derived from his parents – his father was an old-time fiddler and his mother an above average guitar player. It was during his days at Pinson High School that he began playing the guitar (which his mother taught him) and singing in public. His secondary education was cut short by a family crisis and he had to put his fledgling career, and formal education, temporarily on the back burner. Once more he got behind a plough on the family farm, consequently engendering the nickname the 'Tennessee Ploughboy'.

Even as a youth, with no formal vocal training, he was head and shoulders above his contemporaries. Whenever he could steal time away from his farm chores he would sing and hone his onstage techniques.

His big break came in 1936 when he sang on radio for the first time in Jackson, Tennessee. Those who still remember the young Eddy Arnold were not surprised at his meteoric rise to star status. During the late 1930s he was a performer on WMPS, in Memphis, and would take any booking that was offered including local night clubs, in and around St Louis. He returned to Jackson, Tennessee, in 1942 and for six years was a favourite performer on WTJS.

Those six years were a schoolroom for Arnold. Each time he sang he found new ways to refine his singing and entertaining skills, and like most successful entertainers he became his own severest critic.

In 1944 RCA Records offered him a contract and he hired a manager – Colonel Tom Parker, who later moved on to manage Elvis Presley.

By 1946 his career had moved into high gear and for the next four years he scored with such classics as 'I'll Hold You In My Heart', 'Heart Full Of Love', 'Bouquet Of Roses', 'Any Time' and 'I'm Throwing Rice'. There were also some novelty tunes – 'Lovebug Itch' was one that caught on.

In 1949 Arnold had 23 singles in *Billboard*'s 'Hot 100' list of national pop hits. He had become a household name.

The 1950s was a landmark decade for Arnold as a performer, recording artist and innovator. He continued his bestselling pace with 'Kentucky Waltz', 'May The Good Lord Bless And Keep You', 'I Really Don't Want To Know', 'That Do Make It Nice' and 'Cattle Call', which became his signature song. The juke boxes gobbled up the nickels and dimes as Arnold hits played endlessly. The music stores had a problem keeping his records in stock. Arnold 78s became the foundation for many valuable country record libraries.

During the 1950s Arnold was active on the touring circuit. He appeared in all 48 states and Canada and his numerous foreign tours were extremely successful. His popularity and drawing power in Europe, especially, was proof positive of the spread of country music around the world. Personal appearances, radio shows and record sales enhanced his popularity. Television was a significant medium for increasing Eddy's identity quotient. He was a regular television guest and shared the camera with such TV stars as Perry Como, Arthur Godfrey, Milton Berle and Dinah Shore. A booking highlight was when he was asked to be guest-host of *The Tonight Show* in the absence of Johnny Carson. He was also the first country star to host a regular network television show, *Eddy Arnold Time*, which drew impressive ratings in national syndication.

Unlike many of his contemporaries, in both country and pop, who saw their popularity diminish with the rise of rock and roll, Arnold kept churning out the hits during the 1960s. The fanatic adulation of fans for Presley and the Beatles impacted record sales and ended many country and pop careers. But for some, like Arnold, the magic was still there and his fans kept buying. 'What's He Doing In My World' and 'Make The World Go Away' were top-ranked hits in 1965.

The same held true for other 1960s releases: 'The Last Word In Lonesome Is Me', 'Tips Of My Fingers', 'Somebody Like Me', 'Lonely Again', 'Here Comes My Baby', 'It's Over' and 'Here Comes Heaven'. In a tough marketplace Arnold's knack for choosing the right material was awesome.

Honours were his and rightly so. He was voted number one male vocalist in country music on a number of occasions, and during the 1960s he was never out of the popularity top ten.

As satisfying and exciting as the honours were, nothing could top being elected to the Country Music Hall of Fame in 1966. It confirmed Arnold as an authentic country legend and justified his move to a more sophisticated persona. In the early days, when he played the 'Tennessee Ploughboy' to the hilt, his act, which at times included baggy overalls and blackened teeth, could only have been termed 'country bumpkin'. Arnold changed all that with a tuxedo and smooth night club stance which complemented his rich upper-register voice. He also appeared at unconventional venues for country music, such as New York's Carnegie Hall and Waldorf-Astoria and Los Angeles' Coconut Grove. They were certainly 'a long way from Chester County', which was also the title of his autobiography.

Some country purists harshly criticized Arnold for what they saw as an abandonment of his roots and his fans. Arnold made no apology, 'My songs mean different things to different kinds of people,' he was quoted as saying.

RCA certainly appreciated Arnold's country and cross-over selling power. On February 23 1970 they recognized his 60 million record sale milestone (the figure is now pushing 100 million) by presenting him with a special award.

Now into his 70s Arnold still records and tours. While age and affluence might have slowed him down his fans still come out and clamour for 'Cattle Call' plus a full serving from his vast repertoire of signature tunes and hits. Most of his bestselling albums have been digitally remastered on CD and the lush orchestrations, which are an Arnold trademark, are a joy to the ear.

In person Eddy Arnold is just like he is on stage. He laughs easily and his modesty and warm personality make him a pleasure to meet.

His living epitaph can be read on a bronze plaque in the Country Music Hall of Fame: 'He has been a powerful influence in setting musical tastes.'

★*The Best Of Eddy Arnold* (RCA 3675-2-R) Digitally Remastered

There are 12 cuts on this CD that, I feel, is somewhat erroneously titled. Any fan would agree that it is impossible to include 'the best' of this legend's work on just one CD.

Arnold is never better than when he is singing country love songs. Some of his best are here to enjoy.

Cut number one is 'Bouquet Of Roses', a chart-topping hit for Arnold in 1948.

Cut number 12 is the classic 'Cattle Call'. This one has become his theme song. It is a masterful exhibition of Arnold's melodic range. The only other singers to match him in the yodelling department would be Slim Whitman, Elton Britt or Roy Rogers.

Arnold recorded 'I'll Hold You In My Heart' in 1948 and by the end of the Korean War it was probably given to more sweethearts by more servicemen than any other 78 of that period.

Arnold fans will never tire of the other numbers. 'Make The

World Go Away', 'Anytime', 'I Want To Go With You', 'The Last Word In Lonesome Is Me', 'What's He Doing In My World', 'I Really Don't Want To Know', 'You Don't Know Me', and two spirited novelty tunes 'That's How Much I Love You' and 'Just A Little Lovin''.

Bellamy Brothers

(born Florida, Howard February 2 1946, David September 16 1950)

Before the Bellamy Brothers – who really are brothers – made a name for themselves in country music their sound was described as a masterful mix of blues, soul and rock. It was an accurate description because prior to moving into the country-pop field the Bellamys cut their musical teeth in the fermenting Florida environment that spawned such popular and successful aggregations as Lynyrd Skynyrd and the Allman Brothers.

Howard Bellamy received his early musical influence from a father who played dobro and fiddle in a bluegrass band. David chose the accordion as his instrument at the age of nine. It was later, when he became enamoured with soul and blues, that he started concentrating on keyboards.

There is a common denominator that binds most creative individuals who play, sing or write: they all began at an early age, and David Bellamy is no exception.

'I began putting words on paper when I was just eight,' he recalls. 'They were short stories and poems. I didn't write my first song until I was seventeen.'

David was also the first brother to perform in public. In 1965 he was organ player for a soul group called the Accidents. That experience ingrained a love for soul music that has never left him. He remembers, with a wistful smile, the great fun he had playing backup for Percy Sledge, Otis Redding and Little Anthony. 'I even had a go-go girl dancing on top of my organ. Those were great days.'

The Bellamy Brothers received their professional baptism in 1968 when they first performed before a live audience with their father at the San Antonio Rattlesnake Roundup. They stood under a tree and played for free.

The Bellamys then formed a family act. Howard played the guitar, David was on the accordion and their father kept the beat lively with some down country fiddling.

By 1968 the brothers had progressed musically to the point that they were invited to join a rock group called Jericho. On occasion they shared billing with the Allman Brothers and Brewer & Shipley.

No one, including the Bellamys, ever thought that the Allmans would become such a major influence in rock music in a few years time.

'When you're playing the local coffee house circuit and headlining at the Bottom of the Barrel you don't have many grandiose stars in your eyes,' said Howard.

The brothers reached a musical crossroads. They could keep on performing other people's music or they could start writing and begin to stamp their own musical imprint.

By 1970, after a disastrous recording session that they'd sooner forget, the brothers concentrated on studio session work which allowed them the time and environment to perfect their musical styles. They also made important and enduring contacts at all levels of the music industry. When not in the studio the brothers filled their time writing and expanding their song catalogue. David penned a song with the unlikely title 'Spiders and Snakes'. He sent it to Phil Gernhard who was producing comedy singer Jim Stafford. Stafford took to it immediately and his recording of it sold over 2 million copies.

'Spiders and Snakes' opened a gigantic career door for the brothers.

Gernhard, and his colleague Tony Scotti, saw great potential in them as an act and made a management offer. Once the contractual details were ironed out the brothers moved to Los Angeles and began working on a series of single recordings.

'Let Your Love Flow' was an early 1976 single for Warner/Curb Records. It was a prominent hit on both the country and pop charts.

Both brothers are in total agreement about the importance of name recognition. They are also in agreement that the best way to build recognition, and a fan base, is to get out on the road and play live concerts. Their active tour schedule sees them criss-cross North America from Canada to the Mexican border. They have also had a number of successful tours in Great Britain, Scandinavia and Germany where interest in country music is intense.

By the early 1980s David Bellamy's reputation as a songwriter was rivalling his reputation as being one half of the Bellamy Brothers. 'If I Said You Had A Beautiful Body Would You Hold It Against Me', 'Sugar Daddy' and 'Lovers Live Longer' added lustre to an impressive lineup of top songs.

'Do You Love As Good As You Look' from 1981 is not a David Bellamy composition (it was written by Rory Bourk, Jerry Gillespie and Charlie Black) but it is one of their biggest hits.

In solo or close harmony the Bellamy Brothers prove that the marriage of strong lyrics to a solid melody is a winning combination. Above average arrangements are a plus.

★*Best of the Best* (Bellamy Brothers Productions BBPI-1-92)

This CD is released on the Bellamy Brothers own label and the 21-song lineup will satisfy any fan.

Larry Williams' 'Let Your Love Flow' kicks off this collection. It was a wise choice as it grabs immediate attention. Following a pulsing intro the brothers take over solo and in harmony.

The shy, or timid, need not be put off by what one might consider to be a suggestive title, 'If I Said You Had A Beautiful Body Would You Hold It Against Me' is just a lyrical love question that follows parental advice: 'But Daddy always told me don't make small talk./He said come on out and say what's on your mind.'

David and Howard got together with Don Schults in 1989 and the result of that tri-level effort is 'You'll Never Be Sorry'. It's a tender love song and in the vocal hands of the brothers it demands many replays.

David confirms his songwriting skills on this album. He wrote 18 of the 21 songs either singly or in collaboration.

Black, Clint

(born Clint Patrick, New Jersey, grew up Houston, Texas, circa 1962)
The next time you see a picture of Leonard Slye from Cincinnati,

Ohio, aka Roy Rogers 'King of the Cowboys', take a close look. He'll remind you of country superstar Clint Black. Better still, Black will remind you of Rogers. The resemblance is uncanny. They both have the same squinting smile, both can sing and both have that dusting of charisma which places them above mere mortal men. In 1991 the two performed 'Hold On Pardner' together at the 1991 Country Music Awards.

Born in New Jersey, Black was the youngest of G. A. and Ann Black's four sons. At a very early age the family moved to Houston, Texas, and Black grew up a Texan from the crown of his cowboy hat to the tips of his cowboy boots. Even his accent is pure Texan.

As a young boy it was evident that he possessed an unusual musical talent and, with the encouragement of his parents, he learned to play the guitar, bass and harmonica. His first public appearances were at backyard barbecues when he was 15 and he was soon good enough to be invited to join his brother Kevin's band where he sang harmony and played bass.

Occasionally, when low on funds, Black would pick up extra dollars by working as a fishing guide or ironworker. However, the majority of his life has been spent singing and playing.

In 1981 he got his foot in the entertainment door when he was booked into the Benton Springs Club in Houston. For the next six years he ground out a living performing in some of the rowdiest honky-tonks and bars in and around Houston. Even though the hours were long, some of the locations dingy and the audiences demanding, Black held his ground and improved with every performance.

It was during this period of professional growth that he met songwriter Hayden Nicholas. The two men hit it off and Nicholas and Black have since become successful songwriting collaborators. Together they have penned many of Black's hit songs.

In the early days, money was always a problem for Black. Though desperate to cut an audio tape and get it to the right people in the recording industry he was unable to finance the studio fees. Through a stroke of good fortune Nicholas had an eight-track home recording studio where Black could cut his demo. The tape finally landed on the desk of Bill Ham, the manager of the rock band ZZ Top.

Though Ham was managing a rock group, he was in fact a

country music fan and liked Black's straightforward, honest approach to his own composition. Before long he became Black's manager.

Black has no hesitation in giving Ham full credit for getting his career off the ground. During one interview he said, 'When I met my manager, that's when I got my first big break.'

One thing that Black does not lack is confidence especially when it comes to furthering his career. One memorable day Joe Galante, the then head of RCA Records, found himself on the receiving end of Black's confidence. Somehow the singer got through reception, into Galante's office and convinced him that it would be in his, and RCA's, best interest to take a few minutes out of a busy schedule and listen to four of his demos.

Galante listened and was so impressed that he flew from Nashville to Houston just to see Black perform. An eight-album contract was signed and Black immediately began the arduous task of working on his debut album.

Black knew full well that his future, as a songwriter and singer, hung on the success of his first album and he had no intention of blowing it. He produced nearly 50 song tapes which were listened to and dissected by the preproduction staff. Nine were eventually agreed upon for *Killin' Time*.

May 1991 is a landmark month on Black's calender. His video 'A Better Man', which was his first single, was released to great acclaim. The new fans were ecstatic about the handsome singer in the Wrangler jeans and cowboy hat who had a devil-glinting smile.

Black's days of languishing in obscurity were over. He was the new country sex symbol and he relished every moment of the adulation. He had reached the rarefied stratum of superstar. His fans couldn't get enough of his legitimate country sound and honky-tonk styling.

Unlike some recording artists, especially the new ones, who prefer to use seasoned session players for backup, Black relies on his own band with implicit trust. This approach paid off handsomely with three Country Music Association Award nominations in the autumn of 1991. Black also scooped up the Horizon Award.

To no one's surprise award after award followed in the short space of a few months. Even a partial list is impressive, two

Grammy nominations for 'A Better Man' (Best Vocal Performance by a Male and for Best Country Song), an American Music Award for *Killin' Time*, plus Male Artist of the Year and Star of Tomorrow.

Country music was Black's oyster and the shining pearl was to be the first artist, in any format, to have five consecutive number one singles from a debut album.

Put Yourself in My Shoes was the title of his second album. It achieved phenomenal success, going platinum within a month of its release. Being named the first winner of the Nashville Songwriters Association International Songwriter/Artist of the Year Award added sheen to his many accomplishments.

A highlight of his career, and one he'll always cherish, was making the 'Hold on Pardner' video with Roy Rogers. It's difficult to say who had the most fun or whose career benefited most. Rogers was on a comeback wave that had not crested; Black only added more lustre to his celebrated career.

Up until Black met actress Lisa Hartman he had dedicated himself to his career with no stops or detours into a serious relationship. Hartman approached her soap opera career with a similar dedication until she met Black. They were married in a quiet ceremony on Black's farm outside Houston on October 21 1991.

If Black's strong points were tabulated, talent would top, closely followed by dedication to his craft and supreme confidence.

★*Put Yourself in My Shoes* (BMG 2372-2-R)

The title song, 'Put Yourself in My Shoes', opens with a devil-may-care harmonica intro before Black launches into the lyrics with a matching devil-may-care air. He wrote the 1990 hit with Nicholas Hayden and Shake Russell and this song alone was one of the major reasons for the album turning platinum in the first month.

Changing pace with 'The Gulf of Mexico', another Black/Hayden composition, Black slows down his delivery and one can almost feel the gentle rocking of a sailboat. Black and Hayden take the theme of lost love for 'Where Are You Now?' and with a masterful mix came up with some of the most imaginative lyrics you'll find in any song: 'And that's the burning question on fire in my mind/You always had the answers for me time after time/So all I'm asking/Is where are you now?'

There are the obligatory ten songs on this album and none short change. It's an excellent CD for anyone who is new to the Black way with a song.

Branson Brothers

(formed 1987, current members – James Fulbright, Dan Britton, Jimmy Ponder, Rick Baird)

The male quartet is an American institution. For generations men have blended their voices to sing every style of music from country through gospel to pop. Those who love quartet singing never fail to be thrilled by the rich harmonies of a dynamic lead singer, mellow baritone, high-register tenor and deep bass. One of the highlights of a Branson Brothers' concert is listening to bass Dan Britton, who is in the *Guinness Book of World Records* as having the deepest bass voice. Britton set the record in 1984, only to break it a few years later. He constantly amazes the audience, and receives prolonged applause, for dropping to E-flat, three octaves below middle C (18.84 Hertz). He can go lower than the standard tuning of the lowest string on a bass guitar.

The Branson Brothers enhance the reputation of quartet singing with a sound that is unique. Hard work, superior voices and close attention to the subtle techniques of quartet singing have resulted in what the industry calls the 'Branson sound'.

When asked why he chose quartet singing over a solo career lead singer Rick Baird said, 'I loved gospel singing as a kid and that has been a profound influence. However, I'm singing in a quartet now because I have such a high respect for the people I work with as vocalists.'

Even though the quartet had its beginnings in Nashville, and the 1982 incarnation was known as the Tennessee Valley Boys, they changed their name to the Branson Brothers in 1987, after the Missouri town that has become one of the prime sources of live country music in the United States. At the time the group were the first artists to come out of Branson with a major record deal.

The quartet has a number of albums in circulation, which were independently produced, but the major one is their debut album for Warner Brothers *Heartmender*.

The Branson Brothers have discovered the right mix for musical excitement: they enjoy singing together, they carefully choose their material, they revel in performing live and are meticulous in presentation.

★*Heartmender* (Warner Bros. 9 26979-2)

Heartmender begins with a driving, pulsating beat that is maintained until the last note. It is a perfect showcase for the group's versatility. Lonnie Wilson's work on the drums deserves honourable mention.

It doesn't hurt to know that GARTH BROOKS wrote 'Everyday It's Getting Harder To Keep Your Memory Alive', in collaboration with David Stephenson. This is another lively up-beat number. The lyrics are interesting and the arrangement sparkles.

All-in-all *Heartmender* is a fine debut album.

Brooks & Dunn

(formed February 1991, Leon Eric 'Kix' Brooks, born Shreveport, Louisiana, May 12 circa 1954, Ronnie Gene Dunn, born Coleman, Texas, June 1 circa 1956)

When you're hot you're hot, and Brooks & Dunn are certainly the hottest duo in country with the most successful debut album ever released by a country duo or group. *Brand New Man* is nearing triple platinum with well over 2.5 million copies sold (and still counting). The album spawned four straight number one singles, including 'Boot Scootin' Boogie' which received a Grammy nomination for Best Performance by a Duo or Group in the country category. To the surprise of no one Brooks & Dunn were named top duo or group by the Country Music Association, the Academy of Country Music, *Billboard* magazine and the influential trade publication *Radio & Records*. *Jukebox* magazine also got in on the act, singling them out for the Rising Star Award.

The only problem with hitting the bulls-eye the first time out is how to top it second time around. Dunn gave the best answer possible. 'We tried to ignore whatever pressures there might have been. We just did what worked the first time around. We tried to come up with the best songs we could and record them as well as possible.'

'As well as possible' translated into their second album *Hard Workin' Man* (released on February 23, 1993) which has the same searing passion and high-level energy as *Brand New Man*.

The amazing thing about Brooks & Dunn is the shortness of time it has taken them to shoot to the top of the heap – they met only a few months before their careers caught fire. And if it hadn't been for Arista Records chief, Tim DuBois, they might still be wandering around the wastelands of country music trying to make it as solo artists. DuBois started the ball rolling by introducing Brooks and Dunn at a lunch date. It wasn't the time, he felt, to suggest that they team up even though he saw their potential as a duo. Instead he suggested that it might be in their best interests to try writing songs together.

'It didn't take us long to realize that we might have a better chance at the golden ring together than separately,' recalls Brooks. 'Once we teamed up the songs kept popping out.'

'Brand New Man' was the first song they brought to DuBois. 'I knew we had something special there,' recalls DuBois. 'It was obvious I had to convince them that they were an act. They both wanted solo careers so badly and had pursued them for so long. It's not the same thing when you have to share the spotlight with someone else.'

Once the two success-driven dynamos hooked up as an act everything fell into place. 'They get along so well together that I think they are brothers and never knew it,' jokes DuBois.

'We've settled into a good, genuine friendship,' says Brooks. 'We're really starting to feel like we have a common goal of longevity.'

If they are going to last one ingredient is needed – unequivocal, total agreement on the music they sing. From all reports so far, it would appear that they are of one mind as to the direction of their music and careers. They leave the weepy ballads to VINCE GILL and the message songs to GARTH BROOKS (no relation to 'Kix' Brooks). Their sole musical goal is, as they say, to 'scar up those hardwood floors with the gotta-dance songs like "Hard Workin' Man".' To everyone's surprise 'Boot Scootin' Boogie' has even crossed over and become popular in disco clubs.

'Kix' Brooks has a more rock edge to his voice than Dunn who is the less flamboyant of the two. Dunn meshes perfectly with Brooks' showstopping manic leaps, duck-walks and near-destructive guitar work.

Brooks grew up in Shreveport, Louisiana, and lived down the street from the late Johnny Horton of 'Sink the Bismark' and 'North to Alaska' fame. His first professional job was performing with Horton's daughter.

After a period of roaming around, including a stint in Alaska and New Orleans, Brooks settled in Nashville and 'spent a couple of years starving'. Songwriting saved him from financial disaster. His credits include three number one hits: Highway 101 took 'Who's Lonely Now' to the top; John Conlee did the same with 'I'm Only In It For The Love' and the NITTY GRITTY DIRT BAND band matched the feat with 'Modern Day Romance'.

Dunn's early claim to fame, and a harbinger of the future, was being thrown out of a 'very' conservative religious college because he wouldn't stop playing in honky-tonks. Moving to Tulsa, Oklahoma, from Coleman, Texas, Dunn got involved with the local, thriving country scene and before long he was heading up the house band at Duke's Country, a large club that booked the stars and drew patrons like flies to honey.

'It was a great time and I opened for everybody who came through,' he recalls.

In 1989 he won the Marlboro National Talent Round-up after his pal Jamie Oldacker, who played drums for Eric Clapton, submitted a tape of his music as a joke. With his confidence buoyed by the win, Dunn moved to Nashville, ready to take on the country music establishment.

It's a classic story of being in the right place at the right time, meeting the right people and having the right chemistry to work together. One of the advantages of being a duo is that one keeps tab on the other and, when one begins to stray musically, the other pulls him back on course. The professional checks and balances keep each artist on the cutting edge. Their high-energy shows remain as fresh for them as they do for the fans who have made them one of the top road draws. Not only that, the duo also design and market their own line of Western shirts for Panhandle Slim.

Brooks & Dunn cleaned up at the 1993 Academy of Country

Music Awards, walking away with three trophies. They captured Best Album of the Year for 'Brand New Man', Top Single Record for their honky-tonk dance hit 'Boot Scootin' Boogie' and to top off a perfect evening they were named Best Vocal Duet.

With tongue firmly planted in cheek Dunn accepted the award, stating, 'We're having so much fun with this we feel guilty coming up here.'

'There's nothing like walking out on the stage,' says Dunn. 'Our shows surpass our albums and singles by far when it comes to pure enjoyment and excitement. It's just a great thing to be part of it.'

★*Brand New Man* (Arista 18658-2)

Released in 1991, the two leads trade off vocals and harmonize like they'd been together for decades instead of just a couple of years. Brooks has the lower, grainier voice while Dunn has a more country tenor.

Some singers rely upon a protracted intro to set the mood, but on *Brand New Man* it's just three lightning drum licks and they're into it. The opening lyrics are near perfect: 'I'm born to love again/ I'm a brand new man.'

'Next Broken Heart' is a number one hit that has become a Brooks & Dunn concert staple. The band is showcased on both the intro and bridge in a masterful exhibition of good old country sound.

No Brooks & Dunn CD collection would be complete without 'Boot Scootin' Boogie', a foot-stomping delight driven by Dunn's bear-down-hard voice. The country inflections are unmistakable.

★*Hard Workin' Man* (Arista 18716-2)

On *Hard Workin' Man* (1993) the duo deliver the goods. One reviewer wrote, 'Every man and woman who wears a hard hat in America will soon adopt this as their national anthem.' One could add that every aspiring honky-tonk piano player and fiddler should pay close attention to the intro and bridges. The musical brilliance exhibited on these two instruments is a benchmark for excellence.

'Boot Scootin' Boogie' is reprised on this album, but with a difference. For the trained, or acute, ear it's easy to spot the remixing. It has become almost a techno dance and will get the two-steppers and line dancers on the floor in a flash.

The duo's positive declaration that, 'We bring a good energy to the stage,' is never in dispute. They also bring the same 'good energy' to their recorded music. Little wonder that they are firmly ensconced as the top country duo.

Brooks, Garth

(born Troyal Garth, Tulsa, Oklahoma, February 7 1962)

A 'chubby kid' by the name of Garth Brooks came out of Oklahoma with the energy and ferocity of the winds that turned that state into a dust bowl. He blew away everything in sight. No performer, before or since, has equalled his impact on both country music and the fortunes of the recording industry.

In 1992 country music fans bought over 20 million Garth Brooks' albums. That astounding accomplishment was unmatched by any recording artist in any other musical field.

Ropin' the Wind was Brooks' third album and it shot to the number one spot on *Billboard*'s pop music charts in its first week out. This landmark achievement is even more amazing when statistics reveal that there are only two other country artists ever to hit the number one spot on *Billboard*'s pop music charts: JOHNNY CASH in 1969 and Kenny Rogers in 1980. The only difference was that it took Cash and Rogers weeks of heavy album sales to capture the top spot. Brooks did it in just seven days. Thanks to him country music was being taken seriously.

Everything about his music and act is carefully thought out, from the skilful blending of country with rock, to his unfathomable ability to pump up the audience into a frenzy of response – anything seems to go, from swinging on ropes to being doused in water or sprinting across the stage at an unexpected moment.

Even though Brooks seemed to come out of nowhere and explode on the music scene he had paid his musical dues. He was the sixth child in a loving family of half-brothers and half-sisters (both his father and mother had been married previously). A better-than-average athlete, he grew up in the small village of Yukon, Oklahoma, not too distant from Oklahoma City. He was a high school quarterback and went to Oklahoma State University on an athletic scholarship.

Brooks probably inherited his musical talents from his mother, who had been a Capitol Records recording artist and performer on the Ozark Mountain Jubilee before settling down to raise a family.

During his college years he was good enough to get night club bookings and he joined a local band. The music they played was a blend of country, rock and folk and one can spot their influence in the music he now sings.

Regardless of where one is born, if country music is in the blood Nashville draws like a magnet and in 1984 Brooks was ready to conquer new worlds. He won an audition at Opryland and was offered a summer job. However his parents, concerned that if he caught the entertainment bug he'd forget about finishing his education, talked him into putting Opryland, and his career, on hold until after his graduation. As soon as he graduated, with a degree in advertising, he left for Nashville, this time with his parents' blessing.

It took one meeting with a country music executive to shatter his confidence and dreams and he headed back to Oklahoma having spent all of 23 hours in the mecca of country music.

It was two years later before he tackled Nashville again. Then he had a wife, Sandy, for moral support. Unlike the first time his confidence and dreams were anything but shattered, meeting someone who was most positive about his chances as a country singer.

At the time Bob Doyle was with the American Society of Composers, Authors and Publishers (ASCAP) but very shortly after their meeting he quit the job to form his own music publishing company, Major Bob Music. Brooks was his first client.

Brooks was signed by Capitol Records and he began working on his first album, *Garth Brooks*, with Allen Reynolds producing. *No Fences* and *Ropin' the Wind* followed to fan reception the like of which country and pop music had not anticipated.

As frantic and energetic as Brooks can be on stage he can handle a ballad with skill and tenderness, thanks to Reynolds. Until Brooks listened to Reynolds' advice his ballad delivery was full-voiced in the Lee Greenwood style. Once he relaxed and began to sing in a soft mellow tone he became a master in the art of subtle communication. 'If Tomorrow Never Comes' and 'The Dance' would never have reach the heights of popularity and become signature tunes had he dismissed Reynolds' counsel.

Brooks hit the jackpot with his first three albums. The days when country music was in dire straits was still a recurrent nightmare for many. At that time a 200,000 album total sale was reason for rejoicing. The ten-day 700,000 sales figure for *No Fences* was therefore a major feat.

Brooks was inducted into the Grand Ole Opry in October 1990, and became its sixty-fifth member. He became the most nominated artist at the 1990 Country Music Awards – of the five nominations he took home trophies for the prestigious Horizon Award and the Video of the Year award for 'The Dance'.

Billboard and *Radio & Records* gave him a hands-down win as Male Country Artist and he had his arms filled with six Academy of Country Music Association awards in April 1991.

He was no slouch in 1992 either. 'The Thunder Rolls' was Best Country Single and *No Fences* scooped up the Best Country Album trophy.

Brooks is in firm control of his career and future. In fact he has such total control and power that he stopped the release of the video for 'The Dance' because it didn't meet his high standards, even though he won the Video of the Year award. He has also been known to dig in and fight directors on points of creativity – battles he usually wins.

Brooks knows full well there are artists on lower popularity rungs taking careful aim and waiting for the day when he'll be knocked off so they can take his place. He also knows that in order to survive one cannot be complacent. If anybody will survive and fight off the challengers, it will be Garth Brooks. He's no flash-in-the-pan and intends to be around for many years to come.

To the surprise, and disappointment, of the BILLY RAY CYRUS camp Brooks won his third straight Entertainer of the Year award at the 1993 Academy of Country Music Awards. When Brooks was asked backstage how he had grown professionally over the past three years his answer was candid and forthright.

'It's [country music] not rocket science,' he said. 'It's about raising hell and having fun.'

Brooks is one artist who is not afraid to change or take chances with his music. He constantly surprises.

★*No Fences* (Capitol C2 93866)

'The Thunder Rolls', which Brooks wrote in collaboration with Pat Alger, opens with an ominous peal of thunder followed by a mood-setting guitar. It has to be the most arresting introduction to a song in recent memory. A haunting fiddle adds to the melancholy story of a woman waiting for her man to return. The vocal pictures that Brooks paints are from the deft strokes of a master. No wonder 'The Thunder Rolls' was Best Country Single and no wonder that this ten-song album will go down in history as a country music hallmark. Listening to it again and again is akin looking at a beautiful landscape – every time you come back to it there's something new to discover and enjoy.

'Two Of A Kind, Workin' On A Full House' is honky-tonk at its very best. The lyrics create mental images of western bars with dancers keeping time to the infectious beat. 'Yea, she's my lady luck/Hey, I'm her wild card man/Together we're building up a real hot hand/We live in the country/Hey, she's my little queen of the south/Yea, we're two of a kind/Working on a full house.'

Brooks dedicated this album to 'all who hear the music and have the courage to dance'.

'When I saw Garth Brooks I thought I'd seen it all,' said WILLIE NELSON when asked to comment on this country sensation.

Brown, Marty

(born Maceo, Kentucky, July 25 circa 1955)

Take a Marty Brown, throw in a soulful bass and mix gently with some old-fashioned backup and what you get is country music like they don't make any more. Back in the 'good old days' of the 1930s, 1940s and 1950s country music was simple, straightforward and unadorned. It was the umbilical cord to the soul of the singer.

At first listen Marty Brown sounds as if he's in a time warp. More than once, to his great pride, he's been compared to the legendary Hank Williams both as a songwriter and singer and not without just cause. 'I cut my teeth on Hank Williams,' he says. 'I can honestly say that I've heard every piece of music he ever wrote.'

Brown is a throwback to the days when men, with an unquenchable passion for an elusive dream, were not afraid to head down the road without a dime in their jeans and live by their wits. More times than he cares to count he would somehow get to Nashville and end up sleeping in alleys because he'd run out of money and gas for his perpetually broken down Chevette. He is sure he holds the record for being turned away from more publishing companies than any other would-be country singer that ever came to Nashville looking for fame and fortune.

Even after he was married with two children, the urge to try one more time was so great that he would strike out again only to be rebuffed, disillusioned and so desperate that he'd walk into bars and start singing in the hope that someone would throw a few dollars in his hat.

You can only take so many doors being slammed in your face before you says 'enough is enough' and settle down with a steady job. Brown honestly tried to give up country music. He got a job at a plumbing service but was laid off and the old Nashville urge resurfaced. It was an addiction stronger than Kentucky moonshine.

The trip to Nashville was a repeat of all the others and Brown was so emotionally, physically and financially spent that he could hardly raise his head as he tramped along the street. Then he saw a 'Trust Jesus' sign. The building closest to the sign was the BMI building – one of the few that Brown had not been thrown out of a few years earlier before he'd had a chance to sing a couple of songs.

'Kurt Denny listened to me once,' remembers Brown, 'so I thought I'd try to get him to listen again. He did. I played eight of my songs one after the other without stopping. All I had going for me was desperation and my guitar for accompaniment.'

Denny was impressed and took Brown off the streets. He paid for his hotel and meals while he made some calls. By the end of the week there were publishers showing serious interest in his songwriting ability.

A euphoric Brown returned home with the good news and before many days had passed Denny called. He told him to get back to Music City as fast as he could because in addition to music publishers there were recording companies sitting up and taking notice.

Brown couldn't believe his good fortune. Before long he had his name on an MCA recording contract. Producers Tony Brown and Richard Bennett rounded up a studio band and got him a recording date. And thankfully no one tinkered with his music or singing style. The raw, undiluted emotion that Denny had spotted as Brown's key to musical stardom was allowed to come through.

Born in that recording session was Brown's debut album *Hit and Dry*. Good music is always doubled sided – strong melody and strong lyrics. *Hit and Dry* is no exception. It captures the singer who has captured the imagination of the country music world.

Unconventional, unorthodox and unpredictable are adjectives that belong to Marty Brown and as long as they do he'll continue to make his mark in country music.

★*High and Dry* (MCA MCAD-10330)

Music critics were not just being kind when they compared Marty Brown's singing and songwriting talents to those of Hank Williams. All anyone who questions the comparison has to do is listen to Brown sing and check out his lyrics. Case closed!

High and Dry is a stellar debut album. Brown stamps out his vocal and songwriting turf on this one. All ten songs are his own composition.

The title cut 'High and Dry' with an ear-catching guitar intro, sounds more like the second coming of Hank Williams than modern-day Nashville. It's a mournful tale of a man who turns to booze after his love leaves him high and dry: 'I've whisky to quench my thirst inside/But this old bottle won't bring her back/ It only makes me high.'

'Your Sugar Daddy's Long Gone' has an engaging bluesy shuffle and will be high on the list of dance favourites in the clubs. On 'Indian Summer Blues' the backup band really shines and provides Brown with the perfect ambience for another heart-breaking song about departed love. It's uncanny how Brown can get the same catch in his voice that made Hank Williams's singing so unique and distinctive.

High and Dry is a splendid kick-off album. Brown is proof positive that the new music coming out of Nashville is a winner.

Carpenter, Mary-Chapin

(born Princeton, New Jersey, February 21 1958)
It's doubtful if there is any other country music artist who can come within a country mile of Mary-Chapin Carpenter for less likely qualifications for Nashville acceptance.

Born in Princeton New Jersey, about as far away from Music City as one could get, she was raised in Tokyo and Washington DC. Her father was an editor for *Life* magazine and she attended Brown University.

Her musical tastes were as far removed from country as her roots were from Nashville. Instead of TAMMY WYNETTE, PATSY CLINE or EDDY ARNOLD she listened to Judy Collins, Woody Guthrie and folk singers Peter, Paul and Mary. The only thing she had in common with country was a love for singing and strumming her acoustic guitar.

During her college days, and with the encouragement of her father, she began singing in public. By the time she graduated she had decided upon music as her career and she was good enough to win several local awards offered by the Washington Area Music Association. Even though she was popular in the clubs she wanted to expand her musical horizons, so she decided to make a tape and sell it to the patrons who came to hear her sing and play. Together with John Jennings, who was her guitarist and who would go on to become her producer and co-songwriter, she cut a tape on his home equipment.

As so often happens with energetic, ambitious performers, fate took over and the tape eventually landed on the right desk at CBS. They offered her a *country* record contract and her debut album, *Hometown Girl*, was released in 1987.

State of the Heart was her second Columbia album and it hit.

Carpenter was artistically pleased with what she had produced because, for the first time in her career, she had had the budget and time to define clearly what she wanted her music to say and to be able to record it her way.

She describes herself as 'a singer with an acoustic guitar fronting a rock 'n' roll band', but country fans enjoy her music and country radio especially likes the 'Carpenter sound' and gives her music above average air play.

The combination of Carpenter and Jennings produced another

winning album *Shooting Straight in the Dark*. At the 1993 Academy of Country Music Awards Carpenter won the Best Female Vocalist trophy. For someone with non-country roots Mary-Chapin Carpenter has carved out a niche for herself and feels at home in country music.

★*Shooting Straight in the Dark* (Columbia CK 46077)

This album, like the earlier two, was co-produced by Carpenter and John Jennings. Of the 11 songs, nine were written by Carpenter and one was written by her in collaboration with Jennings. The eleventh song 'Right Now' was co-written by Al Lewis and Sylvester Bradford.

Carpenter's voice has been described as 'warm alto' and this is certainly an accurate evaluation for her soothing, melancholy handling of 'When She's Gone'. It's a sad, pathetic story of indifference. The listener is eased into the mood-setting by a sensitive lullaby-like piano/guitar intro. The vocal picture Carpenter paints is crystal clear. 'She wore your favourite dress tonight/ And you just sat there getting tight/On double shots of rum.'

'Down At The Twist and Shout', with its swinging Cajun beat, is just the ticket for lifting the spirits. Carpenter really lets fly on this one. Michael Doucet's fiddle is right out of the bayous and the background vocals on the chorus are a perfect blend for Carpenter's voice.

If the three Carpenter/Jenning's albums are any indication of what's to come Carpenter will have no problem holding on to her fans and garnering new ones at an accelerated rate.

Cartwright, Lionel

(born West Virginia, circa 1963)
Lionel Cartwright is definitely country and definitely unique. His songs touch the raw nerve of emotion in a manner with which every listener can identify. There is a distinct thread of honesty running through his songs.

An analysis of country music quickly reveals that, for the most part, it draws its strength and power from painful episodes. Hurting songs like Hank Williams' 'Your Cheating Heart', or

Marty Robbins' 'Beggin' To You' spring immediately to mind. Cartwright, however, zeros in on the positive experiences of life, even when he sings about lost loves.

The West Virginia of Cartwright's adolescence and youth was the perfect place for an impressionable musical talent to absorb traditional country music. Before completing high school Cartwright was a regular on a country music show in Milton, West Virginia. The next rung up the ladder was taken when he graduated to the popular *Country Cavalcade* show on WMNI in Columbus, Ohio, as featured singer and musician. The WWVA Jamboree, in Wheeling, West Virginia, was next and it was at this point that his musical maturation took place. He began as backup piano player and ended up a featured performer and the show's musical director.

Nashville was the next musical world to conquer, and conquer it he did in masterful style. Before long he added Music City performer, arranger and musical director credits to his resumé.

Cartwright's songwriting talents have matched his proficiency on the piano, guitar, keyboard and mandolin and the majority of his songs are his own compositions. There are subtly crafted edges to each song and no two are alike in tone, inflection or depth. Cartwright is a performer of constant surprises. He is recognized as one of the most uniquely talented new crop of singers and songwriters in contemporary country music.

★*Chasin' the Sun* (MCA MCAD-10307)

'Real life has to do with individuals as well as relationships,' says Cartwright. To prove his point he has turned his view inward on several introspective songs on this CD. '30 Nothing' is the story of a man who realizes it is time for a change. An attitude of hope and confidence, in a bad and difficult situation, is the theme of 'Waiting for the Sun to Shine' and one of the most positive messages of hope and renewal is to be found in 'Family Tree'.

One pleasant element on this CD is guitarist John Jorgenson, who sparkles especially on 'Great Expectations'. Jorgenson deserves all the accolades he garners for his work. 'He just killed us all in the studio,' enthused Cartwright. 'He's one of the most underrated players in country music.'

Joining Cartwright on close harmony are RICKY SKAGGS, Mac

McAnally, Jim Photoglo, Alison Krauss, Russel Smith, Judy Rodman, Karen Taylor-Good and MARTY BROWN. As Cartwright observes, 'There's some serious talent there.'

Cash, Johnny

(born John R. Kingsland, Arkansas, February 26 1932)
Cash was one of five, part-Cherokee Indian children born into a sharecropper's family. Life became a day-to-day struggle for survival after his family moved to Dyess County, Arkansas in a New Deal resettlement program. His parents were so destitute that as an infant he nearly starved to death.

Cash remembers working alongside his brothers and sister in the fields as they hoed and weeded. The backbreaking work under a blistering sun was a character builder for the pubescent boy. His character was further tempered by his parents who followed strict fundamentalist tenets as their guide for life.

When he was ten Cash was hauling water for the road gang and by the age of twelve he was dragging and hoisting nine-foot cotton sacks.

Somehow, through all the privations of poverty, the family remained united. When two brothers died suddenly Cash was heartbroken but his inner strength helped sustain himself and his devastated family. It was just one more traumatic event in a life of traumas for the over-sensitive young Cash. But he found comfort in music and was beginning to show creative talents even before he reached his teens.

By the time he was twelve Cash was writing songs and trying to pattern his songwriting and singing after some of the country artists he occasionally heard on radio. He began singing professionally during his high school days on KLCN in Blythwood, Arkansas. It was his first taste of performng and he was bitten. Even then he saw it as a way to better himself by doing something he loved.

Home and family, as typified in the music of his later years ('Will The Circle Be Unbroken') had a magnetic draw for Cash and it took the Korean War to push him out of the parental nest. He joined the USAF and following basic training was posted to Germany as a cryptographer.

It was during his military hitch that he bought his first guitar and began learning the rudiments of chording. It was also during this period that he wrote 'Folsom Prison Blues', which was destined to be one of his future hit songs.

'There wasn't much romance in writing it,' he once recalled. 'I saw the movie, *Inside the Walls of Folsom Prison*, liked it and wrote the song. That's all there was to that.'

Discharged in the mid-1950s Cash settled in Memphis, Tennessee. He married Vivian Liberto and in order to keep food on the table and a roof over the heads of his wife and four girls, he got a job selling appliances door-to-door. But Cash was anything but content with life as a salesman. The creative juices were flowing and there was no outlet. In his spare time he took a radio announcing course which helped ease the frustration of being in a job that chafed at every turn.

Fate intervened when he met Luther Perkins and Marshall Grant. Perkins was learning the rudiments of the electric guitar and Grant was mastering the bass fiddle. The three musicians practised together and when they felt sufficiently confident they auditioned for Sun Records' Sam Phillips. He turned them down. Sometimes all it takes to reconsider a decision is a reversal of fortunes. Elvis Presley left Sun for RCA and Phillips immediately became interested in filling the roster gap with new talent. All of a sudden Cash and the 'Tennessee Two' looked promising. Cash was offered a contract and began recording with Perkins and Grant.

In June 1955 'Hey Porter' was released, which Cash had written when he was in the service. It became a hit. It was followed with 'Folsom Prison Blues'. This song is now a country classic. By the end of 1956 Cash had his first major hit 'I Walk The Line', an excellent example of the country/rockabilly blending. It is the ideal vehicle for Cash's baritone-bass voice.

1958 was a banner year. Cash enjoyed a surge of popularity with six top-ten hits including two that reached the top of the country charts, 'Guess Things Happen That Way' and 'Ballad Of A Teenage Queen'.

Besides being one of Sun's most bankable artists Cash was fast earning a reputation as a songwriter and it was during this point in his career that he wrote or co-wrote such fondly remembered songs as, 'You're The Nearest Thing To Heaven', 'The Ways Of A Woman In Love' and 'All Over Again'.

The 'Tennessee Two' became the 'Tennessee Three' with the addition of drummer Bill Holland who enhanced the backup sound.

Cash was not creeping up the ladder of country music success he was taking it two rungs at a time and it was not unexpected when he left Sun Records for a larger label.

His first release under his new Columbia contract was 'Don't Take Your Guns To Town'. It sold well over half a million copies and remained high in the country charts for a number of weeks.

Cash was the complete country music performer. He had an engaging voice and was a skilled guitar player. He achieved his clearly identifiable guitar sound by placing a piece of paper under the strings.

Johnny Cash was his first Columbia album – sales topped 400,000. An impressive total and one which confirmed Cash's solid fan following.

On November 5 1960 Cash's friend, country singer Johnny Horton, was tragically killed in a car crash. Not only did Horton's death leave a gigantic void in country music but it pushed an already highly stressed Johnny Cash into deep depression.

To those who only saw the performer, Cash was riding the crest of a wave; to those who saw the man behind the façade he was a depressed human being sinking deeper into the cauldron of alcohol and chemical dependency. At this time Cash's first marriage floundered and they eventually divorced.

WAYLON JENNINGS, who was Cash's equal when it came to living life on the cutting edge, was also on the marital loose. 'I had an apartment at the Fountain Bleu, in Madison, Tennessee,' recalls Cash. 'I suggested to Waylon that we could share expenses and he moved in. We both had a mutual respect for each other as artists and when we got to know each other we had so much in common, including our love for music and, at that time, our love for chemicals.'

The amazing thing about Cash was his ability to churn out the hits and maintain his pre-eminent position in country music at a time when his personal life was in a shambles. Close friends and associates despaired for his life, not just his future. But during this personally tumultuous period he brought out 'I'm In The

Jailhouse Now', 'The Ballad of Ira Hayes', and a number one ranked 'Ring of Fire'.

In the late 1960s he began recording with June Carter, daughter of the legendary Mother Maybell Carter. Their professional relationship evolved into a personal one, though marriage did not come about until Cash acceded to June's demands that he seek professional help, get free from drug dependency and get his life back in order.

In addition to throwing the 'monkey off his back' Cash returned to his fundamentalist beliefs and became a born-again Christian. Many times he has publicly credited God and June Carter for saving his life and career.

Following his marriage, Mother Maybell Carter joined the Cash show along with June and her two sisters, Anita and Helen.

With his personal life in order Cash began to live up to the potential many had predicted would be his when he first burst on to the country music scene as a fresh new talent. 1968 was a banner year for Cash and his wife. They recorded two smash singles, 'If I Were a Carpenter' and 'Daddy Sang Bass'. Cash was named Country Music Entertainer of the Year in 1969 and was the acknowledged king of country music.

Cash became as skilled at playing to a television camera as he was at playing to an audience and in January 1970 he had his own show on ABC. It ran until 1971.

One of the all-time Cash favourites, and a song that confirmed his popularity across the entertainment spectrum, was the highly popular novelty tune with the unlikely name of 'A Boy Named Sue'. This song gained gold record status along with his critically acclaimed albums *Johnny Cash At Folsom Prison* and *Johnny Cash at San Quentin*.

Over the years Cash has starred in a number of movies, and movies for TV, including *A Gunfighter* with Kirk Douglas, *Thaddeus Rose and Eddie* and *Gospel Road*, which was distributed by Billy Graham's World Wide Pictures. He continues to be a frequent platform guest at the Billy Graham crusades and is a crowd favourite with his gospel songs. He has recorded numerous gospel albums, such as *Johnny Cash Sings Precious Memories* and *Hymns From the Heart*.

'It was my mother who inspired me at seventeen,' says Cash. 'She said, "God's got His hand on you. Keep on Singing."' Even during his darkest period he never lost his affection for his family. He dedicated his 1979 two-LP release *A Believer Sings the Truth* to his mother.

Cash has much to be proud of. He started out dirt-poor on a sharecropper's farm and is now internationally recognized as the 'Man In Black'. He has made an indelible impact on country music. His mark will never be erased.

★*Classic Cash* (Mercury 834 526-2)

Someone once called a good country song 'a three-minute movie'. Nothing could be more descriptive of the songs of Johnny Cash, especially the 20 he has included on this splendid album

'Five Feet High and Rising' is the musical story of the disastrous 1937 Mississippi River flood that nearly wiped out the Cash homestead. 'Ballad of Ira Hayes' begins with 'Call him drunken Ira Hayes/He won't answer any more/Not the whisky-drinking Indian/Nor the Marine that went to war/Gather round me people/There's a story I would tell/About a brave young Indian/ That we should remember well.' It's a song that makes one take pause and think.

It was Cash who first brought Kris Kristofferson's 'Sunday Morning Come Down' to the attention of country music and made it a 1969 hit. The Johnny Cash Band with Jimmy Tittle and Jim Soldi on backup vocals make this song a four-star effort.

Earl Ball on piano, Matt Rollings on organ and Cash on vocals is all that is required to duplicate an old fashioned, fundamentalist church sound that is just perfect for 'Peace In The Valley'. Lovers of gospel music won't be disappointed.

Tom T. Hall wrote, 'Cash gives life a sense of permanence and basic worth.' Truer words have never been written.

★*Country Boy* (CD Charly 18)

Country Boy is an excellent companion for *Classic Cash*. There are a total of 45 cuts on the two CDs. A few songs like 'I Walk the Line' and 'Cry! Cry! Cry!' are repeated but this isn't a major problem; in fact, it could be seen as a bonus.

The evergreen Cash classic 'I Walk The Line', which he originally recorded in 1956, leads off this lineup. It has become his signature song and no Cash collection would be complete without it.

There is a total of 14 Cash compositions on this album. Some are better known than others but all are vintage and he's in great voice.

No one, including Cash, would say that he has a brilliant voice. But what sets his music apart from most of his contemporaries is the simplicity of melody, lyric and delivery – there are no vocal tricks. A example of a straightforward Cash song, that can send tingles up and down one's spine, is the enduring 'Guess Things Happen That Way'.

When Cash performs his songs he scowls, he prowls, he half-sneers and he aims his guitar at the audience like a Winchester 73. His fans love it. From the grin on his face, at the end of the show, so does he.

★*Columbia Records 1958–1986* (Columbia CGK 40637)

It is not uncommon for a collector to buy a complete album for just one or two songs. Any two songs on this twenty-song collection would justify purchase. They are all a collector's delight.

'The Legend of John Henry's Hammer' rivals 'MacArthur Park' in length. It comes in at 8 minutes 25 seconds and is well worth time set aside to listen to it. The clash of cold steel as a sledgehammer connects with a railway spike is so real that, when you hear the grunts of the hammer swinger, you can almost smell the sweat.

This song is special because in addition to Cash on vocals and guitar he is backed by the Carter family with Marshall Grant on bass, Bill Purcell on piano and the marvellous Luther Perkins on electric guitar.

The mariachi intro to 'Ring Of Fire' is courtesy of Karl Garvin and William McElhiney on trumpets. Cash is in rare voice and the enthusiasm of the ensemble pushes him to vocal heights that make this song a favourite. Again June Carter and the Carter family are prominent in backup.

Cash, Rosanne

(born Memphis, Tennessee, May 24 1955)

More than one 'SK' (star's kid) has said that life isn't necessarily easy when your mother or father is an entertainer and a major star. Being superstar Johnny Cash's daughter, and belonging to one of the most famous families in country music, didn't guarantee a smooth road to stardom.

For a natural musical talent, who is also proficient at painting and fiction writing, Rosanne carved out her own niche in country music.

Rosanne Cash came to stardom through country music's back door. Her first album was in fact recorded in Germany and the second in Los Angeles. The Nashville establishment considered her an outspoken country rebel because she never bowed to convention.

In retrospect the early and mid-1980s were not a vintage time for country music. Rosanne's accomplishment of being the only woman to have a number-one country album during those difficult years (especially for female performers) is all the more remarkable. She did it with *Seven Year Ache* in 1981 and again with *Rhythm and Romance* in 1985.

In addition to topping the country charts, her single 'Seven Year Ache' climbed to the twenty-second position on the pop charts at a time when disco, pop and rock were outstripping everything in recorded music.

Her star hasn't waned since those successes. She has been a constant achiever and has topped the country charts over ten times since then.

Rosanne was born just days before her father made his recording debut at the fabled Sun Studios in Memphis. When she was 11 she and her parents moved to Ventura, California, but the family circle was about to be broken apart when her mother, Vivian Liberto, and father divorced. Rosanne was to remain with her mother while her father chased country music's golden fleece.

At the time of her parents' divorce Rosanne had no inkling that she too would be a major player in the years to come. During her formative years she maintained a close relationship with her father and joined his roadshow after high school. She started at the bottom as a wardrobe assistant before graduating to the stage as a backup singer.

During the early years Rosanne was a victim of blinding stage fright. At one point in her career it was so intense that she would become rigid prior to going on stage.

In the mid-1970s she left her father's band and moved to England for a while. On her return to the States she went back to school at Vanderbilt University in Nashville. She also attended the celebrated acting school, the Lee Strasberg Institute in Los Angeles.

She was just 23 when singer/songwriter Rodney Crowell entered her life. His career was beginning to take off with the release of his first album *Ain't Living Long Like This* and his influence on country music was beginning to be felt. A professional association began when Crowell helped Rosanne produce enough songs to record an album for Ariola Records in Germany. They married in early 1979 and Crowell became her producer after she was signed to CBS.

Rosanne's landmark album *Seven Year Ache* not only brought her recognition as a vocal stylist of note, but pushed her into the limelight of songwriting. Other albums followed including *Somewhere in the Stars* and *King's Record Shop*.

With three growing children to nurture Rosanne hit the tour road less and less and enjoyed being a wife and a mother. Unfortunately her relationship with Crowell was at times turbulent, and they separated in 1991 after 13 years.

Although the marriage ended, and Rosanne has entered into a new relationship (with John Leventhal), she says she still loves Crowell and considers him a friend. 'How can I not be friends with him?' she asks. 'How can I not love someone who is related to my children?'

Out of the heartache and understandable bitterness of a broken marriage has come a new awareness which has been translated into Rosanne's latest album *The Wheel*. Rosanne calls her songs a 'turnstile to the emotions' and she is brutally honest about the marriage breakup. It is an astounding body of work and a career pinnacle.

★*The Wheel* (Columbia CK 52729)

The raw emotions of a marriage that began in heaven and ended in hell surge with every word and note as Rosanne bares her soul on *The Wheel*. Critics hail it as her best work and a fitting sequel to her highly acclaimed 1990 album *Interiors*.

Rosanne strips away all vestages of pretence on 'Roses in the Fire' with lines like, 'I throw your roses in the fire/To make the flames a little higher/I watch your roses turn to dust/I know no man that I can trust.'

The backup work of John Leventhal who was also the album's co-producer on 'The Truth About You' is simply amazing. He handles the guitar, harmonica and percussion chores with a beautifully light touch. The mood setting is perfect for Rosanne as she vocally points a finger at her man: 'I know the truth about you babe/I know the stories you tell/I can feel your heart locked up inside you/I swear I know you so well.'

Johnny Cash's well-known Christian beliefs were mildly assaulted, to say the least, when he heard his daughter refer to God as a woman on 'If There's A God On My Side'. Being a strict Baptist, and close friend of evangelist Billy Graham, Cash had always held to the popular belief that God was a He not a She. Rosanne told Peter Howell, of the *Toronto Star*, how father and daughter had accidentally run into each other as they checked into the same hotel. 'First he said he loved the record and then he said, "You know, I just got it why you would think God was a woman. It's because you are a woman." And I said, Right!'

There are eleven songs on this CD. Nine were written by Rosanne and two co-written with Leventhal. The backup and harmony vocals were provided by such stellar artists as MARY-CHAPIN CARPENTER, Patty Larkin, Marc Cohen, Tommy Malone, Bruce Cockburn and the omnipresent John Leventhal.

It's hard to imagine Rosanne topping this album either as a singer or songwriter. But she's a Cash so she probably will.

Chesnutt, Mark

(born Beaumont, Texas, September 6 1963)

When Mark Chesnutt looks back on 1991 he does so with amazement. At the beginning of the year all he had was a single hit, a new MCA album and a lot of people saying he'd make it as a country singer.

By the end of the year he'd had three number one singles. His album *Too Cold At Home* was certified gold and he was savouring a nomination for the Country Music Association's distinguished Horizon Award.

In the space of one year this Texas newcomer, whose singing style is compared to Hank Williams, GEORGE JONES and MERLE HAGGARD, has become an established country star. He has also become one of the most popular artists in any field of music. To prove it all he need do is point to his AMOA (Amusement and Music Operators Association) award for Rising Star of the Year, given for juke box play. His competition for the award included Timmy T, Vanilla Ice and Geraldo.

Longnecks and Short Stories was Chesnutt's second MCA album. One listen proves that this is a new country artist who is no flash in the pan.

Chesnutt is close to obsession about his music and the songs he chooses. 'I want something that every band in the world, every country band that's playing in bars like I used to do, is going to play. I want them to say, "Man this is a great album" and start playing every song off the album, even if it's not a single. I want a song that's a classic, something they're gonna be playing for ever.'

★*Longnecks and Short Stories* (MCA MCAD-10032)

There is a danger in hitting big with a debut album because everyone then waits to see if lightning will strike twice. This album, with ten impressive country songs, proves that it can.

The album has a classic sound, even the string parts were recorded in the old style. The closest way to describe it is to look at an old tintype picture that has been restored by using state-of-the-art photographic equipment, and marvel about how good it looks without sacrificing the beauty of time.

'It makes my hair stand on end to listen to it,' says Chesnutt. 'I love those old Elvis Presley albums that he recorded in '69 and '70, when he had a full orchestra. It just amazes me how strong these singers were back then. Especially when they didn't have the technology we now have in the recording industry. These guys pulled it off with the bare necessities. It's great to have a little bit of that sound in my stuff.'

'Talking to Hank' was written by Bobby Harden and is another flashback to the memory of the country legend. What makes this song worthy of being singled out is the appearance of GEORGE JONES. Jones opens and vocally describes coming across a shack in the woods while hunting wild turkey and sipping on Jim Beam.

Chesnutt joins the master and they slip back and forth on the story line: 'An old red-boned hound that looked older than time/ And an old man who swore he was only 29/Well I swear he looked just like old Hank/I wouldn't bet a wooden nickel that he ain't.' Their close harmony is a pleasure to hear.

Chesnutt returned the favour with a cameo appearance on Jones' hit concert video *George Jones – Live in Tennessee*.

Cline, Patsy

(born Virginia Patterson Hensley, Winchester, Virginia, September 8 1932; died March 5 1963)
She had the voice of an angel, a career fraught with triumph and disaster, and a private life that exceeded any scriptwriter's imagination. Yet, in a blazing career of less than eight years, she recorded over 100 singles (51 for 4 Star Music and 51 for Decca Records) including WILLIE NELSON's 'Crazy' which the Music Operators of America voted the number one juke box song for 1993.

Patsy's voice was a rare instrument and her unique intrepretation of a lyric set her light years ahead of all contemporaries.

Much of her success was due to producer Owen Bradley who in addition to being a superb arranger had an uncanny knack for recording. He instinctively knew how to soothe, prod, enrage or stroke Patsy, at just the right moment. Like no other producer he forced her to rise to the melodic heights he knew she was capable of.

Award-winning songwriter Harlan Howard is eternally grateful to Patsy because over the years her recording of his evergreen classic 'I Fall To Pieces' has paid many bills for the Harlan family. 'I stopped looking for another Patsy Cline because there's not going to be one,' lamented Harlan in a recent interview.

The musical prowess of Patsy was her ability to tear at the heartstrings – 'I Fall To Pieces' and 'Sweet Dreams' – then do a complete turnabout with a torch song like Don Hecht's 'Walkin' After Midnight'. She had a distinct bluesy quality to her voice and could really turn it on when required. Hecht called it 'pure B-flat blues'.

LORETTA LYNN remembers the first time she heard 'Walkin' After Midnight'. 'It was on the car radio,' she recalls. 'I rushed home and told Doolittle, my husband, Patsy's got herself another hit and boy did she ever. It was a smash!'

Many of today's biggest stars still bow to Patsy as much for her courage in bucking the establishment as for her brilliance in a recording studio. Loretta Lynn is one of them. 'Patsy was my idol as well as my friend,' she says. 'She opened the door for all the girl singers, including me.'

Though Patsy claimed that she wanted to be nothing more than a country singer she set the standard for female cross-over artists by hitting the pop charts as well as the country charts. The range of singers who acknowledge her profound influence, in addition to Loretta Lynn, include such major artists as K.D. LANG, Linda Ronstadt, Sylvia and REBA McENTIRE. When listening to any of the above, and many other country and contemporary singers, it is not difficult to spot the Patsy Cline influence.

Surprisingly, Patsy never had a million-selling 78 during her brief eight-year career. The gold and platinum records that line the office walls of her husband, Charlie Dick, came long after her death. It's not just the 'grey' country music lovers who keep her memory alive it's the 'baby boomers' who in increasing numbers have discovered her, on CD. They marvel at the richness of voice and haunting tonality.

Following the collapse of her first marriage to Gerald Cline, Patsy married the ever ebullient Charlie Dick in 1956. Their roller-coaster marriage was severed by Patsy's untimely death on March 5, 1963 in a plane crash along with the Randy Hughes, her manager, and two Grand Ole Opry stars, Cowboy Copas and Hawkshaw Hawkins.

'We only had six-and-a-half years together,' recalls Dick, 'but there was never a dull moment. They were great years. I wish they could have gone on for ever.'

Thirty years after her death Patsy Cline is still topping the charts. In April 1992 her smash album *Patsy Cline 12 Greatest Hits* was number one on *Billboard*'s Top Country Catalogue Album Chart for 81 weeks. Combined with the 197 weeks it was previously listed on the chart the total is an astounding 278 weeks. Even today it is being bought in sufficient quantities to still be at number one on *Billboard*'s chart.

The ongoing popularity and current 'star' status of Patsy is due, to a great degree, to Charlie Dick's relentless promotion of the woman who changed the face of country and western music for ever.

★*Patsy Cline 12 Greatest Hits* (Original Decca MCAMD-12)

This is the perfect Patsy Cline CD for not only is it a collection of her greatest songs it is an impeccable showcase for this remarkable talent.

The first cut is 'Walking After Midnight' which many consider to be Patsy at her very finest. She reaches the highs of emotion and the lows of blues. It's a number to play and replay because there's always something new, even if it's just a note or phrase.

The lineup also includes 'Sweet Dreams', 'Crazy', 'I Fall To Pieces', 'Why Can't He Be You' and 'So Wrong', which no fan would exclude from Patsy's body of work.

Also included are some of her lesser played hits: 'Strange', 'She's Got You', 'Leavin' On Your Mind', 'You're Stronger Than Me', 'Back In Baby's Arms' and one of my all-time personal favourites 'Faded Love'.

Patsy was backed by the melodic Jordanaires (Gordon Stoker, Hoyt Hawkins, Ray Walker and Neal Matthews Jr). She also had some of the finest session musicians in Nashville sitting in. The wonderful Floyd Cramer on piano and organ, Harold Bradley on electric bass, Buddy Harman holding forth on the drums and Randy Hughes making his rhythm guitar sing.

This CD is not only a collector's item, it's a treasure.

Collie, Mark

(born Waynesboro, Tennessee, January 18 circa 1965)

Look up Waynesboro, Tennessee, on the map, and you'll find it about halfway between Nashville and Memphis. Ask Mark Collie to define his music and he'll say, 'It's halfway between the rockabilly blues of Memphis and the country music of Nashville.'

A close listen to the Collie brand of music reveals a blending of styles from gospel to country to blues with a sprinkling of rock thrown in for good measure.

'My musical roots are like the roots of a tree,' explains Collie. 'They go in every direction.'

Collie came by his musical talents naturally. One of six children he quickly expanded an early interest in the piano and guitar into captive performances for his family. There comes a time, in every singer's career, when he can look back and say 'that's when it all began to come together'. For Collie this was the day he collaborated with one of Nashville's hottest producers, Don Cook. Together, they wrote and produced his first single, 'Even the Man in the Moon is Cryin''. It was the artist/producer/songwriting relationship that Collie had been looking for: 'I need someone who will allow me to be myself. I'm only good at being me.'

The one thing that is drawing fans to Collie, like bees to honey, is his musical unpredictability. He is one country artist who rides the razor sharp fulcrum of unpredictability in a most engaging style.

★*Mark Collie* (MCA MCASD 10658)

Collie believes that he has captured what he calls a commitment to artistic integrity with his third album.

'Even the Man in the Moon is Cryin'' was co-written by Collie and Don Cook. It is a spirited song which reinforces Collie's description of his music – it's part rockabilly blues and country and a perfect example of the new sound that is coming out of Nashville.

'Shame Shame Shame Shame' is what the industry terms an audience-responsive song. It's a sultry number that gets Collie more audience reaction than any other song in his concert lineup, its beat and lyrics an infectious combination. For anyone who enjoys rockabilly 'Shame Shame Shame Shame' will more than satisfy.

This CD is a collection of listenable songs that showcases Collie's considerable writing and singing talents.

Cyrus, Billy Ray

(born Flatwoods, Kentucky, circa 1961)

High on the list of remembered moments at the 1993 Academy of Country Music Awards show will be the shots of Billy Ray Cyrus smiling bravely as GARTH BROOKS, VINCE GILL and others were called up to the stage to accept their awards. No one called out Cyrus' name even though he had four nominations.

For many it was astounding that this singing sensation, who set country music on its ear with 'Achy Breaky Heart', was shut out. A brave smile, and applause for the winners, couldn't hide the shock and bitter disappointment.

1992 was Billy Ray Cyrus' year. He burst on to the country music scene and made history with his debut Mercury album *Some Gave It All*. It is the first debut country disc ever to top the country album charts. It was shipped gold and was certified platinum two weeks later. Within two months it was triple platinum. It is the most successful debut album of all time and broke the record previously held by the Beatles.

The 'Achy Breaky Heart' single made the *Billboard* charts prior to its release. The novelty hit of the decade soared to number one on both country and pop charts and became a national dance craze. The 'Cyrus virus', as it was called, quickly reached epidemic proportions.

The latest US census lists the population of Flatwoods, Kentucky, at 8,354. Like most medium to small towns, in the north-east section of the state, Flatwoods hasn't changed appreciably since Billy Ray was born there in the early 1960s. Cyrus' father, Ronald Ray Cyrus, is one of Kentucky's most popular politicians. For over twenty years he has been in the state legislature. He also heads up the local AFL-CIO union.

When Cyrus was six his parents divorced and he and his older brother Kevin (Kebo) lived with their mother Ruth Ann in

Flatwoods. Both parents have since remarried and Cyrus is close to his half-siblings on both sides.

It is hard to believe that the country hunk with the libidinus hip swivels, which drive his female fans so wild that they pepper him with their lingerie, is also the grandson of a Pentecostal minister. He started performing in his father's gospel group and the first song he remembers singing, as a four-year-old, is 'Swing Low Sweet Chariot'.

As a teenager Cyrus was into body-building and pumping iron. He did 500 pushups a day and is still proud that he could bench-press 280 pounds.

Goal-setting has been a life long passion and, early on, Cyrus set his sights on a career in professional baseball like his idol Johnny Bench, the all-star catcher with the Cincinnati Reds. He was confident that he had a chance: he was strong, looked after his body and was a star football and baseball player during his high school days at Flatwoods' Russell High School. 'I used to write down my goals in life and visualize them. I liked to see if they would happen.'

He struck out with baseball during his junior year at Kentucky's Georgetown College.

'An inner voice', as he calls it, kept telling him to get a guitar and start a band. Heeding this 'inner voice' he bought a guitar and the very next day formed Sly Dog. They set themselves a goal of playing in a bar within ten months.

One week short of seven months the band was booked for its first gig at the Sand Bar in Ironton, Ohio. The Sand Bar was where Cyrus first learned what 'packing the house' really meant. It was an excellent musical schoolroom. The audiences reacted enthusiastically as Sly Dog shook the rafters, windows and anything that wasn't nailed down with their eclectic blend of quintessential WILLIE NELSON and Lynard Skynyrd.

While playing in the Sand Bar, Cyrus met Cindy Smith, a sales representative. They fell in love and were married.

Cyrus is a person who takes things to heart and when a fire destroyed his band's equipment in 1984 he took it as a sign that it was time to move on and discover new worlds to conquer. He headed for Los Angeles and formed another band. But music becomes an expensive luxury when there are no bookings so not long after Cyrus became a car salesman.

He laughs about it now. 'I had to sell cars for a living when I can't even change the oil in my own car.' It was a depressing time. 'There I was in Woodland Hills, California, making lots of money but so busy I wasn't having time to pursue my dream.'

It took the sage advice of his father to spur him into another career move. 'Always know where you are and always know where you're going,' wrote Cyrus' father. 'But, don't ever forget where you came from.' Cyrus took the admonition to heart and moved back to Flatwoods so he could be closer to Nashville.

For five years Cyrus headlined at the Ragtime Lounge in Huntington, West Virginia. It was a five-day-a-week grind and on most days off he would be on the road for a six-hour drive to Nashville. By actual count he made the drive an average of 42 times a year.

'I'd get to Nashville on a Monday, bang on record company doors or grab a phone book and call whoever would see me,' he recalls.

Call it luck or being in the right place at the right time, one of the people he met was Del Reeves, the Grand Ole Opry singer they dubbed the 'Dean Martin of country music' because of his relaxed easy stage manner. Reeves listened to one of Cyrus' tapes and was so impressed he introduced him to his former manager Jack McFadden. McFadden's management genius is well known in country music and he has managed some of the biggest names, including Buck Owens, Lorrie Morgan and MERLE HAGGARD. He signed Cyrus to a contract.

The rocket was ignited and Cyrus was on his way to stardom.

Billy Cannon of Mercury Records saw Cyrus on a bill with REBA McENTIRE and Highway 101 at Louisville's Freedom Hall and was impressed. Before long Mercury's A&R chief Harold Shedd caught up with Cyrus in Huntington, West Virginia. When he saw the mesmerizing effect Cyrus had on an audience a recording contract was quickly in the offing.

Cyrus recorded *Some Gave It All* in 1991 about the same time that his marriage, which had begun with such high hopes and star-studded goals, was unravelling. 'Cindy had a nine-to-five job,' explains Cyrus. 'When she came home that's when I was leaving for work. I am sure she often wished that she was married to someone with a normal job.' One legacy of the union was Cyrus' hit song and his own composition, 'Wher'm I Gonna' Live'. He got the inspiration for the song after returning home after a night of carousing to find that Cindy had dumped all his belongings on their front lawn. Cyrus gave his now ex-wife (they divorced in 1981) co-writing credits on the song. She shares equally in the royalties.

Cyrus can't see himself getting married again. 'I don't have time,' he says. 'I can't give to someone something I don't have for myself.'

Fame, fortune and hysterical adulation are goals all performers crave. Cyrus has them in abundance but with a cost. In addition to his failed marriage he has become the centre of a public feud with country star TRAVIS TRITT. While some feel it is a manufactured row for media consumption, others are convinced that Tritt was serious, in June 1992, when he told reporters, 'Cyrus and his single hit song ['Achy Breaky Heart'] don't make much of a statement.'

WAYLON JENNINGS added fuel to the fire by comparing Cyrus to Fabin, the 1950s pretty-boy pop star. 'Fabin couldn't sing,' said Jennings. 'He was a wonderful guy, a good-looking guy.' He closed with, 'Billy Ray, he's not a good singer, but he don't need to be if you look that good.'

Cyrus tries to dismiss the slights, 'I don't make my music for Travis Tritt or anybody else. I make my music for myself and my fans.'

Cyrus answered his many critics who say he is a flash-in-the-pan and a one-album wonder when he released his second album, *It Won't Be The Last*, in June 1993, to moderate to good reviews.

★*Some Give It All* (Mercury 314-510 635-2)

When sales for an album are over 7 million and counting it has to be that album that heads the review list.

'Achy Breaky Heart' is the second song on the list and it's the one that has made Cyrus financially secure for life. Written by Don Von Tress it takes its title line from a George Jones 1962 classic 'Aching, Breaking, Heart'.

The hype for this song was text-book perfection – everything from the 'Achy Breaky' video to an endless exploitation of Cyrus' tight pants and sleeveless shirts, with the neck cut out for comfort.

Cyrus closes off the song by going a cappella and it's the perfect ending to the 3.23 minutes that sent Cyrus' career into a dizzying soar.

'Wher'm I gonna live when I get home/My old lady's thrown out everything I own/She meant what she said/She wished I was dead/So were'm I gonna live when I get home' are the opening lines to the song that Cyrus penned on the break-up of his marriage. Setting aside the tragedy of a broken partnership it's a lively toe-tapping number which Cyrus infuses with just the right inflections of a man totally bewildered by what has happened.

Cyrus' sexy growls, with some outstanding guitar licks in backup, make 'These Boots Are Made For Walkin'' one of the strongest songs on the list.

Cyrus wrote or co-wrote six of the ten songs on the album and, as one critic observed, he 'sings from the gut', especially on his own numbers. Cyrus uses his voice like a finely tuned instrument; when he sings country his voice softens and curls around the notes. When he lets fly and rocks out it's with an arresting edge.

It's hard to imagine another debut album ever eclipsing this one.

Daniels, Charlie

(born Wilmington, North Carolina, October 28 1936)
For someone who is not hesitant to admit that he's 'played every mudhole in this country' Charlie Daniels has learned his craft well and is now recognized as one of the premier masters of the guitar, mandolin and fiddle.

Daniels is a product of rural North Carolina and as a youngster he began to show exceptional musical talents. 'My family wasn't particularly musical,' he recalls, 'but for as long as I can remember music has held a fascination for me.' The mandolin came first, followed by the guitar and fiddle. By his fifteenth year he had mastered all three instruments. He and a few friends who were into music formed a small bluegrass band they called Misty Mountain Boys. Since the part of North Carolina he came from was dry they played high school dances, school proms and local events instead of the rowdy honky-tonks that would come later.

Like most aspiring musicians the necessity of earning a living made music a sideline. Daniels spent his night playing and his days in a creosote plant. A mark of his strong character emerged when management restructured and staff cuts were announced. Daniels asked that he be laid off instead of a black man who had a family to keep.

Turning to music, as a full-time career, he and his fellow band members hit the road. If an early touring map, for their band which they called the Rockets, was highlighted California, Oklahoma, Kansas, Florida and Texas plus most states north, south-east and west would have a pin in them.

It was during a stopover in Fort Worth, Texas, that Daniels crossed paths with Bob Johnston, a local record producer. Johnston liked the Daniels' brand of music and arranged a recording session for the band. The title of the single was 'Jaguar' and it was released on the Epic label in 1959. The band members liked the sound of jaguar so changed their name to the Jaguars.

Johnston and Daniels went their separate ways. Daniels hit the road again and Johnston ended up in Nashville where he quickly became a high-profile producer for Columbia Records.

Songwriting had long been one of Daniels' passions and he scored in 1963 when Elvis Presley recorded a song he wrote entitled 'It Hurts Me'.

Johnston had not forgotten his friend and, when he suggested to Daniels that he could do worse than come to Nashville and try his hand at songwriting and studio work, Daniels jumped at the chance.

For four years Daniels made a better-than-average living as a session player. He gained invaluable experience being exposed to various music styles and some of the top recording artists of the day such as Flatt and Scruggs, Pete Seeger and Leonard Cohen. A personal highlight was working with Bob Dylan, probably the most celebrated rock/folksinger of the times. They became personal and professional friends. Dylan was singularly impressed with Daniels' musical talents and invited him to come on tour as a member of his backup band. It was an experience Daniels looks back on with great pleasure.

The next step in Daniels' musical evolution was producing. He produced two Capitol solo albums for Jerry Corbett and Corbett was to return the favour by producing Daniels' debut album for Capitol.

Daniels looks back, with pride, to his involvement with the

annual Tennessee Jam he helped organize in the mid-1970s. It was a country rock festival that was held every April in Nashville. Epic brought out a two-record set of live recordings from the third and fourth Tennessee Jams and they are now collector's items.

The Charlie Daniels Band was organized in 1971 and until the early 1980s it was on the road over 250 days a year. It was an incredible, backbreaking, criss-crossing of North America for concert dates and one-night stands. The band won the Academy of Country Music award for Best Touring Group two years in a row, 1980 and 1981.

It seems that Daniels' musical progression was leading up to one major body of work that would thrust him, and his band, into the forefront of country music. It was an album titled *Million Mile Reflections*.

While the album ultimately became platinum it is not as well remembered as one song which became a runaway bestselling single 'The Devil Went Down to Georgia'. It's the story of how the devil went to Georgia and fiddled his way back to Hell. It's a classic and was the 1979 Song of the Year. The only adequate word to describe Daniels' fiddling is 'spectacular'. In the opinion of many it's the best that's ever been recorded.

A highlight of the 1980s Grammy Awards show was the Daniels Band and 'The Devil Went Down to Georgia'. It was a performance that was talked about for years to come. To no one's surprise the 1980 Entertainer of the Year award went to Daniels. It was also the year that he won Single of the Year for 'In America', a rebel call to the colours.

Daniels has a basic philosophy about life and performing and he has a clear perspective of what is paramount in life's quest for happiness and success. 'What sets a person off is their individuality,' he says. 'To me the most important thing is being yourself and doing things your way.'

★*Charlie Daniels Band Simple Man* (Epic EK 45316)

One look at the credits and it is not surprising to see Daniels listed for guitar, mandolin, banjo, fiddle and vocals. He's also credited as executive producer.

'What this World Needs is a Few More Rednecks' is a Daniels composition in collaboration with three long-time members of the band. Percussionist Jack Gavin is responsible for keeping the beat thumping, the excellent Joel 'Taz' DiGregorio, the keyboard player since the 1970s and Charlie Hayward, who plays a mean bass, is another band original. It's a song of statement as Daniels makes his case for respect, peace and satisfaction plus a little less talk and a little more action.

'Midnight Wind' is an excellent showcase for Daniels and his band. The instrumental intro and bridges conjure up images of a rolling wind. One almost hunches over for protection when Daniels launches into the chorus 'When the midnight moon is shining/When it's shining down the way/If he blew in on the Midnight Wind/ He may never pass this way again.'

The musical strength of all 10 songs is immediately apparent. Even when Daniels softens his voice on a song like 'Saturday Night Down South' there is an integrity to the lyrics, and his delivery, which makes the song stand out, is extraordinary.

★*Renegade* (Epic EK 46835-2)

One knows that something special is in store on the downbeat for 'Honky Tonk Life'. The bass, guitar, fiddle, percussion and piano are a perfect setup for Daniels as he rips into the lyrical story of 'Bubba and the boys at the uptown bar.'

'Layla' is an Eric Clapton/Jim Gordon composition which gives Daniels, and the band, full licence to let go. The infectious beat is full of surprises especially when Daniels shows his virtuosity on the fiddle breaks. The background vocals are exceptional.

Listen carefully when Daniels' introduces his friend 'Willie Jones' who was doing time when he was a guard. It's a great story and Daniels tells it so well with the aid of his swinging band.

Renegade confirms the Charlie Daniels Band as one of the best entertainment aggregations in country music. Everything is presented with panache and honesty.

'Let Freedom Ring' is an unabashed flag-waver. It's as up-to-date as Tienanmen Square which comes in for special mention. ''Cause the heavy hand of cruel oppression/Is much more than a man can bear/Let freedom ring.'

Diamond Rio

(formed from 1984–1991, current members – Marty Roe, Jimmy Olander, Gene Johnson, Dan Truman, Dana Williams, Brian Prout)

Mix the mandolin magic of Gene Johnson with the lead vocals and guitar of Marty Roe. Add a dash of Jimmy Orlander on lead guitar and banjo. Gently sauté the keyboard artistry of Dan Trueman with a pinch of Dana Williams on bass and vocals. Finally, stir in the drums of Brian Prout for full-body flavour. The result is a scintillating vocal group with six world-class musicians who hit the top of the country charts with 'Meet in the Middle' and made country history. Diamond Rio is the first group ever to take their debut release all the way to number one.

Another ingredient in the astounding success of the group is that each member brings a different influence to the band. This individuality that is as smooth a mix as Kentucky bourbon and water accounts for a contemporary, progressive sound which has caught the imagination of a legion of fans.

There is also a country music heritage to consider as well. Marty Roe was named after fabled country singer-songwriter MARTY ROBBINS and the first song he ever learned was MERLE HAGGARD's 'The Diamond Rio Fugitive'. He was three years old.

Jimmy Orlander was not musically backward as a child either. By the age of twelve he was teaching the banjo. Gene Johnston is a musical magician with his mandolin and few can match his artistry not only on the mandolin but the fiddle and acoustic guitar. Dan Truman is a classically trained pianist who toured internationally with the Young Ambassadors from Brigham Young University. His musical tastes, and talents, are eclectic and he adds a unique shading to the music of Diamond Rio. Brian Prout on the drums is spectacular to watch and his rock influence is instantly apparent. The native New Yorker has no problem engaging his wife, Nancy Given-Prout, in drum talk – Nancy is a drummer of repute for Wild Rose, the all-female country band. Rounding out the roster of musical excellence is Dana Williams who began playing bluegrass music at the tender age of twelve. When you are the nephew of performers Bobby and Sonny Osborne, bluegrass is in your blood.

Once again it was Arista's Tim DuBois – who is becoming

legendary for his uncanny ability to spot talent – who signed
Diamond Rio to a recording contract. DuBois saw the group
opening for George Jones and was immediately taken with their
avant-garde music and crowd-pleasing performing skills.

At the time the group was known as the Tennessee River Boys.
Diamond Rio came later. It's the name of a truck manufactured in
Pennsylvania and appealed to the group as being more contem-
porary and eye-catching than the Tennessee River Boys.

By mid-1993 they had just two albums to their credit, *Diamond
Rio* and *Close to the Edge*, plus runaway singles including 'Meet In
The Middle', 'Norma Jean Riley', 'Mirror Mirror', 'Mama Don't
Forget To Pray For Me' and 'Nowhere Bound'.

'I don't think we ever expected things to take off so fast,' said
Williams, 'even though that's what we've been working toward
for almost a decade now.'

All six members of the group know full well that the fulcrum
upon which their success and future balances is fan loyalty. They
were not hesitant in thanking their fans at the 1993 Academy of
Country Music Awards when they beat Alabama to win their
second consecutive Top Group award.

Prout put Diamond Rio's music in perspective: 'We're out there
picking, playing off each other, having fun and putting on a show
as well.'

★*Close To The Edge* (Arista 87822-18656-2)

'When,' as Jimmy Olander says, 'everybody's made an effort to
bring absolute quality to our writing, and the doors of Nashville's
greatest songwriters were thrown completely open to us this
time,' one just suspects that something special must be in store.
'Special' seems hardly adequate when describing the marriage of
musicianship and lyrics which makes this album a certified
country musical gem.

The instrumental brilliance that has become the hallmark of
this group is glaringly evident on 'Oh Me, Oh My, Sweet Baby'.
The arrangement conjures up images of Buck Owens and HANK
WILLIAMS JR.

'It Does Get Better Than This' gives the art of painting vocal
word-pictures new meaning. Best friends gather for a weekend of
fishing and are enjoying the sunset, clear blue lake, tall tales, ice-

cold beer and agree that this must be the living end until they are told to hold on because it gets better than this: 'If you were me/ You couldn't disagree/'Cause I've held her, oh so tight/She's kept me up all night/I've tasted her kisses sweet as wine/Sure, this is a real good time/But pardon me boys/It does get better than this.'

'Close To The Edge' is not only the title song it's the eleventh one on this album and closes out a genuine stellar list of songs.

It is a hard-driving showcase for what the band does to perfection. The uptempo love song is blessed with rich harmonies and the bluegrass overtone adds a patina to the musical canvas.

If one could, with a economy of words, define the bottom line reason for the surging success of Diamond Rio it would have to be an astonishing mix of influences, world-class arrangements, an uncanny gift for choosing hit songs and the dazzling diversity of musicianship that each member brings to the group.

Dunn, Holly

(born San Antonio, Texas, August 22 1957)

For anybody who doesn't know what 'P.K.' means, they could find out by asking Holly Dunn. She certainly knows, because she is a 'P.K.' – preacher's kid – herself. Her father is a Church of Christ minister in San Antonio, Texas, which is about as far away from Nashville, and country music, as one could get.

The home, church, environment she left to attend Abilene Christian University, to study advertising, still has a profound influence in the way she delivers a song. At times there is a distinct gospel quality to her voice. One can almost hear the hand clapping as the gospel beat comes through on a number of her songs.

In 1978 gospel singer Christy Lane recorded 'Out of Sight, Not Out of Mind', which Holly wrote. Years later, in Nashville, she would be the composer of a top-10 hit for Louise Mandrell 'I'm Not Through Loving You Yet'. A number of other established artists such as Sylvia, Terri Gibbs and the Whites have also recorded her songs.

Songwriting is certainly in the genes of the Dunn family. Brother Chris Waters Dunn, who is a songwriter of no mean reputation, preceded Holly to Nashville and made a name for himself. In 1980 he introduced her to Charlie Monk, of CBS

Songs. Monk offered her a clerical job in addition to being a staff songwriter.

'It was a great place to go to school and learn the business,' recalls Holly.

Producer Tommy West was the next one to push Holly further along the road to stardom. In 1984 West formed a new label, MTM Records, and Holly was one of the first persons offered a contract.

By 1986 she had recorded her debut album, *Holly Dunn*, and out of it came a hit single 'Daddy's Hands', which she wrote. That song has gone on to become a country standard.

1987 was Holly Dunn's year – 2 Grammy nominations for Best Country Song ('Daddy's Hands') and for Best Country Vocal Performance. She also won the Country Music Association's Horizon Award, which is highly prized, and was voted the Academy of Country Music's Top New Female Artist.

Holly is a woman of singular talent and ambition. In addition to being a consummate performer she has made her mark as musician, songwriter, bandleader, businesswoman and co-producer of her albums.

'I feel like I'm just hitting my stride,' she said in a recent interview. 'I think the music that I will be doing from now on will be the most significant music that I have ever done.'

★*Getting It Dunn* (Warner Bros. 9 26949-2)

This is the perky-voiced Holly Dunn's seventh album and without question her best one to date. Though some think that Dunn lays on the sobby emotional bit a tad too much it is just right for some of this material.

'A Simple I Love You', by Karen Brooks and Randy Sharp, demands all the emotion Dunn can muster, and muster it she does in grand style. It is a beautiful number.

Holly's brother Chris Waters Dunn co-produced the album with her and also co-wrote four of the numbers, 'As Long As You Belong To Me', 'Let Go', 'I've Heard It All' and the one that really catches one's ear 'You Can Have Him'.

Loretta Lynn had an interesting counterpoint in 'You Ain't Woman Enough'. She tells her rival to keep her hands off her man.

One thing to consider: Loretta released her song in 1970s; Holly released hers in the 1990s.

Times have changed.

Edwards, Don

(born Boontown, New Jersey, March 20 1939)

When Don Edwards says that 'something has to be good if it lasts that long,' he's referring to authentic western music. It's older than country music and has its roots in the dust-choking cattle drives of the 1870s when bone-weary, saddle-sore cowboys herded thousands of longhorns up the Chisum Trail from Texas to the Kansas railheads. Their only entertainment on the drive would be around the campfire when someone would start picking on a guitar in time with a mournful harmonica. The songs would be about the lonesome prairie, slow plodding cattle or the dark-eyed dancer they left behind in a Mexican cantina. Before they returned to Texas they'd blow off steam, and trail dust, in the rip-roaring cattle towns of Abilene and Dodge City.

Western music is also the vehicle for perpetuating the truths, and myths, of gunslingers like Billy The Kid and John Ringo. The exploits of lawmen, in the mould of Wyatt Earp and Pat Garrett, and the shootouts of fearless gunfighters like Doc Holliday and John Wesley Hardin are enshrined in song.

Lilly Langtree was a beauty who became the fantasy of Judge Roy Bean, the hanging judge, who named Langtree, Texas, in her honour. She owes much of her on-going fame to western lore and song to say nothing of the love-besotted judge.

Edwards comes by his entertainment talents naturally. His father was a vaudeville magician and his boyhood heros were Gene Autry and Tom Mix.

'Tom Mix was a sure 'nuff cowboy,' says Edwards. 'I don't go in much for glitter and glitz.'

By the age of ten Edwards had taught himself to play the guitar in his own unique style, combining flat-picking and fingerpicking to frame concurrently the melody and the chords of a song.

In his early years Edwards followed the rodeo circuit and worked ranches in Texas and New Mexico before deciding that a musical career would have a more promising future with less punishment to the body.

For a while he worked the Six Flags Over Texas theme park as an actor/singer/stuntman. It was a discouraging time and more than once he seriously considered giving up show business. His first love was western music and, at times, it was financially difficult to be true to its roots and not drift into the security of country music.

Settling in Fort Worth, Texas, he became part owner of the White Elephant Saloon. It was a most successful operation and was named, by *Esquire* magazine, one of America's 100 best bars.

Singing, and a devotion to western music, began to pay off for Edwards. He was singled out as one of the finest pure cowboy singers of the day. He also had the distinction of having two of his albums included in the Folklore Archives of the Library of Congress. Edwards is also the recipient of the Wrangler Award for Outstanding Traditional Western Music.

★*Songs of the Trail* (Warner Western 9 26933-2)

Even though Eddy Arnold has a stranglehold on Tex Owen's 1934 classic 'Cattle Call' others have given it a try, including Edwards. He comes closest to matching Arnold in both voice and style and his yodelling bridge is pleasant to the ear.

According to Edwards, 'The Cowboy's Song' is his favourite contemporary, pure cowboy song and he does it justice. It was written by Roy Robinson, a genuine Texas cowboy. The backup is a gentle mix of guitar and fiddle.

Any MARTY ROBBINS fan would be quick to point out that his love for the old west and days of the gunfighter will probably never be matched. Edwards echoes those sentiments and 'The Master's Call', which Robbins wrote, is a homage to the singer who inspired him deeply.

'Springtime in the Rockies' was a hit for Gene Autry. It was also a standard for Wilf Carter (Montana Slim). Edwards' version neither adds nor takes anything away from the earlier recordings. Edwards' pleasant voice is just right for the mournful tale of a lonely lover who is pining for his 'sweetheart of the mountains' and promises to return 'when it's springtime in the Rockies'. The tinkling of an old upright piano adds to the mood.

This CD is just the ticket for western music fans.

Foster, Radney

(born Del Rio, Texas, July 20 1959)

When Radney Foster told his parents that he wanted to take a year off from college and try his luck as a singer/songwriter in Nashville they were horrified.

'You have to understand my parents,' explained Foster. 'My father was born in seersucker. He's a lawyer in a small town and so was his father and his father's father. I was the first boy to want to move away from home after college.'

Home for Foster was in Del Rio, Texas, which bills itself as 'Queen City of the Rio Grande'. Nestled on the western edge of Texas hill country it's about five miles from the Rio Grande River and the Mexican border. Next to Foster its most famous citizen was Judge Roy Bean, the hanging judge, who is buried on the grounds of the Whitehead Memorial Museum. Del Rio is where the rolling green land flattens to a horizon of sagebrush and semi-arid grass. Some say it looks like a place where God ran out of ideas.

After numerous, and at times energetic, discussion Foster was given grudging permission to try his luck in Nashville but with conditions: 'If I didn't have a publishing or record deal within a year I agreed to go back to college and finish,' says Foster.

Lack of confidence is not one of Foster's failings: 'I was twenty years old, full of fire and too much energy,' he said. 'I thought I was gonna be the next Elvis by the time I was twenty-one.' However Foster's universe didn't unfold the way he had planned.

He returned to college, finished his education, and married his college sweetheart Mary Springs. He also moved back to Nashville for another assault on country music.

By 1985 his songwriting career was beginning to take off and show definite promise, especially once he started writing with the likes of Bill Lloyd and HOLLY DUNN. 'Since I Found You' was a Foster/Lloyd collaboration and it became the Sweethearts of the Rodeo's first top-ten hit.

Writing with Holly Dunn was a fortuitous career move. They clicked and turned out 'Love Someone Like Me'. It became Dunn's first number one single.

In a town like Nashville a good songwriting demo can become gold if it gets in the right hands. Foster and Lloyd were no slouches in making demos and shotgunning them to anyone who would listen.

It was a demo that led to their signing a record deal and recording 'Crazy Over You'. It was the first debut single to make it to number one in the music trade magazine *Radio & Records*.

Foster & Lloyd became a hit-making duo. Before their amicable 1990 split they recorded three Foster & Lloyd albums for RCA. They also scored with a number of singles including 'What Do You Want From Me This Time', 'Fair Shake' and 'Texas in 1880'.

Tim DuBois, of Arista Records, once managed Foster & Lloyd and had come to the conclusion that Foster showed more promise as a solo artist than as part of a duo. In a typically candid DuBois analysis of the Foster & Lloyd duo, he said, 'There were definite positives in their press following, but there were a few negatives with radio and a few at retail, because of their less-than-sterling sales performances. They were a little ahead of their time for the mid to late 1980s.'

It didn't take DuBois long to sign Foster once he'd split with Lloyd. He also realized that if Foster was going to reach his potential he needed motivation. He takes full credit for, as he says, 'holding [Foster's] feet to the fire and making him dig deeper than ever before as a writer.'

It paid off and Foster's debut album *Del Rio, Texas 1959* doubled original expectations with initial shipments of nearly 100,000 units. The title is Foster's birthplace and date of birth.

The hard charging 'Nobody Wins' became a hit single from the album and made the critics sit up and take notice.

Foster has no illusions about who he is, where he came from or what influences his music. 'I'm a southern kid from a small town in west Texas who grew up liking country and rock records. They are what I've always loved and they still have a huge influence on what I do today.'

Del Rio, Texas 1959 (Arista 18713 2)

Foster describes the album in its promotional material. 'It's about learning how to two-step at the 4-H barns in Del Rio. It has to do with growing up in a little tiny town and cruising the Sonic on Saturday nights, and with all of the records that accompanied that – the Waylon Jennings, the old Beatles, the Buddy Holly and Rodney Crowell and Emmylou Harris – there was life-changing stuff for me in there.'

The wide influences are still evident in *Del Rio, Texas 1959* and the edges are etched with a decidedly roots-country flair.

'Just Call Me Lonesome' is a classic country shuffle that evokes memories of Buck Owens and Ray Price. Foster has the Bakersfield sound down-pat. The backup is lively. The bass and steel guitar are ably pushed by a solid drum beat and tinkling piano.

MARY-CHAPIN CARPENTER adds her special talents to some fine harmony vocals with Foster for the hard-driving 'Nobody Wins'.

'A Fine Line' is interesting if only for the musical story that Foster weaves. It's the tale of a man on the side of the highway. He's in a real fix as he tries to decide how he's going to tell his wife and children that his girlfriend is pregnant.

An impressive debut album.

Fox, George

(born Cochrane, Alberta, circa 1960)

If Canada was the centre of the music country world and not Nashville, George Fox would be a world superstar because of his Canadian musical accomplishments.

In a relatively short, five-year career this country singer has four albums to his credit (two certified gold), every country music award a singer can win in Canada, two CBC (Canadian Broadcasting Corportion) television specials, three consecutive stints as host of the Canadian Country Music Awards show, three Juno awards, nine RPM/Big Country prizes and a career that has taken him from being a totally unknown rancher, on the eastern slopes of the Rocky Mountains, to one of Canada's most popular and recognizable entertainers. Quite an accomplishment for anyone, let alone a Canadian.

To the surprise of many Canadians, who unconsciously apologize for being Canadian, Fox found that songwriters and producers in Nashville like to hear and talk about Canada and there were no shrugs or raised eyebrows when he recorded his fourth album for Warner Music (Canada) in the studios of Woodland Digital in Nashville.

Not only did this Canadian country singer record in Nashville, he included two songs on the ten-song album that were as Canadian as maple syrup and the RCMP. On 'Daughter of the Rockies' and 'Clearly Canadian' Fox sings about Hudson Bay and the 401, that magnificent highway which runs some 900 kilo-metres between Windsor, Ontario and Montreal, Quebec.

Mustang Heart is a 180-degree musical turnabout for Fox from his third album *Spice Of Life*. On that one he clearly side-stepped the question of nationality.

Fox traces his nationalistic resurgence to the time he spent in Nashville. 'A lot of Canadian artists think we have to sing about taking the train down to Nashville or Texas,' he explained. 'When we played the "Mustang Heart" demo for Roger Murrah, the man who wrote "Don't Rock The Jukebox", he thought "Daughter of the Rockies" was the best thing on it. He just felt the sentiment of the song.'

Fox laughs when he thinks about the contest the CBC Morningside radio show held. 'They used "as American as apple pie" as an example and they asked the listeners to complete, "as Canadian as . . ." The winning submission was typically Canadian. It was "as Canadian as possible under the circumstances."'

Fox says he can identify with that.

★*Mustang Heart* (Warner Music Canada CD 90933)

One doesn't have to be Canadian to enjoy Fox's engaging singing style. While the session players are not spectacular, they are adequate and don't detract from Fox's rich voice.

A plus factor for this album is that it was produced by noted songwriter Bob Gaudio whose name is on page one of the song book *100 Greatest Rock 'n' Roll Hits of all Time* with 'Big Girls Don't Cry'. Gaudio's credits, which are impressive, include working with Neil Diamond and Frankie Valli.

Gaudio co-wrote eight of the ten songs with Fox and steered

him in the songwriting direction he had been seeking for years. Fox had stated that working with Gaudio was 'like a dream come true'.

'Daughter of the Rockies' is the other 'Canadian' contribution and it is probably the strongest song on the CD. Fox is never better in his delivery and the lyrics are above average. 'Daughter of the rockies/Just when I thought you were mine/Caught you dancing with the moon/Enchanting every cowboy's mind.'

Try listening to this song without having images of the chinooks, the Calgary Stampede and springtime in the rockies jump into your mind.

Gill, Vince

(born Norman, Oklahoma, April 12 1957)

When you combine a pure tenor voice with passionate songwriting and inspired musicianship you come up with a Vince Gill. It's been said that Gill was one of the best kept secrets in Nashville. All the forecasts of impending stardom, when he was earning a reputation as one of the best session backup singers and guitar players in Nashville, took a while to come true.

It wasn't until 1990, when he released a single called 'When I Call Your Name,' that his name skyrocketed to the top of the charts.

Gill was the only child of an Oklahoma City appellate judge who was an accomplished banjo and guitar player. He is eternally grateful to his father for kindling his interest in music at an early age. The first instrument Gill remembers playing, as a young boy, was his dad's banjo. Music became a passion and he soon had a thirst that couldn't be quenched. By the time he was in high school he was playing in a local band called Mountain Smoke. He cut his teeth on bluegrass.

Like most successful and enduring country stars he had, as they say in the business, 'paid his dues', long before making it big. His musical talents were being steadily honed as he performed in a number of diverse bands and combos.

In 1975 he and his friend RICKY SKAGGS played together in a band called Doone Creek. Always looking ahead for ways to broaden his musical horizons Gill next auditioned for lead singer with the popular country-rock group Pure Prairie League. He won the audition.

A triple-threat member of any group is a musical treasure. There was no dispute about Gill's vocal abilities. He could also play a mean guitar and banjo and the songs that he wrote were so good that they were recorded by the group and included in the act.

He was also one of the major reasons why the group had two top-ten hits 'Still Here in My Heart' and 'Let Me Love You Tonight'. Gill also wrote five songs which were included in the 1980 Pure Prairie League album *Can't Hold Back*.

The next stop on Gill's professional odyssey was Rodney Crowell's Cherry Bombs which made ever-increasing circles with its innovative and exhilarating music. Gill looks back on those days with great fondness as his most musically exciting time. 'I was playing with musicians I had literally idolized for years,' he recalled in an interview. 'In addition to Rodney Crowell there were Emory Gordy Jr, Albert Lee and Larrie Londin.'

Moving to Cherry Bombs was a wise decision. It was there that he met, and became friends with, Terry Brown. Brown was a keyboard player with the group before he became an executive with RCA. Brown still kept close contact with his musical friends and it didn't take him long to be impressed by Gill's unique singing style and skilled guitar playing.

Brown was astute enough to see great potential in Gill as a recording artist and in 1984 he offered him a contract.

Gill not only signed the contract, he moved to Nashville. Within a short space of time he had recorded and released *Turn Me Loose*, a six-cut mini-album. As a result of the popularity of the title song 'Turn Me Loose' and 'Victim of Life's Circumstances', Gill was voted top new male artist by the Academy of Country Music. A steady stream of hits, from 'Everybody's Sweetheart' to a sparkling duet with ROSANNE CASH 'If It Weren't for Him', however, did not grab Gill a broad enough fan base for him to hang on to his contract and RCA dropped him.

RCA not only dropped Gill it lost Terry Brown who moved to MCA Records. The early faith that Brown had in Gill's potential stardom was not shaken and he signed him to a MCA contract. He also became his producer. It was the best professional move both men ever made.

Through Brown's prodding, and encouragement, Gill dropped all musical shackles and allowed his enormous talent full rein.

The critics, disc jockeys, and fans were more than enthusistic about what they heard on *When I Call Your Name*. The lineup of songs bore the imprint of Brown's recording acumen. There was something to please everyone from rodeo songs to dance hall swing to contemporary pop. It was a masterful mix. The leadoff song was 'Never Alone' which Gill wrote with Rosanne Cash. It became a top-twenty hit.

'Oklahoma Swing' did even better. REBA McENTIRE joined him on the dazzling country swinger. It didn't take long for it to reach the top ten. Gill and McEntire were nominated for best duet by the Academy of Country Music.

Sharing the microphone has paid off handsomely for Gill. PATTY LOVELESS joined him for some electrifying vocal harmony on 'When I Call Your Name'.

Gill started the 1990s off with a bang. He won a Grammy Award for Best Male Country Vocal Performance and the CMA gave 'When I Call Your Name' Single of the Year honours. Few will forget Gill and Loveless singing their hit song on the stage of the Grand Ole Opry on the CMA Awards telecast.

There appears to be no stopping Vince Gill. *Pocket Full of Gold* took off like an arrow out of the bow.

The songs were a more clearly defined country style of music for Gill. He is nothing short of brilliant on every cut. The album went platinum and spawned four singles that became big hits including the number one song 'Take Your Memory With You'.

Next to his wife Janis, daughter Jennifer and his music, Gill's passion is golf. As to be expected, this consummate country performer, who at one time seriously thought about becoming a professional golfer, lives adjacent to a golf course in Nashville. There are few, if any in country music, who can match Gill on the golf course. There are just as few who can match him in a recording studio.

1993 started out where 1992 left off, on a high note. Gill shut out BILLY RAY CYRUS and 'Achy Breaky Heart' at the Grammy Awards, winning Best Country Male Vocalist and Best Country Song 'I Still Believe In You'.

'I Still Believe In You' grabbed the voters' attention for the 1993 Academy of Country Music Awards. Gill won the top song award plus Top Male Vocalist honours. It was Gill's first award since 1985 when he was named Top New Vocalist.

★*Pocket Full of Gold* (MCA MCAD-10140)

Gill's songs, particularly those which ooze sadness, or ride the cutting edge of illicit or sinful behaviour, are a total break with the Nashville tradition. Unlike many top artists who have had their share of divorces or drug problems the songs do not mirror Gill's personal, stable, conservative lifestyle.

'When people listen to my songs they don't want to hear about me,' explains Gill. 'They want to hear lyrics that pertain to how they feel and what goes on in their life.'

'Look At Us' is an excellent case in point. John Hughey's steel guitar establishes a reflective mood before Gill gently jumps right in with 'After all these years/Look at us/After all we've been through/Look at us/Still leaning on each other.' He co-wrote the song with Max D. Barnes.

'Take Your Memory With You' is a story of disquieting love. Even though it paints a musical picture of a love lost it is upbeat and certainly could offer strength to the heartbroken.

Gill's musical strength is in being able to change the message and mood without losing or annoying his listeners. He demands rapt attention when he sings because he touches the heart.

Gosdin, Vern

(born Woodland, Alabama, August 5 1934)

It took forty years but Vern Gosdin remembers his debut on the Grand Ole Opry in 1977 as if it were yesterday. It was a night of supreme satisfaction and an even bigger night of memories. The years and struggles flooded back like a wave as he stood centrestage and heard the applause echoing in the old Ryman Auditorium.

Gosdin grew up on a backwoods farm in Alabama. Every Saturday night he would listen to the Opry on a broken-down radio that was barely operable. The signal was so weak that he had to hold his ear close to the speaker but it was strong enough to make him dream of being on the Opry some day and hearing the audience applaud for him. He knew most of the Opry stars and their songs by heart. By the time he was eight his musical heros were the Louvin Brothers. 'I liked their harmonies and to this day they have influenced my music,' he once said in an interview.

Before he was into his teens Gosdin and his two brothers were doing a better than average imitation of the Louvins when they sang in church and soon they became regulars on the *Gosdin Family Gospel Show* on WVOK Radio in Birmingham, Alabama.

By the mid-1950s Gosdin was in Chicago managing a country music nightclub called D&G Tap. Most of his free time was spent singing and honing his bluegrass musical talents.

Chicago wasn't exactly a hotbed of bluegrass or country music and next to Nashville, California held a major attraction. Gosdin's brother Rex was part of a bluegrass band called the 'Golden State Boys' and he convinced Vern that his musical future lay in Bakersfield, offering him a job with the band.

Early in the 1960s Gosdin made another career change when he and his brother joined the Hillmen. It was a major career step upwards as the band was led by Chris Hillman, a skilled bluegrass musician. Hillman is best remembered as a founding member of one of the best pop-rock bands in the business, the Byrds.

In addition to expanding his musical horizons Gosdin was busily writing songs. 'Someone To Turn To' was the first Gosdin song to gain widespread recognition: Hillman and Clarence White recorded it for the soundtrack of the cult movie *Easy Rider*.

The ultimate goal of any performer is to get a recording contract. Gosdin was more fortunate than most because he signed with a succession of labels, including Liberty, Capitol, Era and Bakersfield International, but all with limited success. Only one single made any ripples: 'Hangin' On' for the Bakersfield label which rose to a respectable 18 in the charts before disappearing from view.

The late 1960s and early 1970s were a discouraging time and Gosdin began to have serious doubts about ever making a decent living as a singer and songwriter. Finally, giving in to the pressures, he and his brother dissolved their musical partnership and he moved back to Atlanta determined to settle down with his wife and begin raising a family.

Music became secondary to the thriving glass business he opened in Atlanta, and for ten long years Gosdin stayed true to his decision to forget about a career in music. With the exception of a few local performing dates, he became the quintessential American husband, father and nose-to-the-grindstone businessman.

It was 1976 when an old friend from the California days, producer Gary Paxton, called. He had run into Rex Gosdin and told him he'd like to bring out 'Hangin' On' as a single and was looking for someone to record it. Rex suggested his brother.

Gosdin was dubious and not quite comfortable with the idea of revving up his musical career. However, the magnet that was drawing him was strong and unrelenting: he cut a recording deal with Elektra Records and went into the studio.

His comeback single was not, however, 'Hangin' On' – instead he sang harmony with Emmylou Harris on 'Yesterday's Gone'. It made it to the top twenty. 'Hangin' On' came next, with equal success.

Though he was on the threshold of stardom Gosdin refused to hit the road and tour. The security of Atlanta and his growing business was too comfortable to walk away from.

June 1977 was a landmark month and year. *Till the End*, Gosdin's debut album, was released and it took off in spectacular form. Before long it was in the country top five.

By the spring of 1978 'Never My Love' was released by Elektra, and Gosdin knew it was time to start touring, so he reunited with his brother Rex for a series of concert appearances. The good times were back.

The hits kept coming. By the early 1980s the Gosdin Brothers were riding a crest of fan popularity and musical respect which they had only dreamed of during the struggling years. Then tragedy struck when Rex died. Gosdin always regrets that his brother didn't live long enough to savour the success that came after fifteen years of hard work and disappointments.

A blending of bluegrass, gospel and country sounds has given Vern Gosdin one of the most admired voices in country music. He has earned, and deserves, the nickname 'The Voice'.

The 1980s and early 1990s have been rewarding years. A string of gospel and country releases, which are constant bestsellers, have made him a near cult figure in the eyes of his fans. However the rarefied level of stardom that artists such as GEORGE JONES and

VINCE GILL have risen to for some reason still continues to elude Gosdin.

★*10 Years of Greatest Hits* (Columbia CK 45409)

'If You're Gonna Do Me Wrong (Do It Right)' is a slow, deftly crafted song. Gosdin comes on solo and then is joined by backup singers. There is a breathless quality to some of his phrasing that is appealing – he can grab a note and hang on to it à la George Jones.

The acoustic guitar work on all eleven songs is excellent and that's not taking anything away from the other musicians on backup. Every instrument, and voice, blends to create a musical tapestry.

Gosdin's songwriting skills shine on the six songs that he co-wrote. He has a remarkable ability to come up with the right word pictures to match the melancholy vein that runs through much of his work. One can readily sense the deep-felt emotions in every line.

'Today My World Slipped Away' is a must for anyone who has gone through a divorce as Gosdin weaves a touching story of going to the divorce court. 'My friends say I'll make it alright/I'll recover and start a new life/But that will be so hard to do/'Cause livin' ain't worth livin' in without you.'

The strength of Gosdin's singing is in his unique gentle way with a song. He makes the listener feel every hurt, every disappointment and every shattered love as few other singers can.

Haggard, Merle

(born Bakersfield, California, April 6 1937)
Being born in a converted boxcar, to Oklahoma dust-bowl parents, and doing time in San Quentin Prison before your twenty-first birthday is not what one would call an auspicious beginning for a country music 'icon'. Somehow Haggard was able to snatch a shattered life from the ashes of despair and, through raw talent, determination, dedication and a smattering of luck, rose up through the ranks of country singers to the top of his profession.

Haggard's early years read like a chapter out of a gritty novel about heartache, deprivation and plain stupidity. His parents migrated from Oklahoma during the Great Depression, hoping to find work and some semblance of respectability in California. They settled in Bakersfield and lived in a converted boxcar.

Haggard's father was one of the lucky ones, as he managed to get a menial job on the Santa Fe Railroad. His mother milked cows to bring in a few extra dollars but had to stop to give birth to a son they named Merle.

In later years much of Haggard's appeal was in his rugged individualism and uncompromising stance in the face of convention and life. Those characteristics were ingrained during the early years of survival.

Poverty, rejection and the death of his father, when he was nine, pushed the young Haggard to the heights of rebellion that he shudders to think about now. By the time he was fourteen he had run away from home, surviving by his wits and cunning. Until he was finally arrested and convicted of burglary, in 1957, there was a litany of odd jobs, incessant wandering and petty crimes.

In retrospect the best thing that happened to him was being sentenced to six months to fifteen years in California's notorious San Quentin Prison. Haggard became a model prisoner: he worked in the textile mill, improved his education, worked on his music, which had become a passion, and played in the warden's band. The turnaround in attitude, and desire for rehabilitation, impressed the officials. In 1960 he was granted parole after two years and nine months behind bars.

Years later, the then California Governor, Ronald Reagan, granted him a full pardon.

Haggard returned home to Bakersfield and sought work as a musician. In prison he had become a respectable guitar player and was improving by the day. Before long he was playing in bars and nightclubs in the Bakersfield area and building a fan following. He was also earning good money as a studio session player, but Haggard was not satisfied to just be a session player for recording artists, even though he was thankful for the work and creative experience. He desperately wanted to record and he was soon to get his chance.

In 1964 he met a brilliant vocalist, Bonnie Owens, the estranged wife of country singer Buck Owens. Haggard and Owens clicked professionally and began recording for Tally Records. While they didn't exactly set country music on its ear they had moderate success with a single 'Just Between the Two of Us'. It was sufficiently impressive for Capitol Records to take notice and sign them both to a recording contract.

1965 was a banner year for Haggard. He had a contract with a major label, he had formed his own band, the Strangers, and had had his first breakthrough single. Bill Anderson recorded his song 'From Now On All My Friends Are Gonna Be Strangers' and made it a top-ten hit. To top off a memorable twelve months, he married Bonnie Owens, who was not only his singing partner but his co-writing partner as well.

Within two years Haggard's name was topping the charts with a number of hits. He had become a major new star with an exploding fan following. A single, 'I'm Gonna Break Every Heart I Can', an album, *Swingin' Doors*, and an LP with Bonnie, *Just Between the Two of Us*, enhanced his burgeoning reputation as a shaker and mover in country music.

Industry recognition also was heaped upon him and Bonnie during that creative period: Best Vocal Group from the Academy of Country and Western Music and Most Promising Male Vocalist for 1965.

Haggard and Bonnie also repeated Best Vocal Group again in 1966 and 1967 for an impressive three wins in a row.

Whenever a list of Haggard's best songs is compiled the 1970 Song of the Year 'Okie From Muskogee' is in the top three. It is a stirring patriotic song that was just perfect for Americans who were growing tired of the anti-Vietnam war, flag-burning protests. With no apology, and great pride in his voice, Haggard vocally extols the virtues of old-time America and turns a thumbs down on pot-smokers and hippies.

Haggard continued to catch the imagination and respect of country music fans. They showed their appreciation and joy when the Country Music Association named him 1970's Top Male Vocalist and Entertainer of the Year.

Unlike some of his contemporaries, who grabbed at television's gold ring by fronting their own show, Haggard preferred to keep on the road and in close personal contact with his fans. 'We do concerts. That's the way I support my band,' he explained in an interview. 'I have to have a good band to make good records. If I sell out, so to speak, on television, people won't have any reason to come to my concerts.'

Haggard's songwriting talents have never been in question and 'Ramblin' Fever', which he released in 1977, only confirmed that he is as deft at writing a winning country song as he is at singing one.

As it so often happens when one enjoys great success in one area, turmoil surfaces in another. Haggard's marriage was in tatters and even though he and Bonnie continued to perform together they headed to the divorce court. Said Haggard, 'We have an obligation to our fans to appear together. You don't go out on a street corner and find a Bonnie Owens.'

Another singer and songwriter, Leona Williams, came into Haggard's life in the mid-1970s to fill the void that Bonnie's ultimate departure left. Together they wrote and recorded 'The Bull and the Bear' and they got married. It was a marriage that was not to fare any better than the previous two (his first having been a teenage marriage).

Haggard expanded his creative talents to acting and received fine reviews for a number of appearances in NBC's 1979 TV adaptation of James Michener's *Centennial*.

Professionally, the 1980s started off where the 1970s had ended, with a continuation of hits. 'The Way I Am' was a 1980 chart-topping single, followed by 'Bar Room Buddies', a duet with film star Clint Eastwood.

MCA had a winner in 'Leonard', which Haggard wrote in tribute to songwriter Leonard Sipes (real name Tommy Collins). Both were kindred spirits and had shared many difficult days in years gone by. It proved to be one of 1981's bestselling singles.

'I Can't Hold Myself In Line' in 1981 was a duet with 'hell-raiser' Johnny Paycheck – it paid off in impressive sales. (Paycheck is notorious for shooting a man in a bar room brawl and getting himself a nine-and-a-half-year prison sentence in 1985.)

Haggard is still performing and bringing pleasure to his fans. Though a new breed of 'hot country' singers have pushed artists of Haggard's calibre out of the limelight, no one will ever argue that his legacy will be hard to eclipse.

★*Merle Haggard's Greatest Hits* (MCA MCABD-5386)

If one looks closely on the back page of the four-page CD insert, one will read the following disclaimer:

'This compact disc contains program transferred from analog tape and therefore may contain some tape hiss and other anomalies that exist with analog recordings.'

Even listening closely to this CD (circa 1992), on an above average CD player, tape hiss or other anomalies are difficult, if not impossible, to hear. There's nothing distracting on this CD.

The ten songs which include six Haggard original compositions from 'I Think I'll Just Stay Here and Drink' to 'Red Bandanna' and 'Ramblin' Fever' are a splendid cross-section of the Haggard skill with a song, both as writer and performer.

Haggard can add one further qualification to his contention that 'one must have a good band to make good records'. One must also have a good band to get the audience clapping in appreciation for a well rounded show.

Haggard's band, the Strangers, is one of the best in the business and he's not hesitant in stepping out of the spotlight to allow the individual musicians a few moments of glory. The ovation at the end of 'Rainbow Stew' is as much in appreciation for the sparkling backup and musical bridges as it is for Haggard himself.

Jackson, Alan

(born Newnan, Georgia, October 17 1958)
Without the female fans country music would not be the entertainment force it has become in the 1990s. And without the 'country hunks' or 'the hats' like Alan Jackson, country music would not have the female fans. It's the sexy, charismatic singers who keep bringing the fans – both male and female – into the concerts and, more importantly, into the record stores.

No male performer has personified the handsome, talented, drive-the-women-mad country singer better than Alan Jackson. Though it would be romantic to think that Jackson and country music were a marriage made in heaven, the truth of the matter is that like most aspiring country singers Jackson came up the hard way. Prior to 1985, when he stormed the battlements of Music

City, he was a jack-of-all trades and, probably, master of none: he waited on tables; he sold shoes and he drove a forklift in a K-Mart store.

Being a country music star was not paramount in Jackson's mind when he was growing up in Newnan, Georgia, the youngest of five. His parents, who were loving and fondly remembered by Jackson and his four sisters, had to struggle to make ends meet. 'My father was a mechanic for the Ford Motor Company,' recalls Jackson. 'There was never enough money to provide much more than the basics.'

Jackson was into his teens before he began singing duets with a friend. A small band was formed and weekend dates kept them busy. He was well into his twenties when the music bug finally bit and he decided that he wanted to become a full-time country singer.

To the disappointment of many female fans, who openly boast about their Alan Jackson fantasies, he is a happily married man and father, and has been for a number of years. If it hadn't been for his wife Denise, he still might be wheeling his forklift around warehouse aisles. Through a fortunate happenstance Denise, who was a flight attendant, was in the Atlanta airport the same day as country star Glen Campbell. Campbell was standing at a carousel waiting for his luggage. Denise introduced herself, told Campbell that her husband was about to take the plunge and move to Nashville, and asked for his advice. Campbell did more than give her polite advice, he gave her the name of his Nashville publishing company, and his business card, and invited Jackson to drop by once they had settled in Nashville.

Getting a job to pay for basic living was number-one on Jackson's priority list and he felt fortunate to get one in the mail room at *The Nashville Network*. He also met and became friends with RANDY TRAVIS who was then paying the bills by working as a short-order cook at the Nashville Palace across the street from Opryland. Travis' success came before Jackson's and, with a slight touch of envy, Jackson began to wonder if it would ever happen to him.

Determined to justify the faith his wife had placed in him, he began playing at night in Nashville hotels wherever he could get a date. He also concentrated on his songwriting. And it was the songwriting that paid off before the performing. Glenn Campbell's publishing company offered Jackson a job as a staff songwriter for the princely sum of $100-a-week. Jackson quit the mail room at TNN and grabbed the opportunity.

He worked there only a matter of weeks before he formed a band and decided that the best way to get attention was by touring. Days and nights on the road, plus a backbreaking workload of five sets a night five nights a week, in honky-tonks and clubs, both large and small, was a physical killer.

But hard as he worked, nothing of any career importance materialized until Australian Barry Coburn became his manager. Coburn saw star quality in Jackson, and his impressive songwriting abilities were a plus factor.

It was Arista Records which proved to be Jackson's window of opportunity. The newly formed country division, which was headed by Tim Dubois, needed fresh talent to record and promote. Dubois found it in Jackson and signed him to a recording contract in September 1989.

His first single, 'Blue Blooded Woman', was released in October and made a respectable impression on country music fans. The obligatory video put a face to the singer: Jackson's blond, blue-eyed good looks, and pleasant baritone voice, took country music by storm and the women went wild.

Jackson's debut album *Here in the Real World* was released on April 6 1990. It quickly climbed to number four on *Billboard*'s country chart. Within six months it was gold and, in less than a year following release, it was certified platinum. It was to remain in the top-ten for twelve months. Alan Jackson had arrived.

Jackson is bemused when, at his concerts, women throw undergarments and hotel keys at him. Some even rush on stage to embrace him. 'I've never had a tag put on me before,' says Jackson. 'When they call me a sex symbol I take it as flattering, in a way, and humorous in another. I would rather people be interested in my lyrics and songwriting than anything else.'

The Academy of Country Music named him 1991's Top New Male Artist and he, and his co-writer Mark Irwin, won the Song of the Year award for their hit 'Here in the Real World'. To cap off a round of industry recognition the respected *Radio & Records* publication named him Best New Artist of the Year.

Hollywood has a saying, 'You're only as big as your last movie.' Country music says, 'you're only as big as your last song.' Jackson had no intention of being a one-season, one-single or one-album flash-in-the-pan. In May 1991 Arista released his second album *Don't Rock the Jukebox*. It went gold in two months and platinum in five.

Success hadn't come overnight for Jackson but, once he made his mark, he'd quickly risen to the top. He's a member of the Grand Ole Opry and has had many celebrated musical milestones, including performing for Former President George Bush, an avid country fan.

Regardless of how technology has changed country music, one thing will never change and that's the song. When it comes to putting a country song across, and pleasing the fans, Alan Jackson has few peers.

★*A Lot About Livin' – And A Little 'bout Love* (Arista 18711-2)

Alan Jackson tries to decide what songs he includes on his albums as though he were a fan not the singer. Though he has to like the songs, the fans have to like them as well, or better, if the album is to succeed.

The album title came from the chorus of the lead song 'Chattahoochee', the story of a Georgia teenager growing up around the Chattahoochee River.

'Tropical Depression' is an Alan Jackson/Jim McBride/Charlie Craig collaboration. At first listen it conjures up images of Jimmy Buffett or the BELLAMY BROTHERS and Jackson admits the style is similar. It's a song about a boy who goes down to the islands because he's depressed and can't get over a lost love: 'This tropical depression's gonna/Blow me away'.

Zak Turner and Tim Nichols knew what they were doing when they wrote 'She Likes It Too' which they wrote for Jackson. He says they took some lines right out of his life and put them into the song. 'I got my first motorcycle when I turned sixteen/ I remember my mama raisin' cane with me/She said "Son, tell me why you wanna ride that thing"/ She didn't know about the blond at the Dairy Queen.' The art for the album is a picture of Jackson sitting astride a green Harley Davidson motorcycle.

Jackson's mellow baritone is letter-perfect for 'If It Ain't One Thing (It's You)' which he co-wrote with Jim McBride. His rare ability to turn a phrase shines through in this number.

Few debate the piano mastery of Hargus 'Pig' Robbins. He rises to new heights of excellence as he sets the stage on the intro and, with delicate caressing of the keys, he frames Jackson perfectly on this moving song about a man who sees his love leave and everytime he turns around something reminds him of her.

One of the best critiques of Alan Jackson comes from Canada's Regina Leader-Post: 'Jackson is arguably the hottest star in country music, and surely the greatest new voice of this generation. It is somewhat hard to describe, but in addition to being musically perfect, Jackson's voice is easy to listen to – warm and sincere and somehow friendly.'

Jennings, Waylon

(born Littlefield, Texas, June 15 1937)
Look up 'renegade', 'outlaw' or 'legend' in a country dictionary and you'd probably see Waylon Jennings' picture. He, along with friend and fellow Highwayman WILLIE NELSON, was a leader of the 1970s Nashville revolt. He is a tough, talented Texan who knows what he wants to do musically and, more importantly, knows how to get it. He shook up the comfortable, staid country music establishment as few others have.

The 1960s and early 1970s were difficult years for Jennings. He was rebellious and erratic, failing to appear for interviews or co-operate with tour plans. During that period he was 'his own man'. He chose his songs and sang them the way *he* pleased.

It took time, but before long Jennings won over the fans. He was hard to ignore – once his music was heard it became infectious. He is now recognized as a true musical innovator. He also achieved his goal of making Nashville sit up and take notice.

Jennings' musical roots were deeply implanted by the time he was a teenager. By 1958 he was an established disc jockey on a Lubbock, Texas, radio station and a backup player in local bands.

Rock legend Buddy Holly warmed to the Jennings' appreciation and style of music and asked him to join the Crickets as electric bass player. Jennings toured with Holly until the fateful day, February 3 1959, when he gave up his seat on a private plane to 'The Big Bopper', J. P. Richardson.

The plane crashed in a farm field near Fargo, North Dakota. All on board were killed.

A shattered Jennings returned to Lubbock to once again become a disc jockey and part-time musician. Tiring of life in Lubbock he then heeded Horace Greeley's advice to 'turn your face to the great west and there build up a home and future.'

Settling in Phoenix, Arizona, he formed 'The Waylors' which won the Instrumental Group of the Year award in 1976. Their music was a combination of rock 'n' roll and country with a smattering of western thrown in for flavour. While some contemporary musicians didn't warm to it the fans did and before long Jennings and The Waylors were headlining at J.D.'s, one of the biggest nightclubs in the Phoenix area.

Waylon's fortunes brightened considerably when singer/songwriter Bobby Bare caught the show. He was ecstatic about the Jennings' brand of music and the new sound he was hearing.

Being one of RCA's brighter stars at the time, Bare's judgements was respected. When he told guitar legend Chet Atkins, who was an RCA executive at the time, about Jennings, Atkins listened. He made a point of hearing Jennings and The Waylors in person and he liked what he heard.

Atkins quickly signed Jennings to a contract in 1965. Studio dates soon followed.

Three singles from the early recording sessions made waves: 'Anita You're Dreaming', 'That's The Chance I'll Have To Take' and 'Stop The World And Let Me Off'.

The industry began to sit up and take notice at this nonconformist – Jennings was being hailed as a new artist with great promise. Basking in the glow of recognition he moved to Nashville in 1965 and as they say in country parlance, he 'hooked up' with JOHNNY CASH. Cash had just separated from his first wife, and had not yet made a commitment to June Carter who, in due course, added Cash to her surname.

It is not surprising that the two high-spirited roommates, with strong individualistic streaks, had the time of their lives. The liquor flowed and the pills popped. Through the haze of excess, both men continued to write, record and perform. A mutual bond of friendship and respect was formed and to this day, the two stars, both dried out, perform together as part of the celebrated Highwaymen.

Jennings did not fit comfortably into the Nashville musical community. He was too much of an individualist. He made the establishment uncomfortable even though his guest appearance on the Opry was a smash. The audience, and those who listened on radio, were captivated by his powerful, deep-throated, gruff voice. His delivery of a country song was a far cry from the smooth, liquid tones of a JIM REEVES or MARTY ROBBINS. And his clothes were as unconventional as his approach to music. Instead of quasi-cowboy suits with sequins and rhinestones, he strode on stage dressed in faded jeans and ordinary sports shirt.

Jennings toured extensively in the 1960s and kept up a flow of recordings, many of which grabbed the ears and dollars of a growing fan following. 'That's What You Get For Loving Me' was a 1966 top-ten hit. He continued to hit the charts with singles such as 'Green River' and 'Only Daddy That'll Walk The Line'.

Jennings proved to the sceptics that he could perform any type of song when he and the Kimberlys hit with 'MacArthur Park' and won the 1969 Grammy Award for Best Country Performance by a Duo or Group.

Though his popularity was better-than-average during the 1970s, and he flirted with superstar status, Jennings still had not had a chart-topping hit. That honour went to his wife Jessi Colter with 'I'm Not Lisa', which was voted Song of the Year for 1975.

In 1977 Jennings scored a home run with 'Luckenbach, Texas' and followed with a major hit 'The Wurlitzer Prize'.

His friendship with Johnny Cash paid off in 1978 when they combined to record 'There Ain't No Good Chain Gang'.

The next decade started off strong with a prophetical bestseller 'I Ain't Living Long Like This'. By March it was number one.

One of the top-rated television shows in the early 1980s was *The Dukes Of Hazzard*. Jennings wrote and recorded the theme song and every week his voice was heard over the opening credits. He also released 'The Theme From The Dukes Of Hazzard'.

The Waylon Jennings/Jessi Colter duo recorded 'Storms Never Last', which Jessi wrote, in 1981. The single was a hit and Jennings followed it with a composition of his own, 'Shine'. It, too, was a top-selling release.

Jennings still tours with Jessi and his Highwaymen buddies, JOHNNY CASH, WILLIE NELSON and Kris Kristofferson. In addition to being a composer of note he is making a name for himself as a children's poet. He appeared with Jessi on a children's video, *Jessi Sing Just For Kids*, that she hosted and read two of his poems: 'I Just Can't Wait', an ode to growing up, and the delightful ditty 'Dirt' which enchanted the young audience.

Though he has toned down his wild lifestyle and is drug-free, the fires of rebellion still simmer. He is, and always will be, a man who marches to his own drum. 'At one time, it was considered too far out if you had a minor chord in a song,' he says. 'We've moved a long way since then.'

★*Waylon Jennings The Early Years* (RCA 9561-2-R)

What is striking about this CD is the artwork. It's a smiling, clean-shaven Waylon Jennings in a sports coat and sweater. His hair combed to a near pompadour.

Jennings was obviously moved by the album because in the liner notes he writes, 'Listening to this album brings back a lot of good memories. What's really hard to believe about it was that the musicians, background singers and artists were all in the studio at the one time. Now days, we come from all different directions on different days to overdub and underdub. Sometimes I wonder if we've quit making records and started building them . . . but that's progress I guess.'

'That's The Chance I'll Have To Take', with its arresting harmonica intro, is a great showcase for Jennings' distinctive singing, composing and guitar playing talents. In spite of his reputation as a rough, deep-throated singer his delivery on this plaintive love song is mellow and at times moving.

'Time To Bum Again' by Harlan Howard is a strong counter-point. At that point in his life it could have been his theme song.

'Anita, You're Dreaming' is another Jennings composition in collaboration with Don Bowman. The vibs give it a pleasant lilt and sharp Mexican flavour.

★*Waylon Full Circle* (MCA MCAD-42222)

The cover for this CD is quintessential Jennings – he's in black hat, black suit, black string tie, black beard and sporting a wicked smile. The lineup is also quintessential Jennings, from 'Trouble Man', with the thumping intro, the marvellous Mark O'Connor on fiddle and the wailing harmonica of Tony Joe White, to what has to be the best title of the decade 'Yoyos, Bozos, Bimbos And Heros'.

Waylon either wrote or co-wrote six of the ten numbers and each one is worth listening to carefully so as not to miss the subtle and sometimes not-so-subtle nuances.

This CD was digitally recorded using the Mitsubishi X-850 32-track system and is an ideal addition to any collection.

Jones, George

(born Saratoga, Texas, September 12 1931)

When JOHNNY CASH was once asked to name his favourite singer, he replied, 'You mean next to George Jones.' Cash is not alone in his admiration for the man who, in the opinion of many, is the quintessential country singer.

Jones' range is phenomenal and few others can sear the heart and scorch the soul with a lyric and melody the way he can.

For many years, far more than Jones would care to remember, he lived a totally undisciplined lifestyle that nearly killed him. The 1970s were a personal write-off from brutal alcohol and cocaine abuse. Coupled with these addictions was a 'to hell with it' attitude which antagonized promoters. He regularly arrived late for a show or couldn't perform due to drunkenness. Many times he just didn't show up at all, with no explanation. 'No Show Jones' was a nickname he earned and deserved.

He also had a reputation for a blistering temper which he could aim at friend or foe without warning. The results were usually devastating.

From 1969 to 1975 he was married to country singing star TAMMY WYNETTE. While the years were a marital rollercoaster they were rewarding for both performers. Setting aside their personal problems their collective professionalism and talents shone through and they became 'the president and first lady' of country music.

Jones and Wynette were a dream pairing. During their tempestuous marriage they teamed up for a number of bestselling singles, including the 1971 release 'Take Me' backed with 'We Go Together', and duet albums which their fans loved. 'Golden Ring' and 'The Battle' documented, in song, the final stages of their relationship.

By the time Jones finally listened to his fourth wife, and his doctors, his addictions had reaped havoc on his body – he was down to just over 100 pounds.

'If it wasn't for Nancy I'd be dead,' says Jones. 'She brought me to my senses and saved my life.'

But the fans loved the rowdy, unpredictable Jones and even at his worst they still remained loyal.

Few other performers can match Jones when it comes to wearing their feelings on their sleeve. He unabashedly sings about his triumphs, disappointments and loves with a remarkable candour.

Honours from the fans and industry have been heaped upon him. Early in his career his potential was recognized by the major music trade magazines. In 1956 he was voted most Promising Artist of the Year and 1980 and 1981 were particularly great years. First it was Male Vocalist of the Year plus Song of the Year and Single of the Year for 'He Stopped Loving Her Today', then a Grammy Award for that song in 1981. If that wasn't enough recognition for this superb talent, he also garnered Male Vocalist of the Year for the second year in a row. Music City News Cover Awards named him 1981 Male Artist of the Year.

The pinnacle of honour for any country performer is to be inducted into the Country Music Hall of Fame. Jones was so honoured in 1992.

George Jones would be the first to admit that, next to marrying Nancy, the best thing that ever happened to him was his partnership with Billy Sherrill. Sherrill became his record producer and together they produced his biggest hits which, in turn, have become some of the biggest in country music history. These include 'He Stopped Loving Her Today', 'The Same Ole Me', 'The Grand Tour', 'If Drinking Don't Kill Me' and 'Shine On'.

WAYLON JENNINGS took the measure of his friend at the close of an authorized video biography *George Jones – Same Ole Me*. 'They counted him down and out nine thousand times,' said Jennings, 'but he just keeps coming back. He'll always be part of country music. Some of us will last a little while. As long as there is country music you'll know who George Jones was.'

★*George Jones Live First Time* (Epic EK 39899)

This CD is classic George Jones. Not only is he in top vocal form it was recorded before a live audience and produced by the incomparable Billy Sherrill.

The mix of ten numbers is brilliant from cut number one, 'No Show Jones', which is a lighthearted flashback to his rip-roaring past, to cut number ten, 'She's My Rock', a paeon to love. They are perfect bookends for such Jones' standards as 'The Race Is On', 'Fox On The Run', 'Tennessee Whisky' and 'I'm Not Ready Yet'.

On 'Who's Gonna Chop My Baby's Kindlin' Jones cheekily plays to the audience as he sets up the number. 'You'd Better Treat Your Man Right' is his musical warning to women.

The classic 'He Stopped Loving Her Today' has to be required listening for any fan who loves the best in country music. It's absolutely amazing what this singer can do to a set of lyrics. His vocal shadings are outstanding.

Jones completely satisfies on cut number seven with a four-part medley: 'I'll Share The World With You', 'The Window Up Above', 'The Grand Tour' and 'Walk Through This World With Me'.

The Jones Boys are in backup both vocally and instrumentally.

★*George Jones – All-Time Greatest Hits Volume 1* (Epic EK 34692)

Another Billy Sherrill production with the Jones Boys in fine form on backup.

Even though 'The Race Is On', 'The Window Up Above' and 'Walk Through This World With Me' were included on *George Jones First Time Live* this CD is worthy of mention and an excellent addition to any CD library.

No George Jones collection would be complete without 'White Lightnin''. It is an uptempoed novelty number in praise of the illicitly distilled whiskey they call 'moonshine'. This humorous ditty became his first number one *Billboard* hit.

'Why Baby Why' was first released as a single in 1955 and caught on. It holds up remarkably well decades later.

'She Thinks I Still Care' is a vintage 1960s hit and one of the reasons why other country performers call Jones 'a singer's singer'.

Also included are some lesser heard numbers which were

genuine hits when they were first released and still are in the opinion of his fans. 'Tender Years', 'She's Mine' and 'I'll Share My World With You' round out a most satisfying lineup.

★*My Best To You* (CBS BUK 50194)

The sliding steel guitar and George Jones' voice are perfect partners. Together they slip from note to note and word to word in a most arresting manner. 'Tell Me My Lying Eyes Are Wrong' is a sterling case in point.

'Nothing Ever Hurt Me (Half As Bad As Losing You)' is not one of Jones' better known songs but it is one that should not be missed. Jones matches the surging beat as he rhymes off all the disasters that have hurt him from a toothache that split his jaw in two, to nailing his index finger to the wall. They were nothing, he sings, to the hurt he felt when he lost his love.

Everyone has memories but there are very few country singers who can rekindle them like Jones. 'Memories Of Us' will give one pause as the joys and sorrows of yesterday flood back like a gentle tide. A perfect phrase in the hands of a master sums up this song, 'Yesterday is something that tomorrows cannot change.'

There are twelve cuts on this CD and two are classics: 'I'll Share My World With You' and 'He Stopped Loving Her Today'. Consider them as bonus songs.

Judd, Wynonna

(born Christina Ciminella, Ashland, Kentucky, May 30 1964)
Mother and daughter, Naomi and Wynonna Judd were the most successful duo in country music history until Naomi was forced to retire due to chronic, active hepatitis. The chart-topping success of the Judds ground to a halt.

When Wynonna announced that she would continue her career as a solo artist, there were many doubters. Some prophesied that without the support of her mother she would not make it, especially on the road. Touring takes great discipline and it was common knowledge that Naomi's steadying hand had saved the day more than once.

But Wynonna Judd is not one to be written off easily. Her solo debut came on January 27 1992 when she stepped on stage at the American Music Awards in Los Angeles.

'I was twenty-seven and felt like I was leaving home for the first time,' recalls Wynonna. 'My primary goal was to maintain the identifiable sound that was a key to the success my mother and I had as the Judds.'

Naomi was in the audience. All she needed to hear, before she breathed a gigantic sigh of relief, were the opening bars of 'She Is His Only Need'.

Music is not only Wynonna's profession it is her passion. At the age of ten she moved back to Kentucky, from California, with her newly divorced mother. It was about then that she discovered the joys of music and the door it opened for personal expression.

By the time she was in her early teens she was so obsessed that, though Naomi encouraged her interest in music, she was very concerned. Wynonna had become a music captive.

'I was wrapped up in my own private world,' she said. 'I didn't go to dances and I didn't date. In fact, I didn't discover boys until I was eighteen or nineteen. All I needed, or wanted, was my guitar and music.'

Naomi had always dreamed about breaking into country music and often practised with her daughter. Realizing that if they were to have a chance it would be in Nashville they moved from Kentucky to Tennessee.

Their big break came through their homemade demo tape and an acquaintance who heard the demo and had great faith in their potential. Their friend used his contacts with RCA and got them a rare live audition. It was their big chance and they didn't let themselves or their benefactor down. Backed only by Wynonna on her guitar, they sang their hearts out. An hour later they had a record deal.

Their first experience on a stage was in 1984 as the opening act for the STATLER BROTHERS and they faced an audience of 10,000.

It didn't take long for the Judds to shoot to the top. In the short space of seven years they racked up an astonishng 23 hits, 7 Country Music Awards, 4 Grammys (the first one in 1985) and album sales that soared over 10 million worldwide.

Wynonna is not one to sit back and bask in past glories. She is a music adventurer and willing to try anything that will grab new fans and improve her performance. A smile must cross her face every time she thinks about those who said she would never make it as a solo performer, especially when she reads the smash reviews for her debut album *Wynonna*.

★*Wynonna* (MCA MCASD-10529)

Wynonna is a musical adventure. The listener is taken on a musical odyssey that stretches from the blues of 'What It Takes' with Wynonna's hard-edged vocals to 'My Strongest Weakness' a tender broken-hearted ballad that demands replaying again and again. This one is a charmer.

On 'Live With Jesus' Wynonna gives a haunting spiritual performance. A Paul Kennerley composition, it's interesting to know that Wynonna's vocals were recorded at Kennerley's home over his original demo track.

Naomi temporarily comes out of retirement to sing once again with her daughter on 'When I Reach The Place I'm Goin''. She has lost none of her skill or charm and greatly enhances the vocal harmonies of this stark mountain melody.

Wynnona paints a moving picture on her musical canvas with 'It's Never Easy To Say Goodbye'. It's the story of children growing up and friends leaving. A ring of sincerity comes through loud and clear – there has to be a parallel between this song and the end of the Judds.

Eddy Bayers is on drums for seven of the ten songs and deserves to be complimented. He orchestrates the pace like a master puppeteer pulling the strings.

This is one of the best debut albums to come out in recent memory.

Kennedy, Joan

(born, Minto, New Brunswick, April 8 1960)
In person Joan Kennedy is refreshing, down-to-earth and a pleasure to be around. In spite of five critically acclaimed albums, a two-season television series and live performances numbering in the thousands, this talented country singer is devoid of pretence.

It doesn't take a microscopic analysis to find out the credos that are the foundation of her career. Music was always a part of her life as she grew up, the youngest of eight children, in Douglas Harbour, a small community in Canada's maritime province of New Brunswick.

It is pretty difficult to have pretences when you are one of eight children. 'It wasn't the easiest of lives,' recalls Kennedy. 'Money was scarce and my dad drove a truck to make ends meet. He was away from home a lot of the time.'

Though life was hard music kept the family together. 'Dad loved music and had his own band. Hank Snow was his musical hero and the songs he wrote had a definite Snow influence. During the 1950s and 1960s he played wherever he could get a booking. He still plays at benefits.'

Kennedy's career has progressed from recognition in 1983, when she won a national talent contest, and a year later released her first album *I'm A Big Girl Now* to *Candle in the Window* and her latest for MCA *Higher Ground*. It's her most impressive body of work to date.

It was country music that first influenced Kennedy as she grew up and it's a tradition that's very important to her.

'I think that I'm moving into a more obvious country sound with *Higher Ground*,' she says. 'It's a way of reaching the people who have been my audience for so many years.'

★*Higher Ground* (MCA MCAD-10779)

Every artist feels that their latest album is their best, a career builder and a potential chart-topper. Joan Kennedy makes no apology for being so positive and confident about *Higher Ground*. From the early reviews she is justified.

This time out the listener is offered a more confident, gutsier Joan Kennedy than on any previous album or single. 'Part of the reason,' says Kennedy, 'is the fact that I chose songs for this album that would support my live shows. These songs are tougher and brighter.'

A prime example of what Kennedy is talking about is 'I Need To Hear It From You'. This is a song to which a singer with Kennedy's range and tonality can do justice. The disc jockeys obviously agree as it is getting strong air play.

Don't listen to 'Circle of Love' without a box of tissues close at hand, the lyrics alone are enough to tug at the heartstrings. Add Kennedy's treatment and one is hit right between the eyes. 'Rob and Anna were the perfect couple so it seemed/Six years married, they had all they'd dreamed of except one thing/There's an empty nursery in a room above/A little heartbeat missin' to complete their circle of love.' A grade-A tear-jerker.

lang, k. d.

(born, Kathy Dawn Lang, Concert, Alberta, November 2 circa 1958)

k.d. lang is a vegetarian and an outspoken opponent of breeding and killing beef cattle for food. Because of her stand, the legislature of Alberta, her home province, the heart of Canada's beef country, refused to congratulate her for winning an American Music Award. When asked to comment on the ruckus she replied with typical frankness, 'I'd be a liar if I said I wasn't hurt at all by it. But I have to realize that I'm pushing the boundaries of people's acceptance.'

Her boundary pushing also covers an androgynous dress style, which initially took country music by surprise and started tongues wagging, and public statements concerning her lifestyle and sexual preferences. All or any would have been enough to finish a career twenty-five years ago but not today. If anything, the career of this multi-talented artist, who has been singled out as 'one of the great vocalists on the planet', is soaring. Her fan following continues to grow with every performance and record release.

Born and raised in Concert, Alberta, Kathy Dawn Lang began playing the guitar at the tender age of ten. Possessing a remarkable talent for both singing and writing, she was performing her own compositions by the time she entered her teens.

Always the innovator, she dropped the capitals in her name and became known as k.d.

By the early 1980s she had formed her own band, 'the reclines'. Reaction to their exciting and emotionally charged stage shows was immediate and enthusiastic. Musical popularity and records go hand-in-hand and 'Friday Dance Promenade' was the band's first single. It was quickly followed by 'A Truly Western Experience', which was released independently.

Sire Records signed the band to a major contract in 1984. 'Angel With A Lariat' was released in 1987 to enthusiastic acclaim from both fans and critics.

Shadowland was k.d.'s breakthrough album and 1988 was her year for industry recognition. She was the *Rolling Stone* Critics' Pick for Best Female Singer in 1988 and Canadian Juno award winner for Best Female Vocalist of the Year in the same year. To top off a near-perfect 1988 she won a Grammy for Best Vocals Collaboration for her soaring duet with the late lamented Roy Orbison on 'Crying'.

k.d. also made fashion news with layouts for *Vogue* and *Elle*.

Appearances with musical superstars like Bruce Springsteen, Sting and Peter Gabriel enhanced her popularity and profile and she was an important part of the celebrated Tracy Chapman 1988 Amnesty International Tour.

The momentum continued in 1989 – k.d.'s next album, *Absolute Torch And Twang*, was a winner and she won a Grammy for Best Female Country Artist. Her album sales soared with her popularity and she made her acting and soundtrack debut in the film *Salmonberries*, directed by Percy Adlon.

For as long as k.d. can remember she has been an activist who publicly supports causes close to her heart. If she passionately believes in something she is not afraid to take a stand and lend her support. One cause, in addition to anti-meat eating, is AIDS research and help for victims. She was one of the featured performers in the Cole Porter tribute/AIDS benefit project. She sang the Porter classic 'So In Love'. It was a moving rendition.

Although Alberta had problems in applauding k.d.'s accomplishments, Canada finally recognized her artistry and musical contributions by naming her Female Artist of the Decade.

k.d.'s fifth album *Ingenue* was a marked departure in both sound and style for this innovative and musically restless performer. It marked her departure from country and her move to pop.

When asked to explain the departure, from what many consider to be her musical roots, k.d. said, 'At the end of the *Absolute Torch And Twang* tour I felt it was time for me to move from country. I had won the Grammy but I still wasn't getting airplay and, even the fact that I had been as creative as possible with country music, I had basically run the course.'

k.d. accepts the fact that some fans doubt her sincerity towards country. 'I've always been very honest and open about the fact that I was interested in different types of music and that some day I would be moving on.'

In thanking those who worked with her on *Shadowland* k.d. ends her album liner notes with a simple 'thanks Patsy'. She readily acknowledges the musical influence and inspiration of PATSY CLINE. She appeared in the *Remembering Patsy* home video and said, 'She had a type of soul that is hard to find in a singer.'

Many k.d. lang fans honestly believe that she is the reincarnation of the legendary star. When asked about it Patsy's husband, Charlie Dick, replied, 'I think her voice has great quality and is close to being equal to Patsy's but she doesn't sound like Patsy. No one sounds like Patsy or ever could. k.d. could sing "I Fall To Pieces" and, while she'd do a great job, no one would ever mistake her for being Patsy. As for being Patsy reincarnated I don't hold much with reincarnation or the psychic. Patsy is Patsy and k.d. is k.d. Let's leave it at that.'

★*Shadowland* (Sire CD 25724)

One prime requirement for a chart-topping album is the right producer and one of the all-time best producers in country music is Owen Bradley. It's redundant to call him a legend because legend is inadequate when it comes to describing the man who made so many 'greats' greater and many 'lesser greats' great. Bradley produced *Shadowland*. He covers it with the same magic dust he sprinkled over Patsy Cline when she recorded mega-hits like 'Crazy', 'I Fall To Pieces' and 'Sweet Dreams'. The Jordanaires backed Patsy in those olympian days and they are here to backup k.d. on this album.

When Frank Lesser wrote 'I Wish I Didn't Love You So', he probably never envisaged it being given a country sound. What k.d. does to this evergreen standard is pure magic. The tinkling piano of Roger Morris is the perfect intro for this jewel. k.d. has never been in finer voice. Add the Jordanaires on backup and you have a near-perfect combination. The pace is easy, relaxed and mood setting.

The infectious 'Sugar Moon' is a rip-roaring western swing number and no wonder, as it was written by Bob Wills and Cindy Walker, two of the best western swing exponents. This time it's 'Tennessee' on vocal backup, and Hargus 'Pig' Robbins adds his keyboard artistry to make the number contagious.

The steel guitar of Hal Rugg, Jimmy Capp's rhythm guitar and Pete Wade on electric guitar cannot go unmentioned. A fine example of musicianship.

'Shadowland' is the title number. The Nashville String Machine in backup with cello, violin and viola is as beautiful a mix as one is likely to hear. This song beckons like a long-lost lover and lures the listener in.

'Honky Tonk Angels' Medley' is 'country' special because BRENDA LEE, LORETTA LYNN and Kitty Wells join k.d. If ever there was a trio of honky-tonk angels it is these three country icons. This song delivers precisely what the title suggests, a medley of 'In The Evening When The Son Goes Down', 'You Nearly Lose Your Mind' and 'Blues Stay Away From Me'. All four singers join in, and claim they had a ball in the recording studio.

One can understand and sympathise with k.d. when she says, 'I would like to broaden my base and move more into the pop genre.' However, if *Shadowland* is the country benchmark one can only observe that k.d. would be hard-pressed to find a better producer than Owen Bradley, a better backup group than the Jordanaires, or a better set of session players than those who helped her make *Shadowland* sheer magic. Finally she'll never have better country friends than Loretta Lynn, Kitty Wells and Brenda Lee.

LeDoux, Chris

(born on an Air Force base in Biloxi, Mississippi, October 2 1948) It's been said that Chris LeDoux's music is 'Roy Rogers meets Led Zepplin'. It's an interesting observation. LeDoux has two large cowboy hats which he has worn on different occasions in his life. One is as the professional rodeo star and the other is as the songwriter/performer. By the time LeDoux was fourteen he was a better-than-average horseback rider and good enough to participate in the finals of the Little Britches Rodeo. For the next fourteen years he climbed up through the rodeo ranks until he won the World Championship Bareback Rider Buckle in 1976.

During his college years LeDoux became known as a writer and singer of authentic rodeo songs and was in great demand as a performer.

LeDoux, and his father Al, founded American Cowboy Songs, a family recording company that is dedicated to the career of Chris LeDoux. A strong marketing program has resulted in impressive sales for the twenty-two albums that LeDoux has recorded on the ACS label.

In 1992 Liberty Records released *Whatcha Gonna Do With A Cowboy*. GARTH BROOKS joined LeDoux on the title single and it reached the top ten chart listing.

LeDoux's music is a combination of western soul, sagebrush blues, cowboy folk and rock 'n' roll. An interesting mix, and this versatile performer is equally comfortable in any genre.

★*Whatcha Gonna Do With A Cowboy* (Liberty Records CDP-7-98818-2)

Of the ten songs on this CD, four were composed by Chris LeDoux, 'Call Of The Wild', 'Little Long-Haired Outlaw', 'Hooked On A Second Ride' and 'Western Skies'. All are good but the best one, by a country mile, is 'Western Skies'.

Superstar Garth Brooks joins LeDoux on 'Whatcha Gonna Do With A Cowboy'. All the songs are well served by the session players, but they really excel on this track. There is a wicked intro by Rob Hajacos, his smoking fiddle setting the pace and tone for what's to come.

LeDoux and Brooks make a good duo. Pity they only combined on one song.

Lee, Brenda

(born Brenda Mae Tarpley, Conyers, Georgia, December 11 1945) The only thing that seems to be in dispute about Brenda Lee is her age – there are several versions of the exact year, ranging from 1942 to 1946. But one thing is certain, this powerhouse of natural talent, who is less than five feet tall, can look back on a remarkable career as she approaches her fiftieth birthday.

As a young child Brenda had a keen ear for music and after hearing a song only twice could sing it almost word perfect. Her first of many awards came when she was five – she sang 'Take Me Out To The Ball Game' at a local spring festival and won first prize. By seven she was a regular performer on Starmakers' Review which ran on a local Atlanta radio station. From there she was booked for guest slots on a popular Atlanta television show called *TV Ranch* on WAGA-TV. Her musical destiny was clearly established before she was ten.

Red Foley was one of the top country performers of the day, his career successfully managed by Dub Albritten. Both saw star potential in the tiny girl with the big voice. Foley took her under his professional wing and Albritten assumed the role of her manager and began orchestrating her climb to stardom.

Sharing bills with Foley was the boost Brenda's career needed and before long Albritten had her booked on most of the major, nationally syndicated television shows.

Entertainment giants such as Ed Sullivan, Red Skelton, Danny Thomas and Steve Allen enjoyed her fresh, uninhibited way with a song. Those early viewers warmed to her immediately and formed the nucleus of her long-standing fan following.

Decca signed her to a recording contact before she was in her teens, her first studio date coming on July 30 1956 in Nashville. Within ten years she had recorded over 250 songs. By the close of the 1950s she was an established recording star with hits like 'Rockin' Around The Christmas Tree', and the pop ballad 'I'm Sorry'. Though her roots were country and the years with Red Foley had firmly established her as a country singer, she began to move away from country. In an attempt to sever all Nashville ties, and confirm her pop concentration, her manager publicly stated that her focus and repertoire were now non-country. Many of her fans were dismayed and felt that the musical divorce was unwarranted and unnecessary.

From the late 1950s to the mid-1960s *Billboard* and *Cashbox* named her Most Programmed Female Vocalist and she held on to the title for five years running.

During her salad days, in the centre of the musical spotlight,

Brenda Lee played most of the best nightclubs, concert halls and auditoriums in North America.

She also toured overseas and became a favourite in Europe. One of her major triumphs was an appearance at Paris' Olympia Music Hall.

In 1963 she married Ronald Shacklett and semi-retired to raise two daughters. She came back to the music scene with a bang in 1969 with 'Johnny One Time' which received a Grammy nomination.

Though she had seemingly turned her back on her Nashville roots her songs were constantly appearing on the country charts and her fans remained loyal. By 1971 she was back in country with 'Is This Our Last Time'. That was followed up in 1973 with two fine songs, 'Nobody Wins' and 'Sunday Sunrise'.

The 1980s were musically rewarding. 'Tell Me What It's Like' was well received and 'The Cowboy And The Dandy' made it to the top fifteen.

Up to 1988 Brenda was averaging over 200 appearances a year but since then has cut back significantly her days on the road. She now appears regularly at Nashville's Opryland and is still recording. Her voice is as good as ever and her stage presentations are an exercise in professionalism. She is a master at reaching her audience and commanding undivided attention. She sings with a clarity and energy that her country fans have come to identify as the unique 'Brenda Lee' sound.

During a 1993 interview with *The Nashville Network*'s Crook and Chase she stated that she was still on the road, she had just returned from performing in the United Kingdom and was planning to go to Japan.

'I'm a "road person",' she said. 'As long as the fans come to hear me I'll keep performing.' When asked about retiring her reply was quick and to the point. 'Some day,' she said. 'I'll know when it's time to say enough is enough. When that day comes I'll quit. But, even though I'd not be performing, I'd still like to do something behind the scenes. Show business is in my blood, it's my life, and I can't imagine ever leaving it permanently.'

★Brenda Lee (Warner Bros. 9 26439-2)

'When He Leaves You' is the seventh cut on this ten-song debut album for Warner Brothers, a 'hurtin'' song in the classical mould. The storyline is simple and to the point, 'I come here as a friend/ Though I really don't know you/I know you're in love with him/ And he's made your world brand new/I know you think he loves you/ And he may believe it too/ Pour some coffee and I'll tell you/ What you'll soon be going through/When he leaves you.' Written by Kent Robbins and Mike Reid, it's a gem, with sensitive background vocals that enhance the mood.

'A Little Unfair' by tunesmith Hank Cochran, in collaboration with Chuck Howard, is neck-in-neck for favourite status with 'When He Leaves You'. Mitch Humphries and Hargus 'Pig' Robbins on piano raise the song to melodic heights. One can just feel the sorrow as Brenda wrings every sob and ounce of pathos out of the brilliant lyrics.

If it's toe-tapping music that turns you on 'You're The One And Only' won't disappoint, and is destined for a lot of play in the country bars.

Little Texas

(formed November 1988, current members – Duane Propes, Porter Howell, Del Gray, Tim Rushlow, Brandy Seals, Dwayne O'Brien)

There's a success story circulating around Nashville and it concerns six long-haired country boys who call themselves Little Texas. In order to get their 'act' together, before taking a shot at the big time, the band bought a $300 1972 Chevy van with a homemade trailer and with determination and confidence undertook a gruelling, two-year crisscross of America, calling on any club, from Myrtle Beach to Los Angeles, that might hire them.

The result of long days on the road, in a car with over 125,000 miles on the gauge and questionable reliability, paid off. They polished their high-energy show in clubs and honky-tonks, some of which they'd just as soon forget. Regardless of the less-than-posh venues, with audiences to match, Little Texas evolved into a tightly-knit aggregation that is hailed for its air-tight harmonies, flawless stage presentations and superb writing abilities.

Little Texas is a hot success story. Now they tour with the big names like CLINT BLACK and Kenny Rogers and confirmed their growing stature in country music with *First Time For Everything*, their debut album. Three of the songs, 'First Time for Everything', 'Some Guys Have All the Love' and 'You and Forever and Me' hit the charts and made it to the top-ten.

What is even more remarkable is the fact that the group made it big with their own songs, the members as adept at writing solid country music as they are playing and singing it.

Little Texas draws its musical inspiration from the legacy of country greats such as MERLE HAGGARD, GEORGE JONES, Jerry Lee Lewis and Lynyrd Skynyrd. Mix pure country with rhythm and blues, some low-down jazz and a touch of the classics and you have the exciting new sound of Little Texas.

This refreshing country sound has captured the imagination of young audiences who respond to the wild, energetic stage presentation with whistles, clapping and shouts of approval. 'If we bring anything new to country,' says band member Dwayne O'Brien, 'it's a young outlook. We don't have life all figured out yet. Rather than looking back on things, we are living them now.'

★*First Time For Everything* (Warner Bros. 9 26820-2)

By actual count the six members of Little Texas are proficient on ten instruments in addition to vocals and songwriting.

'Some Guys Have All the Love' is the leadoff song on this CD and it is strong enough to keep one listening to the end song. Written by Porter Howell and Dwayne O'Brien, it places the instrument and vocal strengths of the band front and centre. It's a tenderly crafted love song that's performed with feeling: 'Some guys have all the luck/There's gold in everything they touch/But all of the work I've done/Never did amount to much/I don't live what some call the good life/But I've got a good life with you.'

'Down In The Valley' is the other side of the Little Texas musical coin. It's ripping, infectious, hand-clapping and a delight. When the instruments are put down for an a cappella bridge the harmony shines.

For a debut album, by six country long-hairs, its as close to a ten as you could get.

Loveless, Patty

(born Patty Ramey, Pikeville, Kentucky, January 4 1957)
There is an old saying that 'All country music roads lead to Nashville'. There's also a Nashville addendum that 'Not all the doors of country music are quick to open wide for young, unproven singers'. Patty Loveless had heard the first saying many times when she was a coal miner's daughter in rural Kentucky. The similarity of her early years and those of LORETTA LYNN's is more than just coincidence. They are cousins.

Singing was second nature to Loveless, and so was writing songs. Like any proud parent her mother encouraged her to sing for visitors – she agreed to, but only if she could hide behind the kitchen door. This streak of shyness at times still comes through on stage.

When she was fourteen she and her older brother travelled to Nashville and opened their own doors. The widest one belonged to country star Porter Wagoner, who was gracious enough to listen to the young girl who had thirty of her own songs under her arm. Wagoner was impressed by such a young talent and introduced her to a young singer that he was promoting. She too was drawn to the young girl with the big voice and they became close friends. Her name is DOLLY PARTON.

Loveless was on her way. Before long she was the opening act at a Knoxville, Tennessee, Wilburn Brothers concert. Doyle Wilburn was as impressed as Porter Wagoner and Dolly Parton and he signed Loveless, and her brother, to his publishing house and took both of them on the road as the opening act.

Patty Loveless was still Patty Ramey – her surname inched to 'Loveless' when, at eighteen, she married the group's drummer Terry Lovelace. For the next ten years it was a series of small hotels and honky-tonks. While it was a tough life for the struggling performer, it was a great schoolroom for learning her craft.

By 1985 Loveless was divorced and back in Nashville with her brother who bankrolled a recording session for her. She and her brother then began knocking on doors once again, demo in hand. Fate shined when she auditioned for MCA talent executive Terry Brown. He signed her to a contract and recommended that she permanently change her surname to Loveless. A change of name, a new contract and a fresh start did wonders for Loveless and her career started to move.

1991 was her breakthrough year. She received a third Female Vocalist of the Year nomination from the Country Music Association and her *Honky Tonk Angel* album broke the 500,000 mark in sales.

The next career progression was joining the Grand Ole Opry and being invited to tour with such superstars as CLINT BLACK, HANK WILLIAMS JR, and ALABAMA.

Loveless describes her music as 'traditional country with a little edge'. *USA Today*'s Dave Zimmerman wrote, 'When it comes to female country singers nobody, but nobody in Nashville sings better than Patty Loveless.'

★*Honky Tonk Angel* (MCA MCABD-42223)

This CD is a showcase for the talented Loveless. It crosses many musical lines from the rockabilly-shaded 'Blue Side of Town' to 'Don't Toss Us Away', a hurtin' song if ever there was one.

'I'll Never Grow Tired of You' was written by Carter Stanley and has the added plus of VINCE GILL and Clair Lynch on background vocals. The session players include Mark O'Connor doubling on fiddle and mandolin, Eddie Bayers on drums and Matt Rollings on keyboards. Listening to them is a pleasure to the ear, especially when they bridge between chorus and verse.

Lynn, Loretta

(born Loretta Webb, Butcher Holler, Kentucky, April 14 1935)
It's hard to believe that someone who came from a 'coal miner's cabin on a hill in Butcher Holler' could rise to the pinnacle of country music and be recognized as 'America's Queen of Country Music'. But, that is precisely what Loretta Lynn has achieved. A string of number one hits and a blockbuster movie, *The Coal Miner's Daughter*, certainly didn't hurt. But it would not have

happened if Loretta had not possessed a remarkable 'country' voice and a knack for either writing or choosing the right material. In her authorized biography *Coal Miner's Daughter*, Loretta is bluntly candid about her early years when, at fourteen, she married 'Doolittle' Lynn. (She didn't even know that his real name was Oliver Vanetta Lynn until he wrote it down on their wedding day. 'Doolittle' is an old Kentucky nickname. Loretta calls him 'Doo' and his friends call him 'Mooney' because he used to run moonshine.) She knew nothing about sex and found herself pregnant with her first child before her fifteenth birthday. She and Doolittle have a total of six children, four were born by the time she was eighteen. Many of the songs that she sang, as she cleaned house and looked after her constantly growing and demanding brood, were her own compositions.

Never one to let an opportunity pass by, Doolittle sensed that she might be able to translate her talents into dollars for the eternally cash-strapped family. An inexpensive guitar was her eighteenth birthday present and she began to master the art of playing basic chords.

One Saturday night, when they were at a local Grange Hall in Custer, Washington, Doolittle got her career kick-started. He badgered the leader of the country band to give her an audition for a local radio show they put on every Wednesday. Not only was she good enough for radio she was invited to join the band live on Saturday nights at the Grange Hall.

Fame and fortune didn't come easy and it was only when a British Columbia businessman financially backed her that 'Honky Tonk Girl' became her first recording on the Zero Record label. It took Doolittle and Loretta as many miles on the road as it took hours of hounding programme managers and disc jockeys to get her record air play. But once audiences heard Loretta sing, in her distinctive style, things started to happen at mind-whirling speed. In 1961 Loretta was an unknown with one record to her credit. By the end of 1962 she was on her way to stardom with 'Success', a top ten for Decca. To top off the year she was invited to join the Grand Ole Opry and *Cashbox* named her 'Most Programmed Female Country Star'.

It was during 1962 that Loretta became close friends with her idol and mentor Patsy Cline. To this day Loretta's eyes brim when she talks about Patsy.

The 1960s were good years for Loretta. The hits kept coming: 'Wine Women and Song', 'Before I'm Over You', 'Blue Kentucky Girl', 'The Home You're Tearing Down', and 'Dear Uncle Sam' kept record store cash registers ringing.

One song of that period has been enshrined in the list of country classics.'You Ain't Woman Enough' is the story of a feisty woman who loves her man and will go to any lengths to keep him. *Billboard* made it a perfect decade by naming her Top Country Female Vocalist in 1967. The applause kept coming in the 1970s and in 1971 she was the first woman to be named Country Music 'Entertainer of the Year'. Further recognition came in 1973 when *Newsweek* put her on its cover.

1977 was a very special year for Loretta, winning Album of the Year for *I Remember Patsy*. She sings all of Patsy's greatest hits from 'Sweet Dreams' to 'I Fall To Pieces'. It's like listening to the ghost of Patsy Cline.

Singles kept pace with albums. 'Fist City' and 'You're Looking At Country' were big juke box favourites. They are still getting air play on country stations.

'Coal Miner's Daughter' was released in October 1970 and was named Song of the Year in 1971. It became the title for a film biography with Sissy Spacek playing Loretta and Tommy Lee Jones as Doolittle.

Spacek gave such a tour de force performance that she won the 1980 Oscar and the film became a smash hit.

Loretta has not confined her recording career to solo performances. Some of her bestselling albums were duos with the late CONWAY TWITTY and the late ERNEST TUBB.

Fame and fortune, as Loretta would be the first to agree, is not all laughter and good times. She has had more than her fair share of personal heartaches, which included Doolittle's failing health. In late May 1993 the 67-year-old suffered congestive heart failure from complications related to diabetes and underwent open heart surgery.

Devastating, chronic, migraines have plagued Loretta for years. On more than one occasion she has passed out on stage due to the blinding pain.

The benchmark for most successful country and western artists is maintaining a close relationship with their fans through personal appearances. Loretta is no exception. Up until May 1993 she was performing regularly at the Loretta Lynn Ozark Theatre in Branson, Missouri.

When Doolittle underwent open heart surgery in Springfield Missouri's Cox South Medical Centre, Loretta cancelled her appearances to be by his bedside. The convalescence has been long and arduous. It has taken its toll on not only Doolittle, but on Loretta as well. She recently announced that she was cancelling all engagements for the balance of 1993.

One well-informed Nashville 'insider' questions whether or not Loretta will ever perform again.

No one questions Loretta's devotion to her husband of 47 years.

'If it wasn't for Doolittle, there would be no career,' wrote Loretta in her autobiography *Coal Miner's Daughter*.

★*Loretta Lynn's Greatest Hits* (MCA MCAD-31234)

This is certainly an interesting package, and a must for any Loretta Lynn collection if for no other reason than to hear Loretta speak out for women as she vocally wags her finger at men on 'Don't Come Home A Drinkin' With Lovin' On Your Mind'. She first recorded it in 1966 for Decca and one could imagine Doolittle wincing the first time he heard it. The title says it all.

Fair-is-fair, as the other woman in a love triangle gets her comeuppance on 'You Ain't Woman Enough To Take My Man Away'. Loretta really lays it on the line. This was another 1966 hit. The honky-tonk 'hurtin' theme that permeates country music continues with 'Before I'm Over You', 'Wine Women and Song', 'The Home You're Tearin' Down' and 'Happy Birthday'. 'Dear Uncle Sam' is a heart-broken plea to the government to send her man home from the war because 'you don't need him like I do.'

'Success' was Loretta's first big hit for Decca and is the story of how a home and love has been shattered by success. It is a fitting title because if ever a country and western singer has savoured success, at the expense of some personal happiness, it has been Loretta. There are three other cuts on this CD: 'If You're Gone Too Long', 'The Other Woman' and 'Blue Kentucky Girl'.

Mandrell, Barbara

(born Houston, Texas, December 25 1948)

A story has circulated around Nashville and it's about a super-talented youngster, not yet five years old, who asked her mother to teach her to play the twenty-four-bars accordion. Her name – Barbara Mandrell. The story continues that one Sunday Barbara, who could read music before she could read English, dragged the accordion up on the church platform. She received a resounding ovation, for playing the only song she knew, 'Guitar Boogie', from a congregation that was more accustomed to 'The Old Rugged Cross'.

No one in Nashville who knows Barbara disputes the stories about her early musical abilities. It is fact, not fiction that by the time she was eleven she was playing steel guitar and saxophone in a Las Vegas show with Joe Maphis.

Between the ages of five and eleven Barbara had moved with her parents from Texas to Oceanside, California. She took to a number of instruments in addition to the accordion, steel guitar and saxophone like the proverbial duck to water. It didn't hurt that her father, Irby, opened a music store in Oceanside. One of his friends was Norman Hamlet who taught Barbara the rudiments of the pedal steel guitar and before long she was playing western swing with an air of proficiency that amazed Hamlet, her father and all who cared to listen.

By the time she had finished eighteen months of lessons and dedicated practice her father took her to a music trade show in Chicago. She was hired as a steel guitar demonstrator at the Standel Amplifiers booth and it was there that Maphis heard her play.

Maphis was instrumental in getting Barbara a regular spot on the Southern California TV show *Town Hall Party*. She was still in her eleventh year and became a show favourite. The next step up the career ladder was a network television debut on ABC's *Five Star Jubilee* out of Springfield, Missouri.

Realizing that in Barbara there was a rare talent bursting to be heard her father formed a family group with his wife, himself and Barbara plus two non-family backup musicians on drums and guitar. The Mandrell Family Band was a better-than-average aggregation with an eclectic repertoire ranging from Beatle songs to the *Beverly Hillbillies'* theme song. Barbara played the sax, banjo and steel guitar.

As Barbara looks back it was a happy time and the band became a close-knit unit. In 1967 she married Ken Dudney, who just happened to be the young drummer. It's a marriage that has been singled out as one of the happiest and most stable in country music. Unlike many in show business, who go through a string of marriages and divorces, Barbara is still Mrs Ken Dudney and proud of it.

After her marriage Mandrell semi-retired to raise a family, and her husband became an airforce pilot. When he was posted overseas Mandrell moved back home and before long found herself living with her parents in Nashville.

Surprising as it may be, Barbara and her father had never seen a live Opry show until they both went to a Friday night performance in 1968. All it took was that one show for Barbara to realize that she desperately wanted to be behind a microphone and not in the audience. Buoyed by her father's encouragement and support, she made a determined stab at becoming a professional performer. Before long she was appearing with the Curly Chalker Trio at the celebrated Printer's Alley in Nashville, playing steel guitar and singing.

At that time Billy Sherrill was one of Columbia Records most prominent producers. Once he heard the talented young woman people were beginning to talk about, he signed her to a recording contract. It was 1969, and her first single was not country but an Otis Redding rhythm and blues song – even though Barbara is classic country, R&B has always been a successful musical genre for her. Her records and albums are constantly well received by the black community.

Her country releases were soon being noticed by the right people and in 1972 she returned to the Ryman Auditorium, not as a spectator but as a proud member of the Grand Ole Opry. For five years she recorded for the Columbia label and had better than average success.

'After Closing Time' was a duet with David Houston and made the top-ten. Other releases that enhanced her reputation, and increased her fan following included, 'Show Me', 'Give a Little, Take a Little', another duet with Houston 'I Love You, I Love You' and 'This Time I Almost Made It'. During the early to mid-1970s albums were the recording order of the day for Barbara, as well as singles. Two sterling releases were 'Treat Him Right' and a David Houston collaboration 'A Perfect Match'.

The old adage 'a change is as good as a rest' proved true for Barbara when she left Columbia in 1975 and signed with ABC/ Dot Records. 'Standing Room Only' was her first release for ABC/Dot and it made the top-ten by early 1976. A constant output of impressive singles made the country fraternity sit up and take serious notice. Before the year was out she had her first number one single with the provocative title 'Sleeping Single In A Double Bed'.

In typical Mandrell style, which espouses complacency, she followed up with another number one single for 1979 '(If Loving You Is Wrong) I Don't Want to be Right'.

One way to make a hot career hotter is to tour and make as many TV appearances as possible. Mandrell embarked upon a killing schedule. In addition to her concert dates she guested on most of the important network shows of the day, including *Merv Griffin*, Mike Douglas, the *Rockford Files* and *Dick Clark's American Bandstand*. 1980 was a gold-star year for Barbara when the Country Music Association named her Entertainer of the Year. She followed up that triumph in 1981 by being named Musician of the Year and Female Artist of the Year by *Music City News*.

A television natural she signed with NBC to host her own show, *Barbara Mandrell and the Mandrell Sisters* for the 1980–1981 season. She shared billing with her two younger sisters, Louise and Irene. A sign of the show's success was a renewal for the 1981–1982 season. Barbara was at the peak of her popularity when tragedy struck in 1985 – she was nearly killed in a car accident and for a while it was feared she would never perform again. In typical Mandrell fashion she fought back and within a year returned to the stage singing better than ever.

The brush with death gave Barbara a renewed zest for life and an appreciation of what is and what is not important. Regardless of her professional success and the pressures of staying on top she puts her husband and children first.

One doesn't have to listen for very long to Barbara sing to realize that she is the master of 'cheating' and 'hurtin'' songs. In reality the songs are the antithesis of her rigid standards and the lifestyle she leads. If Barbara wasn't a country superstar she could have an impressive acting career. A number of roles, on television, confirm her dramatic skills. She can assume a character, totally divergent to her real life personae, and make it believable. Once the performance is over she again becomes Barbara Mandrell, wife and mother.

★*Barbara Mandrell Greatest Hits* (MCA MCAD-31302)

An artist knows that stardom has arrived when nicknames or catch phrases are attached to them. GEORGE JONES is 'country music's living legend', Kitty Wells is 'music's living legend' and Barbara Mandrell is 'country when country wasn't cool'. 'I Was Country When Country Wasn't Cool' is the first song on this compilation of her *Greatest Hits*. It opens to resounding applause from an audience that immediately recognizes the 1981 Single of the Year. And the applause really erupts when George Jones drops in for a cameo appearance on one verse.

Barbara's grip on 'hurtin'' and 'cheating' songs is firm and secure. The lineup of this album confirms her special niche in country music: '(If Loving You is Wrong) I Don't Want to be Right' was the 1979 Single of the Year and one of Barbara's best efforts.

When she sings about there being no future in loving a married man one believes she means every word of it, especially when she launches into 'If loving you is wrong/ I don't want to be right'. Other favourites include 'In Times Like These', 'There's No Love in Tennessee' and 'One of a Kind Pair of Fools'.

McBride & The Ride

(formed 1991, current members – Terry McBride, Ray Hendron, Billy Thomas)
Sparkling three-part harmonies, hard driving songs and unquestionable musicianship are the elements that make McBride & The Ride a most interesting group. Lead singer and bassist Terry McBride, guitarist Ray Herndon and drummer Billy Thomas interpret traditional country music while blending their contemporary, somewhat rock, influence into their music. Their tight vocal and instrumental work reflects the dedication they have put

into the long hard days of rehearsing, performing and touring. It's apparent that they enjoy singing and are out to please.

McBride & The Ride was named the 1991 Top New Country Group by *Cashbox* magazine on the strength of their first two albums *Can I Count on You* and *Same Old Star*. Their third album *Sacred Ground* was jointly produced by Steve Gibson and Tony Brown for MCA. The trio looks upon it as a musical turning point and a benchmark for the future. It was recorded using the Mitsubishi X-850 32 track digital.

★*Sacred Ground* (MCA MCAD-10540)

The title-cut and first single 'Sacred Ground' was written by Kix Brooks (of BROOKS AND DUNN) and Vernon Rust. It's the hurting wail of a man who begs a rival to leave his love alone. 'It's a precious thing you don't know nothing about/We were joined in the sight of the Lord/In the eyes of our whole town/ Why don't you leave her alone/You're treading on sacred ground'. It's a great song for those who have suffered the agonies of an outsider slicing through their marriage. It's an even better song for those who treasure what they have. 'Makin' Real Good Time' really spotlights the individual talents of the trio. Their vocal blending is excellent on a song that states its case in a no-frills, straight-forward manner. If the group doesn't let success spoil them and self-destruct, McBride & The Ride will be heard from for some time to come.

McCann, Susan

(born Patricia Susan Mary Heaney, Carrickasticken, Forkhill, County Armagh, February 26 1949)
Just mention the name of Susan McCann at Dolly Parton's Dollywood, in Tennessee, or Tampa, Florida's famous Strawberry Festival. The reply will be, 'You mean that Irish country singer who appeared here and sings like she was born in the Tennessee hills?'

McCann is unique when it comes to non-American country artists. She is acknowledged by many of Nashville's elite to be a quality singer with a pure, unadulterated country sound. Her fan following is international, particularly strong in Ireland, the United Kingdom, United States, Canada and the Continent, where she is singled out as the premier female interpreter of country songs. Following the dictum of most country stars, she gets out of the recording studio to meet her fans and tours extensively with her band The Storytellers.

As a teenager in Forkhill, County Armagh, McCann sang with the local John Murphy County Ceili band. It was during her formative years as a singer that she met fellow musician Dennis Heaney who became her husband. Following the birth of their two children, and a re-evaluation of her future, McCann embarked upon a country music career path that has been a steady climb to international recognition.

In the mid-1970s McCann brought out 'Big Tom Is Still The King', which topped the charts in Ireland and was the beginning of an impressive body of work.

The secret to McCann's success is the material she records and how she records it. 'I love picking songs and am never satisfied until I have the best ones available. There's no sense bringing out a second-rate album. I'd sooner not record than do that,' she says. McCann not only chooses her songs wisely she surrounds herself with the finest musicians available both in the studio and on the road.

Next to her family, her music and fans come first. She readily acknowledges that life, at this point in time, is great. 'I'm doing what I most love doing, singing and entertaining.'

It's the confession of a happy and satisfied performer.

★*Diamonds & Dreams* (Prism Leisure HCD 591)

There are sixteen cuts on this CD but there are many more songs because McCann does a country medley the like of which one hasn't heard in a long time. It's her tribute to country music and what a tribute it is: one song after the other with hardly a breath. The McCann musical magic comes through loud and clear. There is no slurring of notes or words.

She begins with 'What I've Got In Mind' and like bullets out of a gun she covers 'Stand By Your Man', 'Send Me The Pillow That You Dream On', 'Honky Tonk Angel', 'Take The Chains From My

Heart', 'Your Good Girl's Gonna To Go Bad', 'Your Cheating Heart', and 'Bobby McGee', to name but a few.

It's a cornucopia of country music served up in banquet style. This cut was produced by Liam Hurley and he deserves a tip of the leprechaun's hat for an emerald effort.

If there were nothing more on this CD it would be worth the purchase price. It's an excellent addition to any country music collection.

McEntire, Reba

(born Chockie, Oklahoma, March 28 1955)
November 14 1985 is indelibly stamped in Reba McEntire's memory. If you ask her why it is circled on her calendar of memories her eyes will fill up. 'When Opry announcer Grant Turner introduced me as the sixty-first roster member of the Grand Ole Opry twenty-five years of waiting and yearning were over,' she'll tell you. 'It was a dream come true. It was the night I came home.'

There is a circle of wood implanted in the centre of the new Opry stage. It was cut from the stage floor of the old Ryman Auditorium and has become a hallowed icon for country performers. Before she began singing that night McEntire had a few words for a hushed audience. She looked down at the relic and began, 'You know, this little piece of wood has probably heard more sad songs than I'll be able to sing all the rest of my life. But if you'll let me, I'd like to sing one more song just for it.' With a catch in her voice, which has become a trademark, she began to sing the Harlan Howard/Chuck Rains 1984 masterpiece 'Somebody Should Leave'.

At the end of the song a deeply moved audience began to clap. The applause built to a crescendo and McEntire received a prolonged standing ovation. Many in the audience, that night, commented on how fortunate country music was to have young, new, sparking talent like Reba McEntire who was bound to inject a fresh verve and life into the music scene. They were right about one thing. This Okie from Chockie was destined to bring a new perspective to country music.

There's no other country artist who can come close to McEntire when it comes to vocally defining the heart-rending, emotional, roller coaster many modern women are forced to ride. She has earned a singular reputation, and fame, for putting into song the voices of women who are trapped in soul-destroying relationships and sabotaged by love. McEntire's life and career reads like a Hollywood movie script. It has all the ingredients needed for a hit – love, divorce, tragedy and skyrocketing success.

McEntire is the daughter of Jacqueline and Clark McEntire. Her father was a champion steer roper and, as a youngster she was a first-class barrel racer in local rodeos. Along with her brother Pake and sisters, Suzie and Alice, she grew up touring the rodeo circuits. To break the monotony of long drives her mother taught the children how to harmonize and sing together. By the time they were in high school they were earning between $10 and $20 a night singing in Oklahoma clubs.

She had an early single 'I Don't Want To Be A One Night Stand' around the time she graduated from Oklahoma State University. The title was enough to get it heard and played. Her first album was *Reba McEntire* for Mercury/Polygram Records in 1977. McEntire and her new husband Charlie Battles did what Loretta Lynn and Doolittle did to get noticed. They took to the road, visiting radio stations. The only difference was they started out on their honeymoon. It was a slow journey with many rebuffs along the way. Gradually McEntire's records began appearing on the charts. 'Three Sheets to the Wind' hit the top twenty in July 1978. Serious recognition came in 1980 when 'You Lift Me Up to Heaven' and 'I Can See Forever in Your Eyes' began to move up in the charts. Both songs were from her *Feel The Fire* album. The snowball began to roll. She had another chart hit 'Can't Even Get the Blues'. It became her first number one song.

McEntire has a unique quality to her voice. She can be hard and bluesy on one song, sweet and gentle on the next and vocally outspoken on another, especially when she is singing about lonesome, heartbroken, love-starved women.

A change of labels from Mercury/Polygram to MCA Records and a new producer, Norro Wilson, lit a fire under her career. *Just A Little Love*, her first album for MCA and 'Every Second Someone Breaks a Heart', a single from the album, made the industry sit up and take notice. For the first time McEntire edged close to rock 'n' roll. It was a calculated ploy to grab the attention of the young fans and thus increase her following.

From 1984 through 1987 McEntire won the Country Music Association's award for Vocalist of the Year. No other female, in the history of country music, has won the honour four years in a row. It was only a matter of time before McEntire was crowned Entertainer of the Year. She got that award in 1986. It was a memorable year as she also won a Grammy for her blockbuster single 'Whoever's in New England'.

While her career and popularity blossomed there were distracting personal problems that took the edge off her success. After 11 years of marriage, to Charlie Battles, she left their cattle ranch in Oklahoma, moved to Nashville and filed for divorce. To the surprise of her friends and associates she married Narvel Blackstock in 1989. Blackstock was a former steel-guitar player in her band before he became her manager. In February 1990 she gave birth to her first child, a son she named Shelby.

Not content just to be in the top echelon of country stars McEntire pursued and nurtured a promising acting career. She has garnered positive reviews for her roles in a number of productions including *Tremors*, a science-fiction movie, which has become a cult favourite, and for playing opposite Kenny Rogers in the mini-series *Luck of the Draw – Gambler IV*.

An horrendous tragedy devastated McEntire in 1990. A plane crash took the lives of her road manager and seven members of her band. If she had not been suffering from an attack of bronchitis, and hadn't listened to her husband, she would have been on the plane. With an inner strength, that won the admiration and support of her colleagues and fans, McEntire publicly shared her anguish and kept on performing. The sorrows of the past were dramatically captured in *For My Broken Heart* which she released in October 1991. 'Singing sad songs, is a way for me to get the hurt out into the open,' said McEntire. 'I hope this album heals all our broken hearts.' *For My Broken Heart* went platinum just two months after its release.

★*For My Broken Heart* (MCA MCASD-10400)

Released in 1991, *For My Broken Heart* is the saddest album McEntire has ever recorded. It's also her bestseller and third platinum-plus album. Two million copies were sold within nine months of release. McEntire now accounts for more album sales than any other act signed to MCA Records' Nashville division. Such sales figures are a remarkable achievement for an album that has such grim topics as marital breakups, infidelity, murder, missed opportunities, mercy killing and neglect of the aged.

The intro for the title song, 'For My Broken Heart', is almost a requiem but it fits in perfectly with the opening lyrics: 'There were no angry words at all/As we carried boxes down the hall'. McEntire gives it all she's got and one can feel the pent-up emotion as she closes the door on a relationship with a resigned finality, 'I guess the world ain't gonna stop/For my broken heart'. The other 13 songs are just as moving. It's an emotional album from an emotional artist who makes no apology for what she sings or how she sings it. 'It seems your current emotional status determines what music you want to hear. That's what happened on the song selection for this album,' says McEntire.

★*Reba McEntire's Greatest Hits* (MCA MCAMD-5979)

McEntire's voice was once described as 'refreshing as a spring prairie breeze'.

This CD confirms that the assessment was dead on. There are 10 songs to enjoy and they take the listener on a musical ride to remember. On 'Little Rock' McEntire is full of fun and frisky. Confirming her distinction as being probably the most emotional country artist of the day she jolts the emotions with 'He Broke Your Memory Last Night'.

Line dancing and the Texas two-step are all the rage. For those who enjoy a work out on the dance floor McEntire offers 'One Promise Too Late'.

Many artists believe that they sing their own songs best. McEntire wrote 'Only In My Mind' and one could not imagine anyone else doing this heart-wrencher proper justice except the composer. Two lines that recur in the song show McEntire's brilliance in composition. 'He said have you ever cheated on me/ And I said only in my mind'. The consensus around Nashville is that this iridescent star is just hitting her stride.

Murray, Anne

(born Springhill, Nova Scotia, June 20 1945)

Most small towns which have a famous son or daughter prominently advertise it as 'the birthplace of . . .' Springhill, Nova Scotia is no different.

Anne Murray not only has her name prominently displayed, she has her own museum, the Anne Murray Centre. It is filled with Anne Murray memorabilia and country fans from across North America, and overseas, make it one of the most visited tourist attractions in the area. The other tourist attraction is the Miners' Museum which is a memorial to Springhill's sons who also made the town famous. Springhill, which had the deepest mine in North America before it was closed, is the site of three disastrous mine tragedies that decimated the male population of the small town.

Anne was not 12 when the second disaster struck in 1956 and just 13 when the third and last one took the lives of 75 coal miners in 1958. Her strong, independent, spirit was forged in the small town where most of her friends' fathers were coal miners. Her father, Carson Murray, was a doctor and practised medicine in Springhill. The tight-knit Murray family included five brothers, three older, two younger. Living among coal miners who faced death every time they went below had a lasting impact on Anne. In an interview she was quoted as saying 'Coal miners are a solid stock. There have been so many disasters in Springhill and they just bounce back. I'm sure that has had an influence on me.'

Superstar status, and international acclaim, has never dimmed Anne's focus on the importance of a stable private life. Her roots in Nova Scotia are deep and enduring.

When Anne was growing up, Nova Scotia was a hotbed of country music. One of the most popular television shows was the CBC's *Sing Along Jubilee* which was produced in Halifax. Every country fan in Canada watched it. Anne's love for music came naturally and even though she leaned more to pop and rock during her high school days, and at the University of New Brunswick, where she was studying to become a physical education teacher, she decided to give country a chance and auditioned for *Sing Along Jubilee*.

William Langstroth was the show's co-host and associate

producer. He was the man who didn't hire Anne when she first auditioned and he is also the man who eventually married her.

Langstroth remembers the audition well. 'She perched on a stool and with only her baritone ukulele as accompaniment she sang "Mary Don't You Weep".' Even though he didn't hire her, because there wasn't an opening in the show for an alto, Langstroth was sufficiently impressed to ask her to keep in touch, which she didn't. Returning to university Anne dedicated all her time and energy to her studies. She was resigned to a teaching career not a singing one. After a bit of detective work Langstroth finally tracked her down and asked her to return for another audition. She flatly and unequivocally refused. Langstroth is just as strong willed, and determined, as Anne. He finally talked her into the audition. She was hired and for four seasons was a featured member of the *Sing Along Jubilee* cast.

Langstroth's colleague and friend was Brian Ahern. He was taken with Anne's singing and sensed that, with a bit of grooming, this vivacious woman with the soft alto voice had star potential written all over her.

Ahern became her producer for a number of productive years. The breakthrough for any artist is never easy and it took great perseverance on Ahern's part to finally get Ann into a studio and complete her first album *What About Me*. It was released by Arc Records, a small Canadian label.

There is usually one song on each album which stands head-and-shoulders above the others. In this instance it was 'Snowbird' – a cross-over song that delighted both pop and Anne Murray country fans. It became a top hit in both Canada and the United States and catapulted Anne into the limelight.

The brighter Anne's star shone the more in demand she became as guest star on most of the major television shows. Capitol Records knew they had a winner in Anne and began an extensive promotional and publicity campaign complete with the Hollywood star treatment. She was on a hectic treadmill of recording and appearances, and hated every moment. 'I felt like Dorothy in *The Wizard of Oz*,' she said in a 1979 *Billboard* feature. 'All I wanted to do was go home.'

Because she didn't follow up 'Snowbird' with a back-to-back hit, industry interest began to cool and there were those who began openly to wonder if Anne was going to be another one-hit marvel.

During a two-and-a-half year dry period, with nothing making the charts, Anne played some of the worst clubs in the States in an effort to keep her career rolling. Asked what it was like playing those clubs during what some like to call 'paying your dues time', she has a one-word response. 'Rotten!' But the rotten times faded into memory when Capitol released Anne's single of Kenny Loggins' beautifully crafted composition 'Danny's Song' in 1973. The song shot up both the country and pop charts as did her album of the same title.

Anne Murray was no 'one hit' wonder. Other impressive hits followed, including 'What About Me', 'He Thinks I Don't Care', and 'Son of a Rotten Gambler' that was a country top five.

1975 was a watershed year because she won a Grammy for Best Country Vocal Performance by a Female for her *Love Song* album and because she married Bill Langstroth and put her career on hold to start a family. In August 1976 she gave birth to a son, William Stewart Langstroth Jr.

Capitol still kept her profile high by releasing a series of new recordings during the mid-'70s. 'Sunday Sunrise', and 'The Call', came out in 1975. 'Golden Oldie' followed in 1976 and 'Sunday School to Broadway' kept the momentum going in 1977. While none made it to the charts they kept her name alive. By 1978 Anne was ready to resume her career but with a major difference. This time she would be in total control. She would decide what booking to take. She would decide what music she would record and she would have the final say on all career decisions. In the same year Capitol released her comeback album *Let's Keep It That Way*. The decision to include the old Everly Brothers' hit 'Walk Right Back' was a career winner. It became a smash single and is still a concert favourite. Another single from the album was 'You Needed Me'. It quickly climbed to the top-five on both the country and pop charts and has remained one of Anne's most requested numbers. Within a year of release 'You Need Me' went gold and by 1979 the album was platinum.

To add a further glow to 1979, Dawn Joann Langstroth was born on April 20. Never one to settle back in a comfortable cubbyhole and savour success Anne released a children's album. *Hippo in My Tub* was co-released by Sesame Records in the States and Capitol Records in Canada to excellent reviews.

The 1980s started off where the 1970s ended with a Grammy

for Best Country Vocal Performance by a Female for 'Could I Have This Dance'. She also won in four categories in the 1980 Canadian Juno Awards (the Juno is Canada's equivalent of the American Grammy).

Anne is not only in total control professionally and privately, she has a refreshing, candid approach to life. She no illusions or contradictions about what comes first in her life. It's her family. This remarkable artist, with her 4 Grammys, 15 Juno awards for Best Female Vocalist or Country Female Vocalist (1970 to 1986), 36 albums and sales topping 25 million, is still a Canadian and resides in a Toronto suburb.

On March 22 1993 Anne was inducted into the Juno Hall of Fame in honour of her 25 years in show business. She ended her acceptance speech with, 'It's the most important Juno I've ever received – but it won't be my last.'

Anne Murray's Greatest Hits (Capitol C2 46058)

This CD delivers precisely what it advertises. It's a collection of Anne Murray's greatest hits and it doesn't cheat – some greatest hits short-change by including one or two lesser known songs, or downright clinkers, just to pad out the list.

It's only right that 'Snowbird' leads off this album. It was this song, which was written by fellow Canadian Gene MacLellan, that thrust Anne into the country music spotlight. 'Danny's Song' is the perfect vehicle for Anne's throaty alto. It's a beautiful song picture of birth and love. 'You Needed Me' confirms her mastery with sensitive lyrics. The guitar work is outstanding and the chord progressions are most arresting. It's difficult to pigeonhole this classic song as either country or pop. Regardless, everyone who loves 'You Need Me' is unanimous. It's the perfect marriage of words and music. The album concludes with 'Could I Have This Dance'. It's the ideal coda to a most compelling and satisfactory CD.

Nelson, Willie

(born Willie Hugh, Fort Worth, Texas, April 30 1933)

If ever there was a country entertainer who personified 'what you see is what you get' it is Willie Nelson. The only conundrum about Willie Nelson, who went by the name of Hugh when he first hit Nashville in 1960, is why he languished in virtual obscurity during the '50s and '60s. He didn't make his mark as a performer until the '70s.

During those barren performing years he nevertheless earned himself quite a reputation as a composer of merit. What PATSY CLINE did with his 'Crazy' and Faron Young did with 'Hello Walls' is proof positive that even if Willie had never stepped on a stage he would have left an indelible mark on country music as a song writer.

Like so many other country greats such as ERNEST TUBB, and his fellow Highwayman WAYLON JENNINGS, Willie is a Texan who came from humble beginnings. Following a brief air force stint he knocked around Texas, Oregon and California as a disc jockey until boredom and the desire to try and make it in country music took over. It was during this restless period that he began writing and penned 'Family Bible' and 'Night Life'. Short of ready cash, and with a family to feed, he sold the rights to 'Family Bible' for $50 and 'Night Life' for $150. He claims the money went for milk for the baby. Both songs became hits and made others rich.

Every town has an 'in place' and in Nashville, during the heady days of the '50s and '60s, when the Ryman Auditorium housed the Grand Ole Opry, it was Tootsie's Orchid Lounge. A small alley separated the watering hole from the hallowed Opry. Tootsie's became a convenient hangout for singers and instrumentalists. They would slip out of the Ryman, which was not air conditioned in those days, for a light libation between acts. There to meet them would be the song writers and hangers-on. Willie will always remember the many hours he spent at Tootsie's with pleasure. It was there that he met singer, songwriter Hank Cochran who helped him get a writing contract with Pamper Music. Country star Ray Price was a partner in Pamper and he saw more potential in Willie than just his writing talents. He gave him a job in his band as bass guitarist.

It was during 1961 that Willie got a demo tape of 'Crazy' to

Patsy Cline. She recorded it and it became one of the top-selling singles of the year. Willie could have retired in modest fashion, at thirty-four, on the royalties he has received from that masterpiece. 'Of all the artists, including me, who recorded "Crazy" none topped Patsy's single. Her's was the best,' says Willie, without reservation.

Willie also gave Billy Walker a top ten hit with 'Funny How Time Slips Away'. Faron Young will forever be in his debt for 'Hello Walls'.

The lineup of those who, by the early '70s, had recorded Willie's material is a roll call of musical giants. Bing Crosby, Frank Sinatra, Perry Como, Roy Orbison, Stevie Wonder and even Lawrence Welk mined the Nelson mother lode.

The days of Willie writing songs for others, and seeing someone else get the applause and royalties, were coming to an end. He began to record his own songs and make giant ripples on the charts. While he did not have an especially high profile during those early performing years he was building a respectable fan following. He played the small clubs, and honky tonks, where he could let his hair down and play the music he liked for the people who liked it, especially the younger crowd. In Willie, with his long braided hair, bandanna, stubbled face and sneakers, they saw an anti-establishment icon and relished what they saw. They certainly liked what they heard. His concerts soon became sell-outs and his singles, and albums, shot up to the top of the charts.

As his career blossomed and he became recognized as one of country's certified stars his personal life was in chaos. Divorce followed divorce, affair followed affair, personal tragedies were the rule rather than the exception. His multi-million dollar tax problems and bankruptcies became headlines for the tabloids.

In spite of all his problems he has never lost his wry sense of humour or the support of his loyal fans. In their eyes he can do no wrong. This is especially true of the farmers of America. His annual 'Farm Aid' concerts have raised public awareness and multiplied thousands of dollars. Many farmers would have lost the family farm to the banks, if it had not been for Willie and his fellow performers.

There are very few artists who can orchestrate an audience to the degree that Willie can. He moves effortlessly from tender ballads like 'Blue Eyes Crying In The Rain' to rousing beat-driven numbers such as 'If You've Got The Money, I've Got The Time' or 'Whisky River'. No country performer comes close to matching the Willie Nelson 'devil may care' style.

Being inducted into the Country Music Hall of Fame, on the 27th Annual CMA Awards telecast on September 29 1993, was the pinnacle of fan and industry recognition for Willie. When friend Waylon Jennings first heard about the induction he said, 'I think it's long overdue. You've heard of all-round cowboys, well I think Willie is an all-round artist because he does it all great.'

★*Willie Nelson Stardust* (Columbia CK 35305)

When Willie first suggested that he do an album celebrating some of his favourite pop songs, from decades past, the prophets of doom were sure his country fans would turn their backs on it. To Willie's delight, they had to choke on their scepticism. The album spawned a number of top ten singles including 'Blue Skies', 'Stardust' and 'Georgia On My Mind'.

One can sense the joy Willie must have had when he recorded 'September Song'. With an intoxicating piano intro by Brooker T. Jones Willie launches into some of the most beautiful lyrics ever written. His vocal tenderness enchants. Brooker T. Jones again adds his indelible piano signature to 'The Sunny Side Of The Street', and Mickey Raphael is a joy to hear on the harmonica. Willie and his friends get swinging on 'All of Me'. The guitar, drum and organ work on this cut is spectacular. In addition this sterling CD offers the melodic 'Unchained Melody', 'Don't Get Around Much Anymore', 'Moonlight In Vermont' and 'Someone To Watch Over Me'.

Willie would be the first to admit that in order to reach great musical heights one has to have the best session players in the business. This is certainly true for *Stardust*, it sparkles.

★*Willie Nelson's – Greatest Hits (And Some That Will Be)* (Columbia CGK 37542)

The established hits like 'Good Hearted Woman' and 'On The Road Again' make this CD a musical bargain. 'Blue Eyes Crying In The Rain', the sad tale of broken but undying love, is a personal favourite. It was written by Country Hall Of Famer Fred Rose and, even though it was recorded by many others, it took Willie's 1975 rendition to make it the number one country song of the year. Kris Kristofferson, who is unstinting in his praise for his 'Highwayman' buddy, says that one only has to listen to Willie to realize that he 'phrases like a jazz singer by singing behind the beat'. 'Whisky River' is an excellent example of how he does it.

Willie has long been recognized as a crafted guitarist who offers a clean, uncluttered style of playing. Most arrangements are built around his battered guitar. Kristofferson's 'Help Me Make It Through The Night' is a prime example of his virtuosity.

Which numbers fall into the 'some that will be' category? Give a listen to 'Angel Flying Too Close To The Ground', 'Heartaches Of A Fool' and 'If You Could Touch Her At All'.

★*The Best Of Willie Nelson* (EMI-Manhattan CDP 7 48392 2)

This CD delivers. It could have been titled 'Willie Sings Willie 13 Times' because he wrote every number.

From the opening cut, 'Funny How Times Slips Away' to 'Darkness On The Face Of The Earth' it's the perfect marriage of singer and composer, along with the Anita Kerr Singers who back up each number.

Each of Willie's songs starts off with a single word or phrase which grabs immediate attention and keeps the listener's attention right to the end of the ballad. 'Crazy' is a prime example and so is 'Touch Me'. The first begins with the single word 'crazy' and the other with the melancholy phrase 'touch me, touch the hand of the man who once owned all the world'. The listener is immediately engrossed and can't wait for Willie to carry on and spin his musical tale. 'Hello Walls' is a real treat and Willie the singer does Willie the composer proud.

Trying to define the Willie Nelson musical mystique is like trying to catch mercury between one's fingers. Just as you think you have the mystery unravelled Willie surprises with something totally unexpected, either vocally or musically, as he plucks his Mexican flavoured gut-string guitar like no other in the business.

Nitty Gritty Dirt Band

(formed May 1966, current members – Jeff Hanna, Jimmie Fadden, Jimmy Ibbotson, Bob Carpenter)

It was May 1966 in Orange, California, so the story goes, and a group of five young men were killing time by hanging around a local guitar shop. They were desperately trying to figure out how not to have to work for a living. Out of their profound deliberations is conceived the idea of forming a band – not a conventional band but a band with a difference. The Nitty Gritty Dirt Band was born and gave its first concert, in Orange, on May 13 to an appreciative audience that was drawn to the innovative sound and high-level energy. Nearly three decades later the Dirt Band continues to make musical waves.

Two of the original members, Jeff Hanna and Jimmie Fadden, are still with the band. Jimmy Ibbotson came on board in late 1969 and Bob Carpenter added his name to the credits early in 1980. In 1971 the Dirt Band came to Nashville for a recording session. Nashville's ultra conservative establishment was not quite ready for the ragged bunch of young pop musicians, with a strong liking for real Appalachian music but by the time the establishment had recovered its composure the Dirt Band had recorded a landmark three-LP set *Will The Circle Be Unbroken*. The music was a magical blend of the Dirt Band with such leading country artists as Roy Acuff, the Carter Family, Merle Travis and Earl Scruggs. The album stayed on the pop charts for an astounding 32 weeks and the country music critics were unanimously ecstatic. It even garnered high praise reviews from the rock press. The fact that the country music community finally embraced this most unlikely of bands is proof that love and respect for excellence in music will bridge cultural and generational gaps.

During the '70s and '80s the Dirt Band toured ceaselessy. They were selected by the Soviet government to be the first group to tour the USSR. The band spent a month inside Russia and on one occasion played on a massive TV hookup that gave them 145 million viewers.

Deciding that it was time for lightning to strike again the band once more descended upon Nashville. For a memorable nine days, in early December 1989, a steady stream of country stars gathered in the Scruggs Sound Studio to lay down the tracks for *Will The Circle Be Unbroken - Volume Two*.

Circle II went gold in the US and Canada. It won three Grammys, Country Music Association Album of the Year and spawned a long-form video documentary.

The Nitty Gritty Dirt Band has survived and become an American institution because the members have steadfastly remained true to their music. They make their music for the sake of the song and the sheer joy of playing.

★*Will The Circle Be Unbroken - Volume Two* (Universal Records UVLDX-12500)

This 20-song CD deserves all the praise it has received since its release in 1990. Brought together, on one album, are such Nashville musical giants as the late Roy Acuff, JOHNNY CASH, Earl Scruggs, John Denver and Chet Atkins. There is also a strong supporting cast from the newer voices who are making their musical marks - Bruce Hornsby, John Hiatt, Chris Hillman, Roger McGuinn, Emmylou Harris, Levon Helm and others.

The opening number is 'Life's Railway To Heaven' with Johnny Cash showcased on the vocals and guitar. He is ably assisted by the Carter sisters, who include wife June with sisters Anita and Helen. The song opens with a fade-up of voices as Cash discusses the intro with banjo player Earl Scruggs before he launches into the lyrics. It's a novel touch and it brings the listener right into the studio at the very start. The same approach is heard on other numbers. On some songs like 'Don't You Hear Jerusalem Moan' a number of performers walk into the spotlight. Sam Bush handles the first verse with vocal and some great banjo plucking. John Cowan takes over on the second verse. Bob Carpenter finishes off the third and is ably assisted by Dirt Band member Jimmy Ibbotson in his own inimitable style.

Song 19 is 'Will The Circle Be Unbroken', the title song. It features Johnny Cash, Roy Acuff, RICKY SKAGGS and Levon Helm with Emmylou Harris. The first thing one hears is a cacophony of voices as everyone greets everyone else in the studio. Following the opening chorus, which everyone joins in, sounding like the choir from the 'Church In The Wildwood', Cash takes over for verse number 1. Acuff comes in on verse number 2 and so on with the other featured artists. Each verse is bridged by a chorus from the assembly.

The album closes with a moving guitar solo of 'Amazing Grace' by Randy Scruggs.

Oak Ridge Boys

(revamped 1987, current members – Duane Allen, Richard Sterban, Joe Bonsall, Steve Sanders)

When country music fans discovered the Oak Ridge Boys there were those who excitedly exclaimed 'what a great new quartet'.

If they had cared to check they would have learned that this edition had already won four Grammy awards and fifteen Dove Awards (the Dove is the gospel music equivalent of the Grammy). Further checking would have revealed that the original quartet was formed in Knoxville, Tennessee in 1945 and started out as the Country Cut-Ups. Often they would perform for the employees at the atomic energy research centre at nearby Oak Ridge.

Wisely deciding that the Country Cut-Ups was not the best of names they became the Oak Ridge Quartet and began to build up a following with their country/gospel music.

When it became obvious that the gospel numbers were the most popular they built their repertoire around southern gospel music. By the autumn of 1945 they were regulars on the Grand Ole Opry and a programme favourite. They became one of the top-drawing quartets in the '50s and their picture appeared on the front cover of *Time* magazine. But by the middle of the decade the group had disbanded.

In 1957 a new version of the Oak Ridge Quartet was formed. The long hard climb back to popularity began. The group changed their name to the Oak Ridge Boys in 1964. To grab younger fans they had to project a more youthful image. Their appearance also changed with the times. 'We were the first gospel group to wear long hair and beards,' recalls Joe Bonsall. 'When we added a rock drummer to the band the criticism and gossip really began to heat up.' There was bitterness on both sides. The conservative wing of gospel music fought the Oaks at every turn. In an interview with *People* magazine (May 28 1979) a gospel music spokesman was quoted as saying, 'We're serious about Christian ideals and morals. The Oaks made it quite clear that religion was not their concern.'

Duane Allen shot back by suggesting that the spokesman was a hypocrite. 'Gospel acts on-stage might come on as the ministry,' he said, 'but backstage they look for who's going to pay the check. I feel less hypocritical now.'

Making the decision before it was made for them, they began to ease out of gospel music but straddling the gospel/country fence proved disastrous. They nearly went bankrupt. They probably would have been finished if it hadn't been for JOHNNY CASH who offered them a loan and booked them as his opening act for a Las Vegas appearance. Paul Simon was also a rescuing angel. He booked them for session work on his pop hit 'Slip Slidin' Away'.

Fortunes took an upswing when Jim Halsey Inc. started to manage the Oaks. A country-music act was packaged and in August 1975 the group were booked as headliners at the Landmark Hotel in Las Vegas. Things stabilized in 1977 when MCA (then ABC/Dot) signed them to a recording contract. Their debut release was a winner. *Y'All Come Back Saloon* climbed the country charts to third position and gave birth to two chart cracking singles, 'Y'All Come Back Saloon' and 'You're the One'.

The recording success was a confidence builder as well as a financial boon. The Oak Ridge Boys were back in the business of making hit singles and albums and selling out their concert dates. The hits came, one after another. The pop smash 'Elvira' went platinum and 'Bobbie Sue' shot up to gold. Sales figures are eye-popping. The Oaks have over a dozen number one country singles, nine albums that went gold and two that reached the magical platinum figure.

The honours they have racked up are equally impressive. In addition to five Grammys, the Country Music Association awards range from Best Vocal Group, Best Instrumental Group to Record of the Year.

Another major upheaval hit the group in 1987. In the space of a few months they completely restructured their business operation, revamped the band and replaced William Lee Golden, who had joined the Oaks in 1964. He was the longest serving member. Steve Sanders took over the baritone slot. He was a child star in gospel music under the name of 'Little Stevie' and recorded both gospel and pop for MGM.

The musical talents of the quartet are without question and the packaging of their shows is spectacular. Another talent they have is in choosing the right material. 'Let's face it,' Bonsall explained. 'It's not rocket science here. All you have to do is find good songs that move people, take them onstage and put on a great show.'

★*The Oak Ridge Boys Greatest Hits* (MCA DIDX-386 MCAD-5150)

As long as the Oaks have existed, even in the days of the Country Cut-Ups, one of their strengths has been the individuality of each member. Those who have attended a concert, or have seen them on television, are immediately aware that each one is his own man, from the way they dress to the way they express themselves on stage. It's impossible to imagine anyone trying to place restraints upon the irrepressible Joe Bonsall. Many fans come just to see him two-step and jump with the beat.

If you listen to 'Trying To Love Two Women', with a critical ear, you will hear a textbook example of how a lead and a quartet can slide back and forth like well oiled pistons. The Oaks band, which was 1978 Instrumental Group of the Year, adds many musical threads to the tapestry of this number.

'Y'All Come Back Saloon' holds a special place in the hearts of the Oaks. It was their first country hit and signalled their permanent crossover from gospel to country. A tambourine with 'a silver jingle' enhances the vocal images of 'faded love and faded memories'.

★*Greatest Hits Volume Three* (MCA MCABD-42294)

The best description of 'Bobbie Sue' came from Joe Bonsall. 'It's an off the wall fun tune that you don't have to put in your church hymnal. It's not meant to affect one's personal psyche or morality. It's just meant to make you feel good.'

Make one feel good it does. It was written by Dan and Adele Taylor with Wood Newton and became a million plus seller for the Oaks. A driving drum beat starts the group off and keeps up the pressure until the final note. Richard Sterban hooks the chorus with a booming, glass shattering bass vocal. He's the anchor on this song.

'It takes a Little Rain to Make Love Grow' is romantic, inspirational and moving. The four-part harmony reinforces the consensus that the Oaks are about the best quartet recording today. There may be better tenors than the kinetic Joe Bonsall but no one is his equal when it comes to playing to an audience. On 'Little Things' he reaches up and grabs an upper range that is truly amazing.

This CD is worth adding to any collection.

O'Connor, Mark

(born Seattle, Washington, August 5 1960)

While it may sound like a scriptwriter's fertile imagination, what happened is absolutely true. It was 1972 and Roy Acuff was in his dressing room, back stage, at the Opry. He took the time to listen to an impromptu performance by a 12-year-old child prodigy from Seattle. 'I asked him to play "Tom and Jerry", an old fiddle tune,' recalled Acuff. 'He was amazing. Then and there I decided to put the boy on the Opry, with me, that very night.' By the end of the next week Mark O'Connor had his first record deal.

What O'Connor has accomplished in the short space of 20 years is incredible – session player on over 450 Nashville albums, 12 albums of his own plus impressive Country Music Awards. In addition to being one of the finest violin masters in country or pop music he is an accomplished composer and virtuoso on both guitar and mandolin. He is totally versatile in his music. Regardless of whether he's playing old-time fiddle, classical string, or jazz, O'Connor never ceases to amaze his contemporaries and music critics. 'I believe Mark O'Connor and Itzhak Perlman are two of the greatest musicians on the planet today,' says Chet Atkins.

★*Mark O'Connor The New Nashville Cats* (Warner Bros. 9 26509-2)

During the past years, as one of the most in-demand session players in Nashville, Mark O'Connor has had the pleasure of working with some of the finest musicians in country music. For *The New Nashville Cats*, which O'Connor produced and wrote all the songs for, he chose some very special musicians to help him showcase the instrumental side of the Nashville recording scene.

In the spotlight, on the 10 cuts, is a cross-section of musical excellence from the likes of Matt Rollings on piano, Brent Rowan, electric guitar wizard, Eddie Bayers on drums, Jerry Douglas on lap steel, Terry McMillan adds harmonica shadings, Roy Husky plays a marvellous upright bass, Jim Horn doubles on baritone and alto sax and Charles Rose shines on trombone. O'Connor is of course front and centre on fiddle.

Each cut has its attraction but cut number two deserves high praise not only for the artistry of the instrumentalist but for the vocal work of VINCE GILL, RICKY SKAGGS and STEVE WARINER. All are nothing short of mind-blowing.

The recording sessions were a musician's dream. 'We had a blast', says O'Connor. Those who listen to this CD, time after time, will be in total agreement. It's a gem.

O'Donnell, Daniel

(born Kincasslagh, County Donegal, Ireland, December 12 1961) For any country music fan in the United Kingdom or Ireland no introduction of Daniel O'Donnell is necessary. In fact, it's not really necessary in Nashville either because this country singer with the easy, laid-back voice, is fast establishing himself on both sides of the Atlantic.

In the short space of four years he has sold over one million albums and 250,000 videos. Not bad for someone who was on the verge of chucking it in and emigrating to Canada to start all over again.

All it took to kickstart O'Donnell's career was a carefully worked out marketing and promotion programme. Before too long word of mouth on the Irish circuit was making O'Donnell a household name. His fans warmed to the clear diction and melodious turn of a lyric. By 1991 the UK charts were beginning to look like O'Donnell's bailiwick; seven albums were in the top twenty. It didn't take long for the international country music community to take notice.

O'Donnell made his American debut at Nashville's Country Music Fare in 1988. He also played the Grand Ole Opry as guest of George Hamilton IV. *The Last Waltz* is O'Donnell's best selling album to date and was recorded in a Nashville studio. It has a pure country sound and great lineup of songs. O'Donnell has the voice and skill to really put over a country song. His phrasing is as close to perfect as one will hear. O'Donnell is certainly going to be heard for years to come, especially if he continues to stay true to the roots of country music.

★*The Very Best Of Daniel O'Donnell* (Ritz BCD 700)

When you are named Daniel, and you come from County Donegal, it would be sacrilegious not to include 'Danny Boy' in a CD entitled *The Very Best Of*. O'Donnell slips 'Danny Boy' into ninth place in this 20 song lineup and does justice to this Irish classic. He also stakes out his turf as a certified country singer, with 'Stand Beside Me'. His traditional Nashville sound is gentle, clear and moving. The piano bridges are as pure country as one could wish. 'The Old Rugged Cross' is a highlight. This evergreen hymn has graced the lineup of more country singers than there are stars in the sky. In the gentle hands of O'Donnell it receives new shadings.

In the liner notes, O'Donnell 'hopes that this collection is something special'. He also hopes that some personal memories will be revived. He should have no fears. It's a most pleasing collection and anyone who listens to all 20 cuts, and doesn't have any memories revived, just can't have any memories to revive.

Oslin, K.T.

(born Kay Toinette, Crossitt, Arkansas, May 15 1944)

When K.T. Oslin was 13 she genuinely disliked country music. She thought its focus was too male oriented. Now into mid-life, with a country music career that has won her a host of fans and industry respect, she is still outspoken about country music. 'Old men singing about drinking and cheating on their wives didn't turn me on as a kid and it doesn't turn me on now,' she said. 'They sing about men asking their women to take them back. If my man cheated on me, I wouldn't take him back.'

At a time in life when many entertainers have had their fifteen minutes in the sun and are but a distant memory K.T.'s career was just beginning to get up a head of steam. This late-blooming star has made up career time at an astounding pace.

When she was a teenager growing up in Mobile, Alabama, and

Houston, Texas, rock and roll and good 'ole Texas music were her passion. She was also drawn to the theatre and was carving out a career with national companies in Broadway musicals. She toured with Carol Channing in *Hello Dolly* and appeared with Betty Grable in the Broadway production of the same show. She also appeared in such theatrical blockbusters as *West Side Story* and *Promises, Promises*. Had she not become jaded with singing commercial jingles about everything Madison Avenue had to peddle she could have had a very successful and lucrative career.

K.T. can trace the beginning of her songwriting career back to the day when she was in a ladies' washroom and read some graffiti on the wall. The scrawl 'I ain't never gonna love nobody but Cornell Crawford' caught her eye and stirred her creative juices. She and a friend from her jingle days, wrote a song, 'Crawford, Crawford'. It was enough to attract industry attention and she began recording on her own.

K.T.'s talent and determination finally paid off when Joe Galante, of RCA, was sufficiently impressed by the quality of her lyrics and the conviction in her voice to offer her a recording contract. 'Wall of Tears' was her debut single. While it didn't exactly set the country music scene on fire it did respectably well by rising to number 40 on the charts. An '80's Ladies' single and a video of the same title came next. The '80's Ladies' cycle was completed in rousing fashion by an album that was eagerly bought by K.T.'s fans. No one quarrelled with the Country Music Association when they presented K.T. with the much coveted Song of the Year award for '80's Ladies'. She became the first female songwriter to win it. As pleased as K.T. was by being voted top new female vocalist by the CMA in 1988 and winning a Grammy for best female country performance she was overwhelmed when her *80's Ladies* album went gold. She became the first female to have a gold debut album since Canada's Anne Murray took one home for *Snowbird* in 1973.

K.T. kept churning out the hits. 'Do Ya' was her next big hit and further cemented her grip on stardom. *The Woman* album was a 1988 smash and resulted in two more Grammys – one for best country song and the other for her performance of the chart-topper which she composed. Her two biggest albums *80's Ladies* and *Hold Me* were platinum by the close of 1989. Needing to recharge her creative batteries K.T. took off for two years to reflect and write. The result was a third album, *Love in a Small Town*. As was to be expected the songs are typical Oslin. They have a message and all the froth is stripped away. The story lines are about common people with believable experiences. 'Come Next Monday' became the hit single from the album. There has always been a strong feminist bent to K.T.'s music and, while it is applauded in some circles, it has negatively influenced some radio programmes who are leery about offending male listeners.

K.T. is an interviewer's dream. She is opinionated and forceful. She also possesses a delicious, self-deprecating humour that endears her to the audience.

★*80's Ladies* (RCA 5924-R)

Of the nine tracks on this CD, Oslin wrote four and co-wrote one. Each of her songs stands out, especially 'Younger Men'. Following a pulsating, mood-setting intro, Oslin launches into the song and leaves little or nothing to the imagination – 'Women peak at forty, men at nineteen'. Before long into the song she gives fair warning with 'And the very next opportunity I'm gonna give a younger man a try./Cause younger men are starting to catch my eye'. If you want to hear a throaty deep, suggestive, vocal growl don't miss this one. Oslin is fantastic.

A dramatic change of pace, and ambience, is to be found on 'I'll Always Come Back'. Oslin delicately weaves a nursery rhyme about a little girl and some sheep she couldn't find. 'But don't you worry I'll come back'.

'80's Ladies' is about three little girls from school. 'One was pretty, one was smart and one was a borderline fool.' You'll have to listen to find out which one Oslin is.

A tip of the hat to the musicians and singers in backup. They're excellent.

Parnell, Lee Roy

(born Abilene, Texas, December 21 circa 1958)
If Nashville has one failing it's in trying to clone success. When GARTH BROOKS burst on the scene, and became the hottest country star in history, nearly every record company and producer began

a feverish search for another Garth Brooks. History has proved two things: there is only one Garth Brooks and Lee Roy Parnell will never be a clone of anyone. He is his own man, own singer and own songwriter.

When Parnell was six he sang 'San Antonio Rose' with Bob Wills, the pioneer of western swing, on WBAP in Fort Worth, Texas. Wills was a friend of Parnell's father and an early musical influence. The Texan, out of Abilene, was seriously into playing and writing in his mid-teens and by 19 he had formed his own band. For ten long arduous years he was on the road playing a unique style of kicking music in the honky tonks of Texas. In 1987 Parnell moved to Nashville with his wife Kim and two children, Blake and Allison. Music City was introduced to the Parnell style of music when he was booked into the celebrated Bluebird Café for a series of Monday night shows.

Because of a reputation which preceded him the 'in' crowd attended his first show and were an appreciative and enthusiastic audience. Word of mouth quickly spread and he never performed to anything less than a standing-room-only audience.

Parnell is a master of the guitar and slide guitar. His playing has been likened to a laser which cuts through a song with arresting effects. In addition to performing Parnell has been a staff writer for PolyGram Publishing for several years. His writing credits are impressive. He co-wrote six of the 10 songs on *Love Without Mercy*.

Country music's unprecedented new popularity is mainly due to the integration of exciting new sounds like Parnell's into an existing formula. Even though it is difficult for some country music purists to admit, if it hadn't been for artists like Parnell, who constantly break new musical ground, country would not now have a solid base of young fans – and that base is growing by the day.

Parnell's tenor voice has shades of STEVEN WARINER but with a more cutting edge. Regardless of what he sings, be it rhythm and blues or ballads, there is a bell-like clarity in the way he handles lyrics. There is also a snarl in his voice which is without doubt one of the sharpest in country music. It's impossible to listen to Parnell and be indifferent to his music.

★*Love Without Mercy* (Arista 1864-2)

This album is like a musical train that makes all the right stops at country, pop, soul, gospel, rock, blues and ballads.

'The Rock' has a definite GEORGE JONES flavour to it, with gospel undertones. It was the song that Parnell chose to build the album around. It is a sad song, 'I was a rock standing for you/There was nothing I wouldn't do'. The powerful message demonstrates that the human condition survives all. 'Yes I'm your rock/But I'm rollin' away'.

'Road Scholar', with a play on Rhodes Scholar, is a hurricane-like song. Delbert McClinton joins Parnell in a duet and the two musically paint a picture of an unrepentant honky tonk musician who pays tribute to Jerry Lee Lewis and Elvis Presley, 'My teachers were the killer and the hound dog man'. There is no missing Parnell's celebrated snarl on this one. The lyrics are imaginative and bring a smile to the face of the listener. Every one of the ten songs starts with just Parnell on his guitar followed by his voice. The backup is lean and simple – a couple of guitars, a bass, drums and some piano.

Parton, Dolly

(born Dolly Rebecca, Locust Ridge, Sevier County, Tennessee, January 19 1946)

When you are the fourth of twelve children and start out life in a two-room shack, with an upstairs loft, you do one of two things. You either grit your teeth and, with monumental determination, climb out of the pit of abject poverty or you accept your lot in life with quiet resignation. Dolly Parton did the former and the end result was super stardom for this petite, overly endowed entertainer.

Childhood, while happy, was a day-to-day struggle. Try as he would, Dolly's father could not scrape the bare necessities out of the land for his king-sized family. He finally gave up and took a job in construction to make ends meet. Many of Dolly's songs like 'Coat of Many Colors' and 'The Bargain Store' have strong undercurrents of growing up in rural Tennessee in the foothills of the Smoky Mountains. She knows what it was like to be the butt of ridicule because her parents were dirt poor. Dolly can't remember how old she was when she started to sing but it was long before she could read or write. She would make up songs and get her mother to write down the words for her. When she was seven she made a guitar out of an old mandolin that had two bass strings. It was her greatest treasure until she turned eight and her uncle replaced it with a small Martin guitar. 'I knew from the time I was seven that I wanted to be a singer. I also wanted to become a star and live in a big house,' recalls Dolly. During her pre-teen years, and up until she graduated from high school, music was the passion of her life. She sang constantly, regardless of where she was or what she was doing.

At eighteen she graduated and immediately left for Nashville where she hoped to break into country music. Fortunately she had relatives in Nashville and her uncle Bill Owens took her into his family. He was a respected songwriter and, probably just as important, he had contacts in a city where contacts are all important. Realizing that his niece was a budding songwriter he began writing with her. Together they composed 'Put It Off Until Tomorrow'. Through a stroke of good fortune, country singer Bill Phillips recorded it and the song became a 1966 top-10 hit. On the strength of this song she was offered a contract by Monument Records and her debut album *Hello, I'm Dolly* was released in July 1967.

The next rung on Dolly's ladder of success came when she met Porter Wagoner. At the time Wagoner was one of the biggest country music stars around. He had his own television show and touring act in addition to an impressive recording career. He was looking for a female singer and when he heard Dolly sing he offered her the job. She joined the cast of his television show and began touring.

Wagoner was under contract to RCA at the time. He was instrumental in getting her to switch from Monument to them. Within a short time Dolly was a valued RCA artist. She and Wagoner began to record some of the most popular duets of the day. Even though their costumes were equally outlandish, with rhinestones and sequins, to say nothing of Dolly's wigs and Wagoner's pompadour, their voices were complete opposites. Dolly's high register leads meshed like well oiled gears with Wagoner's masterful soft, deep, harmony. Together they turned out a string of singles including 'Yours Love' and 'Always Always'. Cash registers rang as fans made the hit album *Just The Two of Us* a shattering success. Today their duets are considered to be country classics.

Dolly was on a tight and hectic schedule during the early to mid-'70s. It was a series of one studio session after the other, and endless days on the road touring. She drew the fans who were as enamoured with her singing as they were with her kewpie-doll, sexy stage presence. Her popularity began to overshadow Wagoner's and she started to become restless. She wanted to chart her own destiny instead of having Wagoner make decisions for her and keep her under his control. In 1973 she left the show but did not totally leave Wagoner. For the next three years he still produced her records. They even cut records together. 'Is Forever Longer Than Always' is memorable and so is 'Please Don't Stop Loving Me', which she wrote with him.

Dolly's star was iridescent in 1975. The Country Music Association voted her Female Vocalist of the Year and most of the major trade journals like *Billboard* and *Cashbox* voted her top female country vocalist. Still not completely satisfied with the direction her career was taking, and confident that there were new worlds to conquer she broke completely with Wagoner in 1976. She went out as a single with her own backup band. The break was bitter. An enraged Wagoner slapped Dolly with a law suit and the acrimony sizzled for many years to come.

In 1977 RCA released 'New Harvest . . . First Gathering'. It was a trial balloon to see if the country fans would remain loyal to a new pop sounding Dolly. Not only did the country fans stay loyal, Dolly broke through the pop barrier with resounding success. Next came the album *Here You Come Again* and the title single. It was virtually impossible to turn on a country or pop radio station without hearing the song.

Only the biggest stars in the world are signed to multimillion dollar Las Vegas contracts. Dolly knew she had made the inner circle, in 1979, when the Riviera Hotel got her to sign. She was committed to six weeks a year for two years. Hollywood also jumped on the Parton bandwagon. She was signed to star with Jane Fonda and Lily Tomlin in *9 to 5*. Following the success of *9 to 5*, and a chart-topping single with the same title, Dolly inked her second film contract. She and Burt Reynolds shared star billing in

The Best Little Whorehouse in Texas. Dolly played the madam and
Reynolds the sheriff who is in love with her. The film opened to
less than enthusiastic reviews and did little to enhance either star's
career.

The only entertainment mountain that had not been scaled was
television. In 1987 ABC budgeted a whopping 40 million dollars
for *Dolly*. It was trumpeted as the biggest and best variety show to
hit any network. In spite of Dolly's enthusiasm, talents and
pairing with mega stars like Burt Reynolds and Kenny Rogers the
show bombed. It was a bitter pill for Dolly to swallow.

She returned to root-country sounds with Emmylou Harris
and Linda Ronstadt on a collaborative album *Trio*. It racked up
sales of a million plus and spun off four hit singles. The success of
Trio, in 1987, helped to ease the pain of her venture into prime
time television. The success of her Tennessee theme park
'Dollywood' was added balm for her bruised ego.

Dolly is pragmatic about her successes and failures. 'I've had bad
times, but I've always tried to maintain a good outlook. I've had
headaches and disappointments, but never so great that it blocked
my vision of the future.'

★*Dolly Parton in White Limozeen* (Columbia CK 44384)

This CD was released in 1989. From the CD cover picture it
would appear that Dolly Parton has got about as far away from
Nashville, Seiver County and Porter Wagoner as she could get.
Here she is, all decked out in a shimmering white dress, stole,
platinum wig with arms outstretched. Behind her is the 'white
limozeen' of the title under a theatre marquee with her name in
bright lights. But not to worry. This is still the same old Dolly who
made tacky popular and glitz acceptable.

On 'Why'd You Come in Here Lookin' Like That,' Dolly wags
her vocal finger at a rival with a demanding 'Why'd you come in
here looking like that/In your cowboy boots and your painted-on
jeans'. The beat is honky tonk and Dolly lets loose with all her
pent-up vocal energy.

'What is it My Love' is a hurtin' song that Dolly delivers with a
soft plaintive tone. David Huntsinger's piano intro and accompaniment is just perfect.

Her duet with Mac Davis on 'Wait 'Till I Get You Home' makes this song a stand out. The Parton/Davis lyrics are anything but laid back. 'Wait 'til I get you home/Wait 'til I get you alone/Wait 'til I get my hands you.'

The backup is superb, including the Christ Church Pentecostal Choir on the chorus of 'He's Alive'. It's a soul-stirring anthem.

Reeves, Jim

(born James Travis, Galloway, Panola County, Texas, August 20 1924; died July 31 1964)

If it hadn't been for a leg injury, Jim Reeves' name might very well have been listed on the roster of baseball's St Louis Cardinals instead of on a plaque in Nashville's Country Hall of Fame.

Unlike most country music stars, music was not Reeves' main passion; baseball was. He had eight older brothers and sisters and was brought up on a farm in rural East Texas. Athletics was a way to break the monotony of farm life. He was a better than average player and dreamed of a pro career. With fierce determination he played his way up, through high school and university, until he was spotted by a scout and drafted by the Cardinals. The Cardinals assigned him to Marshall and later Henderson in the East Texas League before the leg injury ended his baseball career.

With his sports dreams shattered Reeves turned to entertainment as a way to make a living. Even though he played the guitar and sang he did not seriously consider himself a musician or performer at that point in his life. He got a job as an announcer and disc jockey on KWKH in Shreveport, Louisiana. On occasion he would take his guitar into the studio and sing for his listeners. He was great with a hymn or old standard such as 'Have I Told You Lately That I Love You'. Little did he know, at the time, that one day this song would be one of the favourites on his top-selling album *The Country Side of Jim Reeves*.

Shreveport was on the country music map as the home of the popular country programme *Louisiana Hayride* and, in 1953, Reeves joined the show as announcer. Before long he had graduated to performer. He began appearing at local clubs and for a while he was a sideman with Moon Mulligan, in Beaumount, Texas. He also had a stint as bandleader/singer at one of Texas' most celebrated honky tonks, Longview's Reo Palm Isle.

Reeves began recording singles in 1949 but it wasn't until he started recording on the Abbott label that he made an impact. 'Mexican Joe' was his second release for Abbott and, to his pleasant surprise, it took off in 1953. That song established Reeves as a country singer to be reckoned with.

In those days he was not known as 'Gentleman Jim Reeves'. That appellation was seven or eight years away when he dramatically changed his singing style. Early in his career his delivery was hard-core country. His voice was high register with an edge that bordered on strident. One listen to early releases like 'Bimbo' in 1954, or 1955's 'Yonder Comes a Sucker' shows that back then, his sound was the antithesis of his best remembered days. By the late '50s and early '60s he began lowering his voice to its natural level and the velvet tones, that his fans so relish on classics like 'He'll Have To Go', came through loud and clear.

Reeves moved to Nashville near the end of the 1950s and became a regular on the Grand Ole Opry. He also toured extensively, including USO tours overseas where he entertained the troops. In 1960 he crisscrossed the states plus Africa and Europe. His tours were sold-out successes and he is partly responsible for the enduring and constantly building interest in country music overseas. In an amazing career, which was cut short in by a plane crash during a violent thunderstorm in July 1964, Reeves scored more top-10 hits, as of early 1970, than any other country artist with the exception of EDDY ARNOLD and Webb Pierce.

Like PATSY CLINE, who met the same early tragic death, his voice was not stilled. His widow, Mary, saw to it that the legend of Jim Reeves is kept fresh by issuing previously unreleased recordings and repackaging the standards. Thanks to state-of-the-art electronics and remastering techniques fans were amazed and delighted to hear Reeves in duet with Patsy Cline on 'Have You Ever Been Lonely'. The single was assembled electronically from the two singers' versions of the same song.

Someone counted and found out that there have been more than 30 hits by Jim Reeves since his untimely death. That's more than he had when he was alive.

★*The Best Of Jim Reeves* (RCA 07863-53678-2)

The hallmark of a classic Jim Reeves song is luxuriant strings and sophisticated guitars in the hands of session players who deliver what they call a muted Nashville sound to backup his soothing baritone. This is precisely what the listener receives on this 12 song CD. It really delivers the best of Jim Reeves.

The opening number is 'He'll Have To Go'. This mega hit showcases Reeves' velvet styling as probably no other song. Released in 1959 it is a melancholy plea to a lover to get rid of the person she is with so they both can pretend. 'Put your sweet lips a little closer to the phone/ Let's pretend that we're together all alone/ I'll tell the man to turn the juke box way down low/ And you can tell your friend there with you he'll have to go'.

A close favourite in popularity, and a song that Reeves wrote, is 'Am I Losing You'. Reeves the singer does justice to Reeves the songwriter. The chord progressions, which are so much a part of the Reeves' musical stylings, are evident and certainly enhance the enjoyment.

Some criticize Reeves' singing as being too syrupy and dated. They may have a point but, for his fans, he'll never be dated. It's a pity he left the music scene so early in life and career. One wonders what he'd be singing today.

Robbins, Marty

(born Martin David, Glendale, Arizona September 26 1925; died December 8 1982)

Marty Robbins' love and interpretation of country and western music didn't come second-hand. He knew and identified with the cowboy as probably few other singers in his field. Of mixed Italian and Indian heritage, he came to a natural love of music at an early age. His grandfather, who was a travelling medicine man, taught him cowboy songs and regaled him with tales of gunfighters and desperados. His father added to his musical knowledge by teaching him the finer points of the harmonica.

As a young boy Robbins grew up in the desert region of Arizona and would pick cotton all day in dry, dusty, fields to earn enough money to see the latest Gene Autry picture. Many times he told interviewers that in Autry he saw the epitome of the singing cowboy. Autry became his idol and inspiration. Robbins never lost his love for the Old West and, during a brilliant career he was to achieve his greatest applause for singles like 'El Paso' and albums such as *Gunfighter Ballads and Trail Songs*. He had a remarkable talent for musically painting vivid tableaux.

The family moved to Phoenix in 1937. Robbins attended high school until he enlisted in the navy and spent a three-year hitch. It was his first time away from home and, while on Pacific duty, he learned to play the guitar and started writing songs. Discharged in the late '40s he returned to Phoenix and gave serious thought to making music his life's career. Through hard work, perseverance, and a bit of luck he landed a spot on a local country radio show. It was more than luck when Little Jimmy Dickens guested on the show. He was immediately impressed by Robbins' easy way with a song. For a young performer he had a unique manner of phrasing and a smooth tone.

At the time Dickens was with the Columbia label, and he suggested that someone should hear this exciting new singer. A Columbia executive decided to heed the suggestion and flew east to Phoenix. Before long Robbins had a contract. 'Love Me Or Leave Me Alone' was his first release and while it didn't exactly set country music on fire it showed promise. That promise was justified when his second single 'I'll Go It Alone' hit the top-10.

Good country songwriters are always in demand. When Fred Rose, of Acuff-Rose Music Publishing, heard 'I Couldn't Keep From Crying', and discovered that Robbins had written it, he flew west to Phoenix to get his signature on a writing contract. With all the interest Robbins was generating, in both the writing and performing fields, it was only natural that he was invited to become a member of the Grand Ole Opry in 1953.

'Knee Deep In The Blues', 'The Story Of My Life', 'White Sports Coat' and 'El Paso' made the '50s memorable for Robbins and brought him a fan following that was the envy of many country artists. 'El Paso' is a brilliantly crafted musical saga of a cowboy who dies for the love of a cantina sweetheart in the badlands of New Mexico. It begins with the haunting line 'out in the West Texas Town Of El Paso I fell in love with a Mexican girl' and ends with 'one little kiss and Falino goodbye'. There is unanimous Nashville agreement about 'El Paso'. It is one of the songs that moved country music back to its historic roots. No one was surprised when Robbins won a Grammy for it in 1960. It was the odds-on favourite to win the first Grammy ever to be presented for a country song.

Robbins' fans were shocked when he was stricken with a massive heart attack near the end of the '60s. He underwent cardiac surgery, which was successful, and before too long he was back writing and performing. 'My Woman, My Woman, My Life' was the perfect therapy. It was a stellar hit and he won another Grammy for Best Country Song of 1970.

Next to his family, and music, Robbins loved fast cars and competitive racing. Prior to his near-fatal heart attack he began racing stock cars on dirt tracks. He was as adept behind the wheel as he was behind a recording studio microphone. Before long his driving skills and coolness in the face of danger, won him the admiration of seasoned drivers. He worked his way up through the ranks, at local events, and graduated to the National Association NASCAR Grand National Division. He won 'Rookie Of The Southern 500' honours in 1972 and was soon challenging such giants of the sport as Cale Yarbrough and Richard Petty. He named his car 'Devil Woman' in honour of one of his biggest hits.

Three potentially fatal crashes brought his professional racing career to an end in 1973. In one harrowing race at Charlotte, North Carolina, he intentionally slammed into a concrete wall rather than broadside a fellow driver's stalled car. When he hit he was doing over 145 mph. Finally, he listened to the pleas of his family, friends and associates and quit driving. With great reluctance he became just a spectator of the sport he loved so dearly.

Robbins was a recording artist for nearly four decades and during that period he amassed an impressive body of work which totalled over 60 albums, many of them award winners. He was as active on the touring circuit as he was on television and his film work included parts in ten movies. In *Guns of a Stranger* he played a singing cowboy.

Country music was shocked and saddened when this giant of the industry succumbed to a third heart attack on December 8 1982. A saddened Gene Autry summed up his feelings. 'He not only was a great singer, but a great writer as well and I think that he would also have been a western star in pictures had he concentrated on it. We shall always miss him but his music will live on forever.'

Marty Robbins A Lifetime Of Song 1951–1982 (Columbia CK 38870)

This is one of the most satisfactory CDs you could find if Marty Robbins' smooth, mellow, style of singing is your cup of tea. There are 20 songs in this collection. Every one is worth serious listening, from 'Singing The Blues', an up-tempo number that still appeals to young people and just cries out for a full dance floor, to 'Ribbon Of Darkness' which made country fans sit up and take notice in 1965. It opens with a whistling intro by Robbins. Some arresting guitar plucking adds to the pleasure.

One of the most enjoyable cuts is 'Don't Worry About Me' which Robbins recorded in 1961. It has one of the most ear-arresting low-down, deep-throated sax bridges one will ever hear.

There was industry trepidation, in 1959, when Robbins recorded 'El Paso'. It came in at 4 minutes 38 seconds.

'Much too long for radio play,' complained programmers.

'Nonsense,' replied the fans, who demanded that it get air time, and air time it got. It's still near the top of request programmes. 'El Paso' was Robbins' all-time personal favourite. This CD is a gold-plated treasure for country fans.

Marty Robbins Singin' The Hits (CBS A2165)

This CD merits more than passing notice if only for two cuts. 'Have I Told You Lately That I Love You' allows Robbins full range for his deft musical shadings. A marvellous steel guitar intro sets the mood. The backing is subtle as befits this vintage western love song. 'Beggin' To You' was a 1963 release and while it enjoyed above-average popularity it never reached the lofty heights of his biggest hit 'El Paso'. However, if a poll were taken of today's fans, it would be near the top.

When Robbins slides up to what is termed a 'head voice' on 'Beggin' To You' first-time listeners will do a backward search on their CD players. They'll want to be sure they really heard what they thought they heard. For Robbins has a remarkable ability to raise his voice to a high melodic note on the tail end of a word or phrase. Robbins weaves a plaintive story of a shattered man who walks out the door and then comes back begging to his love. By the time he reaches, 'You don't want my lovin' but you let me stay around/I guess just to walk on so you won't touch the ground', one can feel the heartbreak with every note. This is what country music is all about.

Seals, Dan

(born Rankin, Texas, February 8 1948)
You'll never catch Dan Seals riding around town in a stretch limousine hoping to get noticed. In private he'd rather be inconspicuous. He much prefers to let his music be the centre of attention when he's on stage performing for SRO audiences. 'Some people are more in love with being a star and driving around in a car than they are in actually doing the work and having great songs and great material,' he says.

Seals and country music go together like black-eyed peas and grits. His father grew up with ERNEST TUBB and Seals was raised in West Texas where country music is king. Seals' brother, Jim, was Texas State Champion Fiddler at the age of nine and went on to become a musical partner with Dash Crofts. They became famous as Seals & Crofts. Seals made his musical impact when he and John Ford Coley became partners. They became famous as England Dan and John Ford Coley. Seals and Coley hit with 'I'd Really Love To See You Tonight'. It was a smash and sold well over two million copies.

As a solo artist Seals has been consistently topping the country charts since 1985. A reviewer once likened Seals to mild-mannered Clark Kent who becomes Superman after stepping into a phone booth. Once the gentle, introverted Seals steps on a stage, with guitar in hand, a dramatic change takes place. He becomes the magical, uninhibited dispenser of highly energetic dance music and memorable ballads. It has been written that 'note for note, there are few concerts, or records, that offer the range of human drama, wisdom, pathos and excitement that is to be found in those involving Dan Seals.'

Seals is a perfectionist when it comes to his music. 'I'm always looking for lyrics that knock me out and in turn, I hope, will knock other people out,' he says. A disciple of the 'quality not quantity' school, Seals takes a year and a half to turn out an album. 'We do less material than some artists,' he explains, 'but we're happy working at that pace and the audiences seem to be happy.'

Seals' first impressive country single came in 1985 with 'Meet Me in Montana'. It was a duet with Marie Osmond and kicked off a remarkable chart-topping run of albums, and singles, up to his latest Warner Bros. album *Walking the Wire*.

With typical Seals' understatement, *Walking the Wire* deals with the fleeting nature of time and its effect on love and commitment. His fans love it.

★*Walking the Wire* (Warner Bros. 9 26770-2)

The secret of Seals' success is his ability to take rich scenarios, which swing between the joyful and the sorrowful, and cause his listener to pause and reflect. 'Someone Else's Dance' is the forthright musical story of a family formed and sustained by fate and circumstances. It has the added plus of the marvellous Hargus 'Pig' Robbins performing his witchcraft on the acoustic piano. The harmony vocals of Dennis Wilson, Curtis 'Mr Harmony' Young and Cindy Richardson-Walker are perfect.

'Sneaky Moon' is an up-beat number that get's one swaying. A nice touch that catches the ear, and imagination, is the splendid harmonica work of Terry McMillian who ties everything together. One will go a long way before a better intro to a moving song is heard. 'We Are One', opens with 'In a bombed out room in Belfast/A young boy is crying/He's alone and don't understand'. Some of the lyrics are drawn from the writings of Baha 'u'llah in the teachings of the Ba'ahai Faith. One doesn't have to understand Ba'ahai teachings to be stirred by this song which Seals wrote.

Skaggs, Ricky

(born Cordell, Kentucky, July 18 1954)
By the time Ricky Skaggs was five years old he was playing the mandolin and amazing the radio audience of WTCR, in Ashland, Kentucky, with his dazzling musical talent. When he was seven he

astounded Flatt & Scruggs, of bluegrass fame, when he appeared on a television show they hosted. Great things were predicted for the precocious youngster with more talent than any child his age deserved. The predictions were neither unfounded or extravagant.

1969 was a watershed year for Skaggs. Sandy Hook was his boyhood friend and they shared a mutual passion for country and bluegrass music. The more they played together the more determined they became to make music their career. One of their accomplishments was being able to do a wicked impression of the Stanley Brothers, who were their bluegrass idols. After seeing them perform, Ralph Stanley was so impressed that he offered the two extraordinary talents a job with his band. Skaggs was only fifteen.

Sandy Hook changed his name to Keith Whitley but Skaggs kept his. For the next few years the two young friends toured with the band and enhanced their musical skills. Skaggs left the Stanley band in 1972 in order to widen his musical horizons by playing in a number of outstanding bluegrass bands such as New South and Country Store. The experience gave him the musical confidence to organize his own band in 1975 which he called Boone Creek and he quickly earned the reputation for being able to play both traditional and progressive bluegrass with equal skill.

Emmylou Harris entered Skaggs' musical life in 1977, when he joined her Hot Band. His mastery of many instruments made him an invaluable asset to the band. The audiences loved his singing and playing and quickly made him a show attraction. His voice, which has been compared to the clear expressive tenor of an Ira Louvin, was soon heard in duet with Harris.

All the while he was playing with other bands, and learning the musical ropes, he was making a modest impact with solo albums for small record labels. 'That's It', 'Sweet Temptation' and 'Skaggs and Rice' are valued additions to many bluegrass collections.

He has never been content with the *status quo*. Eager for new skills he began to learn the intricacies of producing albums. He played a major production role in Harris' hallmark album *Roses in the Snow* and is credited with much of its success.

He signed with Epic records in 1983 and *Waitin' for the Sun to Shine* was his debut album. The sales, which far exceeded industry projections, earned him Country Music Association Best Male

Vocalist of the Year award for 1982. Major honours were quick to come. In 1985 he was voted Entertainer of the Year. It is country music's most coveted award.

Skaggs and his wife Sharon share more than a mutual passion for bluegrass. Before her marriage to Skaggs, Sharon had her own musical career as Sharon White of the bluegrass musical family, The Whites. Skaggs and his wife often perform together. They won the 1987 Vocal Duo of the Year award.

In addition to being a solo performer Skaggs is one of the few superstars who manages his own career, and runs his own music publishing company and booking agency. This multi-talented singer, musician and businessman is also a producer of note and has worked with many major artists. He produced DOLLY PARTON's successful album *White Limozeen*. Skaggs is modest about his triumphs and talents. His goal is to bring country music back to its traditional basics by reinstating the banjo, fiddle, mandolin and steel guitar in the mainstream of country and bluegrass music. He feels very strongly that these instruments have been shunted into the background, the victims of innovators who believe that it is time to shuck off the old and move on with the new.

★*My Father's Son* (Epic EK 47389)

The superb sound on this CD is courtesy of a Studer America 48-track digital tape machine that was used for the mixing. Skaggs was so pleased with the results that he singles it out for special mention.

The piano work of Barlow Jarvis on 'Life's Too Long (To Live Like This)' is worth the price of admission. The beat drives and Skaggs soars with an infectious set of lyrics.

One of the joys of listening to a new CD is discovering a song that just has to be shared. 'You Don't Count The Cost' is an excellent case in point. The opening verse is the story of what happens to a mother when she gives birth and holds the baby to her breast. 'When it comes to love/You don't count the cost'. The second verse tells of a soldier who is fighting for his home and, as fear swells up inside him, he still goes on. 'When it comes to love/ You don't count the cost'.

'Somebody's Prayin'' is a hymn of faith and praise. When Skaggs sings, 'Lord I believe/Lord I believe/Somebody's prayin' for me', there's no question about him believing what he sings. Skaggs is a born-again Christian with deep beliefs that guide his life and career.

This album shines and it's all due to the talent of Skaggs, the strength of the songwriters and the musical skills of those on backup.

Sons of the San Joaquin

(formed circa 1989, current members – Joe Hanna, Jack Hanna, Lon Hanna)
If there is a similarity in names between The Sons of the Pioneers and The Sons of the San Joaquin, it's not coincidental.

Cowboy star Roy Rogers used The Pioneers as a springboard to cowboy movie stardom and the music of that outstanding western group has been the inspiration for The Sons of the San Joaquin. 'Our dad became a fan of The Pioneers way back in the '30s,' explains Jack. 'He'd sing a lot of those songs and we learned our first ones from him. We became great fans of their music too.' The great depression was wreaking havoc in America when the Hannah family packed all their possessions into a 1935 Ford and headed west to California, in search of work. They settled in the beautiful, lush Sierra Nevada foothills and were surrounded by cattle ranches and western ambience. It was the perfect location for the nurturing of a life-long love affair with cowboy music.

Weekends turned into singalongs as the family joined in songs of sagebrush, cattle and cowboys. It was a great musical classroom for the young Hannah boys who honed their singing skills on such classics as 'Tumbling Tumbleweed' and 'Cool Water'. Joe and Jack started out singing Pioneer classics in public at church and local events with their father, who can still carry a tune even though he's into his early 90s. Over a period of time they became so proficient that they expanded their act into a weekend travelling band.

It was really Lon who can take credit for the formation of the Sons. He kept at his father and uncle until they joined him in a trio. Their first professional break came when Lon met cowboy singer Gary McMahon at a Western Music Association convention. When the Sons were invited to perform at the 1989 Elko

Cowboy Poetry Gathering, they ended up singing with Michael Martin Murphy. He was sufficiently impressed to invite them to join him on his *Cowboy Songs* album.

The diverse musical training of the Sons ranges from western to classical. Joe and Jack have sung opera and Lon sang with Bennett Consort, a vocal group with the styling of the Manhattan Transfer. But as much as they enjoy other musical styles, it's the songs of the cowboy that hold their musical love, and interest. Jack explained it best. 'We like the text, we like the outdoors and we like the lifestyle.'

The Sons sing the same bright, cheery songs as the Pioneers and their close harmonies are musical clones. While hesitant to call themselves authentic cowboys, Joe and Jack still train horses and work cattle in addition to their other jobs as teachers and singers.

★*A Cowboy Has To Sing* (Warner Western 9 26935-2)

There are 10 songs on this delightful CD. Six were written by Canadian born Bob Nolan who, along with Leonard Sly and Tim Spencer, formed the Pioneer Trio. When Sly became Roy Rogers and went on to film glory, Nolan and Spencer became the mainstays of the Sons of the Pioneers. Spencer wrote three songs and co-wrote one with Nolan.

'Cool Water' was originally recorded on Electric Transcriptions in 1941. It's Nolan's most famous composition and is an enduring western classic. In the safe hands of the Sons it is given a melodious stroking that would put a smile on Nolan's face. 'Blue Prairie' is the only Spencer/Nolan collaboration in this lineup. It was first recorded in 1934 and is an eloquent expression of western songwriting excellence. The word 'blue' is repeated 20 times throughout the song and it becomes the catalyst upon which the vivid imagery of the prairie is built. 'Moonlight on the Trail' is Spencer's invitation to ride with a night herding-hand over the trails of the past. The Sons weave the words and music into a resplendent cowboy tapestry.

This CD is a certified, gold plated, four star, winner. It's a must for lovers of pure, simple, unadulterated, cowboy music.

Statler Brothers

(formed 1963, current members – Don Reid, Harold Reid, Philip Balsey, Jimmy Fortune)

If it hadn't been for JOHNNY CASH, and a box of face tissues, there would never have been the Statler Brothers. On the verge of breaking into country music's 'big time', and touring with Cash, they needed a new name for their quartet. Harold Reid saw a box of Statler Tissues and suggested Statler Brothers. 'It was a good as anything,' he recalls.

All the original Statlers came from the Staunton, Virginia, area and even though they call themselves brothers only two, the Reids, actually are. During the mid-'50s, Lew DeWitt, Phil Balsey and Phil Reid formed a trio and sang gospel in local churches.

Gospel quartets were popular during the '40s and '50s and none were more popular than the Blackwood Brothers and the Statesmen. These two groups had a profound musical influence on the Statlers during their formative years as gospel singers. The group stayed together until 1958, when they disbanded.

In 1960 they regrouped and Don Reid, who was in his teens, joined them. At various times they were known as the Four Star Quartet and the Kingsmen. They built a respectable fan following by touring and singing in churches, at all-night gospel sings, Christian banquets and on local Christian television shows.

1963 was a watershed year for the group. Johnny Cash was performing in Roanoak, Virginia, and Harold Reid badgered the promoter until he introduced him to Cash. With no apology, or embarrassment, he enumerated the merits of the quartet with typical Reid bravado. Cash was suitably impressed and invited them to open his next show. It was a real gamble because Cash had never heard the four brash singers perform. Once he did, he knew his instincts were right.

Harold Reid had no intention of letting their one appearance with Cash be their last. Reid was either persuasive or Cash's resistance was gradually worn down. Cash finally asked them to join him on tour and for eight years they were one of the featured acts. It was a mutually beneficial association.

Country music began to take serious notice of the Statlers in 1966 when they hit with Lew DeWitt's 'Flowers on the Wall'. It shot up to the top-10 on the country charts and made number one on the pop charts. It also won two Grammy Awards. The Statlers were naturals for television and in the '70s were regulars on Cash's prime-time show. The 1970s were vintage years for the quartet. Top-10 hits became the rule rather than the exception as singles such as 'Bed of Roses', 'Do You Remember These', and the Grammy Award song 'The Class of '73' kept the cash registers ringing. 'Whatever Happened to Randolph Scott' was another mid-'70s hit and it still receives resounding applause from those who remember the film cowboys.

Don and Harold Reid are not only superb singers, they are hit-writing tunesmiths. They have a wry gift for comedy, with a dash of poignancy, in such songs as 'I'll Go To My Grave Loving You' and 'Thank God I've Got You'.

Leaving Cash was not an easy decision. It was, however, an understandable one as the Statlers were confident and secure in their abilities to make it on their own. Up to 1982 Lew DeWitt wrote songs and sang tenor. Reluctantly, because of poor health, he had to leave the quartet and Jimmy Fortune replaced him.

The Statlers have a tried and proven format. Don is lead singer and master of ceremonies. Brother Harold sings bass. He is a deft comedian and keeps the show moving with asides and comic turns. Phil is baritone and Jimmy holds up his end as tenor. They have never altered their basic four-part gospel quartet sound which is probably their greatest asset. The Statlers have had remarkable success with their albums. *The Best of the Statler Brothers* was on the charts for an astounding four years and sales are pushing 3 million copies. They are show headliners around the world. They have appeared with evangelist Billy Graham, in his crusades, and sang at the White House.

The Country Music Association recognized the star stature of the Statlers by naming them the Top Vocal Group for an unrivalled seven years in a row. This run of awards was broken in 1979 when the Oak Ridge Boys won but the Statlers were back in the winner's circle the following year. Their syndicated specials, and prime-time weekly show on *The Nashville Network*, are fan favourites and always earned high ratings.

When Kurt Vonnegut called the Statler Brothers 'America's poets' he was not being kind nor patronizing. He was just echoing what the legion of fans, around the world, think of these four multi-talented men who dispense humour and songs in their uniquely winning style.

★*The Statlers Greatest Hits* (Mercury 834-626-2)

With 'Let's Get Started If We're Gonna Break My Heart' the Statlers bring the art of painting pictures in song to a high level of excellence. And one doesn't have to be in love with 'Elizabeth' to appreciate what it is like to miss the woman one loves – it is a beautiful love song. 'Atlanta Blue' is the perfect coda to a masterful 10-song collection. The album was in the charts for a remarkable 4 years and has sold around 3 million copies.

Strait, George

(born Pearsall, Texas, May 18 1952)

George Strait reminds one of the successful actor who was asked 'Who do you want to thank for your success?' The answer came back like a bullet, 'The man who said I'd never make it.'

In the early '80s the prevailing attitude of the country music establishment was that Strait's blend of music and dress were too old-fashioned to make it in Nashville. He was told to dress like the '80s, deep-six the steel guitars and fiddles and 'get with it'. It was the decade of synthesizers, strings and flashy clothes. Strait turned a deaf ear and by 1990 the scoffers had changed their tune. The quiet, clean-cut singer, with the mellow deep-register voice had reached the pinnacle of stardom. Not only could Strait sing up a storm, he looked like a real cowboy, which he is.

Strait is yet another transplanted Texan. He was the second of three children. His father was a maths teacher at a junior high school. He was also a part-time rancher near Pearsall, a small community in the brush country of south Texas. As a youngster Strait learned to ride and rope with the best of them. He wet his feet, musically, while in high school by singing with a group of buddies who formed their own rock band. If you asked him what song he first sang he'd reply, without hesitation, 'Louie, Louie'.

Following a Mexican elopement with Norma, his high school sweetheart, Strait joined the army. He was stationed in Hawaii and it was there that he taught himself to play the six-string guitar. All he had was his guitar and a Hank Williams song book to learn the basics of chording from, but that was enough. Today he is an accomplished guitar player. He caught on quickly. He impressed his base commander sufficiently to be asked to recruit and lead a country band. The last year of his army hitch was the best as he toured military bases, performing country music. The year was well spent. By the end of it he was adept and comfortable on a platform. Upon discharge he returned to Texas and enrolled in Southwest Texas State University in San Marcos. His goal was a degree in agriculture and a return to full-time ranching which he loved. He reached his educational goal but the allure of country music was also strong. He pinned a note to a campus bulletin board announcing that he was a country singer looking for a country band. As luck would have it a group called Ace in the Hole were looking for a lead singer. They found one in George Strait. Following a brief rehearsal and shakedown period the band began getting dates in honky tonks within a 200 mile radius of San Marcos.

Life was hectic for Strait following graduation from university. From sun up to sun down he was manager of the family ranch, with over 1,000 head of cattle to ride herd on. Most nights he was on stage, with the band, singing.

Strait's early dedication to country music was rock solid. His repertoire included the best of MERLE HAGGARD, GEORGE JONES and Lefty Frizzell plus a liberal sprinkling of good old country music. To this day that dedication has not altered.

By 1979, after three tries at breaking through in Nashville, Strait was becoming tired and discouraged. He was on the verge of accepting a job in Texas, designing cattle facilities, but thanks to the faith and insistance of his wife he decided to give country music one more year of his life. Fate can have such strange twists.

Erv Woolsey was the manager of the Prairie Rose, a night club in San Marcos. On a number of occasions he had booked Strait and the Ace in the Hole band. He liked their music and especially liked Strait's singing. Over the years they kept in touch. When he left San Marcos for Nashville, to become a promotion manager, Woolsey was instrumental in getting his friend a recording session with producer Blake Mevis. The session paid off. Less than six months after deciding to give music one more year of his life Strait had a record contract with MCA Records. His first album was *Strait Country* and from that album came his first hit single 'Unwound'. Even though 'Unwound' hit the top-10 in the charts there were detractors. They were convinced that Strait's traditional, raw, country style would be too much for contemporary radio and he would quickly fade from the music scene because his records would not get air play. The highly respected country music critic John Morthland wrote, 'I have to wonder how long he'll last.' He wonders no longer because Strait has lasted and silenced every critic.

Since 1981 only Alabama has racked up as many number-one country hits as Strait. He had a blockbuster album *Ocean Front Property* in 1987. It became the first country album to debut at number one on *Billboard*'s country music chart. He further silenced any questions about his longevity in 1990 with 'Love Without End, Amen'. It became the first song since 1977 to hang on to the number-one chart position for five consecutive weeks. He made an astonishing repeat of the feat with 'Famous Last Words of a Fool' in 1991. Adding to his lustre and star status was his acting debut in *Pure Country*. He played a country singer who packed it in, in mid-career, and returned to Texas to become a working cowboy. The cowboy and country singer role was type casting. The soundtrack has become another top album for Strait. His fans liked the clean-cut masculinity, natural acting ability and quiet strength that came across on the screen. The critics liked him as well. They made favourable comparisons with classic film cowboys in the vein of Roy Rogers, Gene Autry and Gary Cooper.

Strait is a quiet, introspective, individual. He jealously guards his private life, especially after his 13 year old daughter, Jennifer, was tragically killed in an automobile accident in 1986. Strait was devastated and retired from performing for a year. He has steadfastly refused to allow television cameras into his home in San Antonio or onto his ranch where he raises cattle and indulges in his hobby of breeding and raising race horses. Strait is also a man of steadfast loyalty. After 20 years of marriage he and Norma are still together with George Junior. Erv Woolsey, the man who remembered Strait and got him his first recording session, has been his one and only manager. One of the original Ace in the Hole members is his road manager and he still has the same booking agent, publicists and fan club president that he started out with.

'I record the songs that I like and I do them the way they feel right to me,' he says. 'It's worked so far, I guess I'll just keep on doing it the same way.'

★*George Strait Ocean Front Property* (MCA MCABD-5913)

ERNEST TUBB has been gone for over 10 years but just one listen to the opening bars of 'All My Ex's Live In Texas' and his memory will be rekindled. It is almost eerie to hear George Strait sing 'All my ex's live in Texas/And Texas is the place I dearly love to be/But all my ex's live in Texas and that's why I long to be in Tennessee'. It's pure, unadulterated Ernest Tubb, and it's wonderful.

Strait is constantly grateful to Dean Dillon, Hank Cochran and Royce Porter for 'Ocean Front Property'. Who ever heard of having 'ocean front property in Arizona'? Crazy as it sounds the lyrics work. The lyrics also work on the other eight cuts. 'Am I Blue', 'Someone's Walkin's Around Upstairs' and the foot-tapping 'Hot Burning Flames', which the renowned Hank Cochran wrote in collaboration with Mack Vickery and Wayne Kemp, are enough to make the album worthwhile.

Ocean Front Property is an excellent foundation upon which to build a George Strait CD collection.

★*George Strait Pure Country* (MCA MCASD-10651)

Before one lays any praise on this CD, one discouraging note: Whoever is responsible for the artwork can take a bow for the front because it is eye catching. However, the back is another matter. The list of songs is printed in very small, light grey type on a midnight-black background. The song titles are nearly unreadable. Obviously, the designer does not wear bi-focals.

Now the praise. *Pure Country* is the original motion picture soundtrack. The 11 songs are an interesting blend of western swing, romantic ballads and traditional honky tonk. Strait was offered a musical challenge and he met it head on.

'Heartland' is rollicking country-rock. 'Cross My Heart' is in the lush style Strait fans have come to expect. 'She Lays It All On The Line' is classic driving rockabilly with a thumping beat. 'The King Of Broken Hearts' and 'When Did You Stop Loving Me' are two new honky tonk songs that grab the ear. A personal favourite is

'Thoughts of a Fool', a 1961 Ernest Tubb hit. Strait has Tubb's phrasing down pat and does honour to the country music legend. Those who saw *Pure Country* will enjoy this collection. Those who didn't are in for a musical treat.

Stuart, Marty

(born Philadelphia, Mississippi, September 30 1958)
Country music roots are deeply imbedded in Marty Stuart's soul. He draws his inspiration, motivation and strength from the past, the present and the future. On stage he plays a 1954 Telecaster guitar with a steel-guitar-like string bender on the B-string. A Martin D-45 guitar, that was once owned by Hank Williams Sr., is a highly-prized addition to his instrument collection and Lester Flatt's D-28 keeps alive the legacy of the bluegrass great when in the hands of such a skilled player. On the road he travels in ERNEST TUBB's old bus which has vivid and enduring memories of learning how to play poker from Tubb, Porter Wagoner and a band of cronies.

Stuart was influenced and taught by some of the greats of country music. At the tender age of 12 he was hired by a gospel-bluegrass band called the Sullivan Family to play mandolin. He had just entered his teens when Lester Flatt, who had just severed his long association with Earl Scruggs, hired him. Following Flatt's death on May 11 1979 Stuart began to spread his musical wings with what he terms a bluegrass-fusion style, with fiddle player Vassar Clements and acoustic guitar wizard Doc Watson. JOHNNY CASH was his next employer and he played with Cash until 1985. Many times, when asked about those early days, he will say 'The years with Flatt were like getting a high school education. The years with Cash were musically equivalent to earning a university degree.'

From his early days, growing up in Mississippi, Stuart was a rebel and that streak of independence was nurtured alongside his musical maturation. He never lost sight of the fact that some day he wanted to be captain of his own fate and create his own music.

In 1978 he recorded an album, *Marty: With A Little Help From His Friends*. It was followed up with another in 1982. Sugar Records released 'Busy Bee Cafe' which garnered better than average acceptance and reviews. CBS signed Stuart in 1986 and released *Marty Stuart* which spawned a top-20 single 'Arlene'. The next stop on Stuart's recording road came in 1989 when he signed on with MCA Records and released *Hillbilly Rock* which he described as 'hillbilly music – with a thwump'. It was what the industry would term his breakthrough album. The single, 'Cry, Cry, Cry', did almost as much for Stuart as it originally did for his mentor, Johnny Cash, and 'Hillbilly Rock' became his signature song.

Tempted followed hard on the heels of *Hillbilly Rock*. The album is the ideal showcase for this multifaceted talent who excels with bluegrass, gospel, honky tonk and is constantly expanding his country rock frontiers.

Understatement is not in Stuart's vocabulary, whether he's on stage performing or in an office negotiating a new contract. He owns one of the largest collections of cowboy suits, boots, jackets and shirts with rhinestone-studded patterns and elaborate embroidery. Whenever he strides on stage he is noticed, even before he begins performing, and that is just fine with Stuart.

He has also made an indelible mark on country music through his songwriting. The list of country artists who have recorded his music include Buck Owens, Emmylou Harris, Mark Collie, TRAVIS TRITT and GEORGE STRAIT plus many others of their stature. Travis Tritt and Stuart joined forces to record 'The Whisky Ain't Working', which Stuart wrote. It became a runaway hit in 1992 and had the fans clambouring for more.

Stuart once had a vision which he related during a reflective moment. 'It was a perfect musical world in which the work of the masters of hillbilly music lives on in the music of the new young artists.' He is coming closer to seeing that vision a reality every time he enters a recording studio or steps on a stage.

★*Hillbilly Rock* (MCA MCAD-42312)

Hillbilly Rock wasn't calculated to fit any record-buying demographics. It is raw, uncompromising Marty Stuart.

Stuart tackles 'Me and Billy the Kid' with gruff, barked out vocals that suit the melody, lyrics and thumping backup perfectly. Glen D. Hardin on piano matches Billy Thomas on drums like a musical Siamese twin.

One can imagine the first time Johnny Cash heard Stuart's

version of his hit 'Cry Cry Cry'. He surely must have thanked the good Lord that he recorded it first because Stuart gives his version a run for the money.

Ernest Tubb's ghost hovers over 'When the Sun Goes Down'. The vocal inflections and arrangement are classic Tubb and Stuart does not offend Tubb enthusiasts.

Stuart is lavish in his praise of his honky tonk band and rightly so. They are excellent. The backup arrangements are textbook perfect. This CD is a great cure for the blues.

★*Tempted* (MCA MCAD-1016)

Whenever Marty Stuart is asked to explain just where he fits into the mix of country music he replies, 'I was raised by the masters that invented the music around here. I'm one of their kids.' Johnny Cash's imprint on Stuart's rendition of 'Blue Train' is immediately recognized from the moment one hears the pumping bass intro. Cash co-wrote the song with Billy Smith and his musical child does him proud.

The lyrics and melody of 'Little Things' allow for fascinating vocal inflections. This is a stretch song for Stuart and he is more than ably aided by the splendid work of his backup band. The bridges are as pleasing as the lyrics.

Five of the ten songs on this album were either written or co-written by Stuart and two of them, 'Tempted' and 'Little Things', became hit singles. Stuart didn't have a hand in writing 'Till I Found You' or 'Burn Me Down' but he made them hit singles as well. Four hit singles out of a ten-song album is a remarkable accomplishment.

Texas Tornados

(formed December 1989, current members – Freddy Fender, Augie Meyers, Flaco Jimenez, Doug Sahm)
This group is a whirlwind of energy. Their music is a hypnotic blend of South Texas Mexican and Gringo cultures. Add a liberal infusion of barroom boogie, reggae and '50s rock 'n' roll and you have a mix the like of which is unique in country music. Their fans think it is as refreshing as it is unique.

The professional backgrounds of the four members are as widespread and diverse as the music they play. Augie Meyers and Doug Sahm played with The Sir Douglas Quintet which is remembered for the pop hits 'She's About a Mover' and 'Mendocino'. Freddy Fender, born Baldemar Huerta (his professional name came from Fender, the maker of fine guitars), came into prominence during the late '50s as The Bee Bop Kid. Country music knows him as a splendid balladeer with a couple of million plus sellers, 'Before the Next Teardrop Falls' and 'Wasted Days and Wasted Nights'. Falaco Jimenez is perhaps the best-known voice from conjunto, a form of dance music that borrows from the polka and the waltz.

Fender, Meyers and Sahm have a common bond. They all worked for record producer Huey Meaux and occasionally performed together in the late 1950s. Jimenez came from the same San Antonio area as Meyers and Sahm but it wasn't until 1973 that he joined them in a recording studio. It was 17 years before all four got together again. It happened in December 1989, in San Francisco, at a place called Slims. They were all there for a Tex-Mex Review. The musical strength of each one was apparent when, without rehearsal, they took to the stage and wowed two sell-out crowds. Everything clicked so well that by the following April the Texas Tornados was a formal group and laying down tracks for a first album. All four were totally amazed at how well they meshed musically. 'When the music first came out I thought they'll laugh at us,' recalls Fender. 'Before I knew it, it hit!' Hit it did. The first album grabbed a Grammy award and the second, *Zone of our Own*, received a second nomination.

Just as WILLIE NELSON, early on his career, brought together hippies and rednecks in the formative days of the musical outlaw movement, so the Tornados have successfully blended Hispanics and Caucasians into an enthusiastically loyal group of fans.

Fender shakes his head at the thought of what the Tornados have accomplished. 'Here we are with Gringos and Mexicans singing all at the same time with such flavour,' he explains. 'When you put out a Mexican song and you're a Gringo singing it, with the accordion in back, and you're convincing, if that's not a miracle I don't know what a miracle is.'

Part of the miracle is due to the experience of all four members and enduring friendships that span over a quarter of a century.

There is a definite spontaneity to their music and it isn't feigned. They have such respect and confidence in each other that they don't plan their sessions beforehand.

'Once we're in the studio,' confirms Jimenez, 'we come up with some idea and we create it there. We make things up in the studio. We don't believe in planning and rehearsing for months prior to a session. We have fun and that's the main thing.'

Meyers has a refreshing approach to the music they make. 'Once an album is done and packaged I never listen to it again. I've always done that. But I find myself in my car pullin' this tape out and playing it on the highway. That's a good sign.'

★*Hangin' On By A Thread* (Reprise 9 45058-2)

Hangin' On By A Thread is their third album. The foundation of the album is a mesmerizing blend of South Texas's Mexican Gringo cultures.

'Tus Menturas', with Fender on lead and harmony, has just the right mariachi sound to evoke images of a hacienda under a night sky strewn with twinkling stars.

There is a soulful intensity about 'One and Only' which was written by Sahm's son Shawn and was co-arranged by father and son. Sahm senior joins Fender on the vocals and their voices are a perfect blend.

Nothing more need be said about the bouncy 'A Mover El Bote' than to provide the translation 'move your boodie'. This one's a ton of fun. Any fears Fender may have had about people laughing at the Tornados music are certainly laid to rest with this CD.

Tillis, Pam

(born Plant City, Florida, July 24 1957)

When someone calls Pam Tillis a 'hot country newcomer', the daughter of country music star Mel Tills laughs. She is anything but a newcomer. She's a survivor. At the age of eight she made her first public performance singing with her father in the Grand Ole Opry in the Ryman Auditorium. During the next 20 to 25 years, until she became a certified country star, she led what politely might be called a chequered life. It ran the gamut from teenage rebellion, parental estrangement, a failed marriage to a searching for identity and purpose.

'My dad felt that country was the only musical road for me,' recalled Pam. 'The songs he wanted me to sing were just terrible. I rebelled.' The rebellion included being labelled 'the foremost teenage roustabout in suburban Nashville'. 'I was your basic misfit and professional partier,' she says, without apology.

Since early childhood Pam has been uneasy and defensive about her looks. 'I always thought my appearance was kinda flawed,' she says, with a frankness that has made her a refreshing change from some of the superficiality that surrounds much of show-business. She is still emotionally and physically scarred by a car crash in which her face was shattered in over 30 places from her cheeks down to her chin. Her nose was flattened and her eye sockets were severely damaged. She was just 16. It took over five years, and multiple operations, to reconstruct Pam's face. She still has pain when it rains and is careful about what angles are used for album cover photos or video tapings.

The musical path Pam took from rebellion to stardom included experimentation with pop, jazz, new wave and disco – anything but country. She moved to California and formed a fusion band with a jazz pianist. 'It was really wacky but it was something I had to do,' says Pam in defence. 'I thought it was real avant-garde. I was a young woman making music for the sheer joy of it. It was a time to hang out, play, sing, and not worry about a record deal or the charts.' The record deal materialized in the mid-'80s with Warner Bros. The first album she cut was pop but curiously there was a country song in the lineup – 'It Ain't Easy Bein' Easy'. Musical salvation came when Nashville recognized her as a skilled session singer, much in demand for demos and jingles. All the while she constantly honed her impressive songwriting talents.

Tree International, country music's largest publishing house with an impressive track record for spotting raw talent signed Pam to a songwriting contract in 1990. Pam readily admits that the contract was a watershed in her professional life. 'The game plan was to write for a year. I was at the point in my life where I didn't believe in forcing things any more. I felt I had been swimming upstream for so long.' Tree wasn't the only organiza-tion with an astute sense for spotting talent. Arista Records signed her to a recording contract. The timing was near perfect.

She had songwriting and recording contracts and her confidence was high.

At last country was starting to sound good to her. 'It had all the roots of the cool country of the late '50s and early '60s. It was beginning to sound like the music that I liked when I was growing up,' Pam explains. 'It just started to turn me on. I got real excited about making a country album.'

Put Yourself In My Place, which was skilfully produced by Paul Worley and Ed Seay, was released to resounding critical applause in January 1991. By August 1992 it had racked up sales of over 500,000 and was certified gold. Pam's star was shooting out of sight when her debut single 'Don't Tell Me What To Do' hit number one on the charts. She is one of only four female country artists to reach that height with a debut release.

1991 was a frantic year. It was packed with tour dates opening for GEORGE STRAIT and numerous award nominations from the Country Music Association, the American Music Awards and the Academy of Country Music.

The choice of songs for her latest album, *Homeward Looking Angel*, is in keeping with Pam's eclectic approach to music. She had hundreds of songs to choose from. When the lineup was confirmed there were five songs by other writers and five songs that she wrote with her second husband, Bob DiPiero. 'I wanted this album to have my personal stamp on it and not just be a bunch of unrelated songs,' said Pam.

Pam and her father have come to terms with the musical and personal problems that had marred their relationship. No longer does she feel intimidated by his success and no longer is he trying to run her life. They are seriously discussing a dad-and-daughter duet on a future country album. That suits Mel just fine. 'I tried to get her to cut this kind of music for 11 years,' he told *People* magazine. 'I'm not saying I told you so, but with the Tillis name people just think country.'

★*Homeward Looking Angel* (Arista 18649-2)

The many facets of Pam's musical artistry come into clear focus on this CD. 'Do You Know Where Your Man Is Tonight' is Pam Tillis at her very best. There is a catch in her voice as she asks the question, 'Do you know where your man is/And are you sure that he's doin' you right?' It could have been sung by LORETTA LYNN but one could hardly imagine it sung better than Pam. John Jorgenson on steel guitar and Steve Nathan on piano make their instruments sound like voices in harmony.

'Cleopatra, Queen of Denial' is a perfect anthem for any woman who has problems with a selfish man. 'Well I knew he didn't have any money/Yea that's why he couldn't buy me a ring/ Oh and just because he bought himself a brand new pick-up truck/ Really didn't prove anything'.

'Love Is Only Human' is an album standout. Pam is joined by Marty Roe of DIAMOND RIO. Their duet is heart warming and moving.

The many strata of emotion, and the varied musical styles on this CD not only show Pam Tillis for the superb talent she is, they also illustrate the resurgence and strength of country music.

Travis, Randy

(born Randy Traywick, Marshville, North Carolina, May 4 1959) During the mid-80s country music was in dire straits, the victim of the post-Urban Cowboy syndrome which had virtually stripped it of its roots. One journalist wrote that Nashville was 'down on its side and gasping for breath with a death rattle poised in its throat'. The country and western recording industry was reeling. The benchmark for a number one seller had fallen to 300,000 copies, instead of the million copy sellers of years gone by.

Out of nowhere came Randy Travis. He was ruggedly handsome, and painfully shy but how he could sing. He took Nashville by the scruff of the neck and set it back on its heels with his debut album *Storms Of Life*. He became the first country artist to sell more than one million copies within 12 months of release date.

The fans suddenly had a new musical idol with a lop-sided grin and deep baritone voice. He opened the doors for a new breed of 'hot' country artists like CLINT BLACK, GARTH BROOKS and Kathy Mattea who infused new life and excitement into the recording industry.

Even though some saw him as an 'overnight' success Randy Travis had paid his dues. Born Randy Traywick, in Marshville, a small town in the Piedmont Crescent of North Carolina, he was the second of six children. From the age of eight, when he began to master the art of chording on an acoustic guitar, music has been his life, with the odd detour, as a teenager, towards fast cars, hard drinking and leisure drugs. He nearly wiped out his future when he was arrested for breaking and entering. If fate had not stepped in he was staring at a possible five years in jail.

Travis signed up for a talent contest, at a honky-tonk called Country City USA, in Charlotte, before his court date. The club was owned by Lib Hatcher and her husband. When she heard Travis sing she immediately saw potential stardom for the skinny 17-year-old and, determined that he was not going to jail, she interceded on his behalf with the judge who, impressed with her pleas and sincerity, placed Travis on probation in her custody. Hatcher groomed Travis like a thoroughbred. By 1980 she had divorced her husband, sold her interest in the nightclub, and moved to Nashville with her protégé. It was not easy. Work was as scarce as money and Travis was grateful just to be able to clean offices for $30 an office. Fate was kinder to Hatcher. She got the job of managing the Nashville Palace, a combined club and restaurant, across the road from the Opryland Hotel and she took Travis with her. Inbetween flipping hamburgers and mopping floors, she made certain that he got on stage and sang. With masterful promotional skills she made sure that he was heard by the movers and shakers in Nashville's recording industry. Many of the Grand Ole Opry stars accepted her invitation for a complementary meal and it was no coincidence that Travis was performing on those nights. Even though Travis got more than polite applause, there was no rush to sign him to a recording contract, apparently because his clean-cut, simple, country singing style was not flashy enough for those who were impressed by the rhinestone cowboy approach. Even though they liked his singing they thought he was too dull to attract fans. It took the courage of a top Warner Bros. talent executive, Martha Sharp, to open the door to stardom. In the face of strong opposition she signed him to a recording contract.

After a shaky start his first album *Storms Of Life* took off and held the number one position for 12 weeks. His second album, *Always and Forever*, confirmed his superstar status and justified Hatcher's faith. She continued to manage his meteoric rise and added another title, on May 31 1991, when she became Mrs Randy Travis.

The fans could not get enough of the square-jawed, clean-cut baritone who came on stage with a starched shirt, a crease in his jeans and an embarrassed shrug.

Travis readily admits that GEORGE JONES is both his idol and a major influence. One only has to listen to him sing with simplistic sincerity, especially when he drops his voice to a lower register, to hear the Jones inspiration.

From 1985 to 1992 Travis racked up an incredible total of 58 awards and honours which include: a prestigious Grammy for Best Country Vocal Performance/male; American Music Awards for video, album and single, Entertainer of the Year, Male Artist of the Year and Number 1 Country Album Artist, from *Billboard*, to name just a few.

When the history of country music is updated, years hence, Randy Travis will be singled out as not only a superstar but the artist who singlehandedly changed the course of country music, when it was at its lowest ebb. He brought this American phenomenon back to its historic roots and gave it new life.

★*Randy Travis Greatest Hits Volume One* (Warner Bros. 9 45044-2)

When Travis and his producer, Kyle Lehning, first heard T. Graham Brown's demo tape entitled '1962' they were searching for songs to complete the lineup for the *Storms Of Life* album and agreed that it could be a potential winner. Lib Hatcher wisely suggested that the title should be updated to '1982' to better fit Travis' age.

'An Old Pair of Shoes' is pure country. Travis demonstrates how a simple melody with equally simple lyrics, 'I'm feeling like an old pair of shoes/All worn out from walking through these blues', can combine to produce a song that will drive one crazy. It will keep rolling around in one's head long after listening to it.

To their profound regret a number of country artists first turned down 'I Told You So' before Travis grabbed it and made it a hit. The list of those who took a pass includes CONWAY TWITTY, Gary Morris, Lee Greenwood and Earl Thomas Conley. Travis relishes the time he was working with Twitty on a series of shows. 'Every time Lib would walk up to him she'd just say,"I told you so". It got to the point that every time he would see her coming he'd say "I don't want to hear it."' The work of Doyle Grishan on steel guitar and Kayton Roberts on Hawaiian guitar, especially the chorus, is worth the price of the CD. Both are excellence personified and help make 'I Told You So' one of the strongest numbers in the lineup.

'Too Gone Too Long' needs no introduction or real comment because Travis has made this one his very own. The pace is lively and the session players, such as the magical Mark O'Connor on fiddle, sparkle.

'Heros and Friends' was written by Travis, in collaboration with Don Schlitz, and confirms his love affair with the cowboy. The vocal pictures he paints of simpler days are vivid.

★*Randy Travis Greatest Hits Volume Two* (Warner Bros. 9 45045 2)

Once again Travis is backed by the finest collection of session players in many a year. The musical artistry of Mark O'Connor on fiddle, the scintillating percussion work of Terry McMillan and Kirk 'Jelly Roll' Johnson's harmonica playing give new meaning to brilliant and the toe-tapping banjo of Bela Fleck makes this CD a collector's prize.

On 'Forever and Ever, Amen', Travis secures his position in the galaxy of country stars. The influence of George Jones is abundantly evident, especially when he grabs a word and hangs on. This number has two unforgettable lines that give one pause. Travis pledges his love for 'As long as old men sit and talk about the weather/As long as old women sit and talk about old men'.

There are 11 cuts on this CD including the delightful 'Diggin' Up Bones' with its hand-clapping intro. It's an early Travis hit and one of the numbers that caused people to rediscover the elements that make country music so appealing. Once again the Jones influence is evident as Travis smoothly slides from phrase to phrase. *Greatest Hits Volumes One and Two* will be followed by who knows how many more volumes. One can hardly wait.

Tritt, Travis

(born James, Marietta, Georgia, February 9 1963)

Choosing *T-r-o-u-b-l-e* as the title of his chart-topping album was a typical piece of honesty for Travis Tritt, the Georgia rebel. 'I try to be as honest as I can when interviewed and when asked a question I tell the truth. More times than not it gets me into serious trouble. Like the time I was asked my opinion of Billy Ray Cyrus' blockbuster hit "Achy Breaky Heart".'

All Tritt said was, 'I've never seen the guy perform. Don't know him personally. Never heard the album. I have heard the single and seen the video and frankly I don't care for either one of them.'

The floodgates broke and Tritt went on The Nashville Network *Crook & Chase* show to apologize to Cyrus, his family and fans. In typical Tritt fashion he didn't apologize for speaking his mind. 'I apologized completely but did not apologize for stating my opinion. If I had to do it over again I'd voice the same opinion.'

When Tritt exploded on the country music scene in 1989, with his first single 'Country Club', he became the hero of the working-class man and a sensual sex-symbol for many women. He also became the latest long-haired rebel in a string of rebels going back to the early days of WAYLON JENNINGS, WILLIE NELSON and HANK WILLIAMS JR. 'Country Club' had a refreshing credo for the times – 'have a good time and drop all the pretensions.'

Pretension is not a word in the lexicon of the 'good ole boy' from Georgia who grew up an only son on the family farm. The farm was small and Travis Sr., a jack-of-all-trades, supplemented the family income by driving a truck and school bus. He also earned extra money by working as an automobile mechanic. Understanding and sympathy for the blue-collar working man came naturally to Tritt after watching his father eke out a living the hard way.

At an early age Tritt discovered music. Before he was nine he had taught himself to play the guitar and by the time he was fourteen he was writing songs. He learned to sing in the children's choir of Marietta's First Assembly Church of God.

Family life was a constant gyration of emotions as Tritt's parents wrangled incessantly. Three months after graduating from high school Tritt married – as much to escape from the bickering as it was to embark upon married life. The marriage was short-lived. 'We were just too young,' says Tritt with typical candour. By the time he was 26 he was divorcing for the second time and penning a future smash hit, 'Here's a Quarter (Call Someone Who Cares)', in the wake of his second marital failure.

Tritt can look back on years of professional frustrations that were as emotionally devastating as they were physically draining. During the day he sweated on the loading dock of a heating and air conditioning firm. At night he sang in clubs where management placed more importance on the volume of beer sold than on the quality of the music. His big break came in 1984 when Danny Davenport, a promotion man for Warner Bros. Records, saw some raw-boned potential and took an interest in his career. He offered career-building advice and allowed him to use his home recording studio. After two long years Tritt finally finished recording an album and Davenport got Warner Bros. to listen to it. Tritt got his heart's desire – he was offered a recording deal. But there was just one problem. Warner Bros. already had another Travis under contract – RANDY TRAVIS – but after kicking around names, including his Christian name James, it was decided that country music was big enough to take two singers with the same name.

Tritt's career took a positive upswing when Ken Karagan, Kenny Rogers' manager, agreed to sign on. It was a milestone for Karagan – the first time in two decades that he had become involved with an artist who had no credits to offer and nothing more to show than possible star potential.

Tritt's potential became a reality when his debut album *Country Club* was released in March 1990. By September it was gold and by July '91 it was platinum. Even though he lost out to GARTH BROOKS Tritt was honoured to be nominated by the Country Music Association for its Horizon Award.

It's All About to Change was album number two. The hit single that was instrumental in pushing the album to gold was the song he wrote while signing the papers for his second divorce, 'Here's a Quarter (Call Someone Who Cares)'. There were a number of other successful singles from the album that eventually went platinum – 'If Hell Had a Jukebox', 'Bible Belt', 'Anymore' and 'Nothing Short of Dying'.

Tritt teamed up with MARTY STUART, best known as a 'hillbilly rocker', for a boisterous single with a title that was probably more by design than by accident, 'The Whisky Ain't Workin''. Deciding that it was about time the nose of country music was tweaked, Tritt and Stuart launched a 'No Hat's' tour in late '91. The two rebels refuse to wear cowboy hats like CLINT BLACK and ALAN JACKSON. To them the hats are a sign of conformity and the tour was their way of saying they are non-conformists both in how they dress and how they sing.

★*T-r-o-u-b-l-e* (Warner Bros. 9 45048-2)

Warner Bros. must have known they had a skyrocketing hit with *T-r-o-u-b-l-e* because they launched it with the most expensive and elaborate promotional campaign in history, including radio and retail cross-promotion, saturation television and print advertising, plus the satellite transmission of a 90-minute live show to 25 key markets. The album was produced by Gregg Brown who assembled one of the strongest lineups in recent memory. Every one of the 10 songs would be singled out as the paramount single on any other album. The title song 'T-r-o-u-b-l-e' leaves little to the imagination. 'Well I play an old guitar from nine till half past one/I'm just trying to make a livin' watching everybody else havin' fun/ Well I don't miss much if it happens on a dancehall floor/ Mercy look what walked through that door/Well hello t-r-o-u-b-l-e'. The beat is heel-pounding, not toe-tapping, and the keyboard virtuosity of blind pianist Hargus 'Pig' Robbins is nothing short of spectacular – shades of Jerry Lee Lewis. Just when you think Tritt can't be gentle he strokes the sensibilities with 'Can I Trust You With My Heart?' This is one great CD.

Tubb, Ernest

(born Ernest Dale, Crisp, Texas, February 9 1914; died September 6 1984)

Nashville is a town where egos are large and competition fierce but it is difficult to find anyone who has a bad word to say about Ernest Tubb or 'E.T.' as he was called by friend and fan. Tubb was born on a farm near Crisp, Texas, a dusty whistle-stop town that few ever visited and fewer remember. By the time he was in his teens he had discovered the music of the legendary Jimmy

Rodgers, the Singing Brakeman. It didn't take him long to decide that country music was his ticket out of the Texas boondocks.

He would be the first to admit that he had a near obsession with Rodgers. The highlight of his young life came when he met Rodgers' widow, Carrie. She took an immediate liking to the tall, lanky, laconic Texan and, in addition to giving Tubb one of her husband's cherished guitars, she became his manager for a while.

In early career Tubb sang in a much higher range as he tried to imitate the tone and phrasing of his idol. Listening to his early 78s (he cut his first record in 1936) it's hard to imagine that the deep-throated Tubb of later years could reach such notes and control his voice to such an extent. Voice discipline was not one of Tubb's strong points, nor was hitting notes but that didn't seem to matter to his die-hard fans. He overcame the deficiencies by hitting the mark with his songs and the mark was usually right in the middle of the listener's heart.

Carrie Rodgers told him that there was only one Jimmy Rodgers and, if he played his cards right, there would only be one Ernest Tubb. Finally he took her advice and dropped his voice to its natural level. It was sound advice because the hits began to arrive. He wrote and recorded 'Walking The Floor Over You'. It was this song that catapulted him into super-star status in 1942. Other chart-toppers such as 'Slippin' Around' and 'Waltz Across Texas' made the country music fans sit up and take notice. Soon Ernest Tubb was a radio favourite and getting more than his share of juke box playings. It didn't take long for major stars like Bing Crosby to see the potential of 'Walking The Floor Over You' and record it. It is now high up on the list of country classics.

Tubb also made a mild ripple in movies in a few forgettable B westerns such as *Fighting Buckaroo*, *Riding West* and *Jamboree*. He was a wooden actor but his fans really didn't care. They flocked to the Saturday afternoon matinees to see their idol and hooted and whistled as he got the best of the outlaws, sang a few songs and rode off into the sunset with the girl.

Touring was a priority. Early on Tubb played in some of the most rowdy honky-tonks in the south and south west. The patrons were demanding and unforgiving if they were not pleased. In order to be heard above blaring juke boxes and thundering crowd noise, he used his electric guitars to grab immediate attention and quiet with high-volume spit-out electric leads and riffs.

With a fan club that was growing by the day it was only natural that Tubb was invited to join the Grand Ole Opry in 1943. Not only did he become one of the Opry's most beloved performers, he shook up the establishment. In the face of strong opposition from country music purists within the Opry, he introduced electric instruments to his act. The sound of country and western music in the old Ryman Auditorium was changed forever.

There are many established artists who would not hesitate to say that Ernest Tubb got them started in the business. If he didn't invite them to become a member of his backup group The Texas Troubadours, he'd showcase them on *The Ernest Tubb Midnight Jamboree*. This radio show became a Nashville institution and came on WSM right after the Grand Ole Opry signed off. Fans would pack the narrow store and cluster around the small stage at the rear. It was worth the press of people to hear Tubb sing and introduce a lineup that included many future country stars. It was, and still is, a live show.

From the early '40s until his death, from emphysema, in 1982 Tubb set the standard for touring artists. He played everything from small town Legion Halls to high school auditoriums and county fairs. No one, before or after, has matched his dedication to touring. To him, his fans came first. Singer and guitarist Cal Smith was a Troubadour and recalls a prime example of Tubb's respect and regard for his fans. 'It was a horrendous night. The rain was pouring and the wind was howling. We were parked and some fans banged on the tour bus door. They wanted to meet 'E.T.'

'He got off the bus, stood in the rain, shook hands, signed autographs and charmed the ladies. When he got back on the bus he was soaking wet. We asked him why he would bother on such a night and he replied, "If they can come out in the rain to meet me I can stand in the rain to meet them".'

Tubb was elected to the Country Hall of Fame in 1965 and even when failing in health he still toured and played upwards of 300 dates each year. He had quit his heavy smoking but the damage to his lungs was irreversible. Near the end there were many tears in the audience as loyal fans watched this country legend strain for a note and gasp for breath. Grand Ole Opry star Porter Wagoner summed up his friend and poker-playing buddy best when he said, 'Ernest never thought he was a particularly good singer but he never realized just how good he was.'

★*Ernest Tubb Country Music Hall Of Fame Series* (MCA MCAD 10086)

The Country Music Hall Of Fame considers this CD to be 'the best of Ernest Tubb' and one only has to listen to the 16 cuts to agree with them. Tubb's voice has never been captured better. His first big hit was 'Walking The Floor Over You' which he wrote and recorded for Decca in 1941. It not only became a bestseller, it became his signature tune and won him his first sponsor, the makers of Gold Chain Flour. He became the Gold Chain Troubadour hence the name of his splendid backup group, The Troubadours.

Three other Tubb classics in this collection merit honourable mention: 'Soldier's Last Letter'; the old-time hymn 'Love Lifted Me' and the one song that is close to 'Walking The Floor Over You' in fan popularity, 'Waltz Across Texas'. Other Tubb hits include 'It's Been So Long Darling', 'Have You Ever Been Lonely (Have You Ever Been Blue)', 'Two Glasses Joe' and 'Throw Your Love My Way'.

This CD is for the country music fan who realizes that no collection would be complete without Ernest Tubb. This one fills the bill as no other.

Twitty, Conway

(born Harold Lloyd Jenkins, Friars Point, Mississippi, September 1 1933; died June 5 1993)
If ever there were two words that have been grossly overused, in country music, they are 'legend' and 'institution'. But when an artist had a career that spanned four decades, when he had been a major force in performing, recording, songwriting and business long before many of the 'hot country stars', and had one of the most recognizable faces in country music, 'legend' and 'institution' do not seem overly exaggerated appellations.

Conway Twitty was virtually weaned on country music. Born

Harold Lloyd Jenkins, the son of a Mississippi River boat captain, he taught himself the guitar at the age of five. He often sang to his own accompaniment in the pilot house of his father's boat. By the time he was ten the family had moved, to Helena, Arkansas, and he had formed his own band, the Phillips County Ramblers. It was not just a kids' band. Jenkins and his friends were good enough to get their own radio show on Helena's KFFA.

Even though music was a obsession for the youthful Jenkins, it was not all-consuming. At one time Jenkins seriously considered entering the ministry. Another seduction was baseball. He was a skilled high school player and sufficiently promising to be offered a contract by the Philadelphia Phillies upon graduation. Country music's gain was religion's and baseball's loss.

He was drafted into the army in the mid-'50s and before long was shipped to Japan. Forgetting the ministry, and baseball, he formed another band, the Cimarrons, and began touring army bases in Japan.

Once out of uniform he decided that, if he wanted to be a success he would have to climb aboard the rock 'n' roll train along with the likes of Jerry Lee Lewis, Carl Perkins and Elvis Presley. He also decided that the name Harold Lloyd Jenkins didn't have the panache necessary for a rock performer. There is a town in Arkansas called Conway and another in Texas called Twitty. It didn't take long before people took notice of Conway Twitty. He was on his way to stardom.

In 1956 he began recording on the Sun label. His first single was 'Born To Sing The Blues'. It was unreleased. Five other singles including 'Rockhouse' and 'Lawdy Miss Clawdy' hit the record stores. By the end of the year, the cash registers were ringing.

1958 was the breakthrough year for Twitty with 'It's Only Make Believe'. The amazing thing about 'It's Only Make Believe' was how quickly it broke the million seller barrier. It was Twitty's first mega hit. The next hit to go gold was 'Lonely Blue Boy' for MGM Records in 1960. Television appearances on *American Bandstand* and *The Ed Sullivan Show* helped push his rock releases to the heady sales range of 16 million copies plus.

During his rock period he appeared in six movies, which significantly increased his fan following. Now mostly forgotten, at the time they attracted the high school and college crowd, with titles like *Platinum High, College Confidential* and *Sex Kitten Goes to College*.

The early '60s saw Twitty's career slow down. Taking it as a sign that his days as a rock performer were numbered, he shifted back to country music which was his first love. Moving to Oklahoma City, he formed his first country band, the Lonely Blue.

It was at this point in his career that Owen Bradley came into his life and signed him to a Decca recording contract. Decca also had under contract LORETTA LYNN, by this time an established star. Lynn and Twitty were not to team up as a bestselling duo until later but the idea was beginning to germinate.

Following the path of so many country artists Twitty moved to Nashville in the late '60s. His country career was firmly launched. His records were being bought by a growing fan following. His music was played on radio and in juke boxes around North America. Like Ernest Tubb, touring was always a high priority for Twitty and his schedule was as packed as the halls, clubs and auditoriums he played. The Grand Ole Opry beckoned and he joined the roster of regulars.

'Hello Darlin'', in 1970, was a smash for both Twitty and Decca. Twitty wrote the song and it confirmed his star status as a singer and his brilliance as a songwriter. It not only hit the top of country charts it was a crossover to the pop lists as well. (When an American/Soviet astronaut team was circling the globe in a joint space endeavour, they specifically requested that the song be beamed up to them. There was a Russian language version pressed for the cosmonauts and, when CMA reissued the original song in its 'Oldies' series, the Russian version was on the flip side.)

In 1971 the Lynn/Twitty duo was launched and this brilliant collaboration resulted in a memorable body of work which included singles and albums. The single 'After The Fire Is Gone' became a top chart hit. The cash registers rang sufficiently to make the album *We Only Make Believe* one of the fifty top-selling albums of the year. Another Lynn/Twitty collaboration was 'Louisiana Woman, Mississippi Man'. It became a major 1973 hit for both artists. Twitty the singer was ever grateful to Twitty the songwriter for 'Linda On My Mind'. It was released in 1975 to enthusiastic reviews and was one of his most requested songs.

The '70s closed out with another skyrocketing hit, 'Happy Birthday Darlin''.

Not only had Twitty been amazingly successful with his choice of music, he struck pay dirt when he formed the Lonely Blue Boys. He changed the name to Twitty Birds, another shrewd move by the former Harold Lloyd Jenkins. When the best country music backup groups are discussed the Twitty Birds are always included.

Twitty was an active man. In addition to recording, songwriting and performing he was involved in a number of business ventures and organizations. In the '70s he and Loretta Lynn jointly owned the successful United Talent Agency. Over the years he owned a number of music publishing firms, Hello Darlin' Music, Never-break Music and Twitty Bird Music.

Even though he opted for music over baseball, and never regretted the decision, he never lost his love for the game. He was the owner of the Nashville Sounds baseball team and was very seldom seen, off stage, without his favourite baseball cap perched on top of his luxuriant head of hair.

When theme parks became all the rage in North America, Twitty built 'Twitty City,' about 20 miles east of downtown Nashville. It contains his plantation-style home, a museum, gardens and gift shops. It's a required stop for tour buses and draws thousands of Twitty fans every year. Whenever possible Twitty would personally greet his fans, shake their hands, pose for pictures and sign autographs. Twitty City was also his home. Twitty shared it with his wife Dee Henry, his four children Joni, Jimmy, Kathy and Michael and his mother Velma Jenkins.

While Twitty sang about a sexy world in songs like 'Slow Hand' and 'You've Never Been This Far Before', he was physically circumspect in his performances. There were no hip-swing gyrations that are the trademark of other country and rockabilly performers. In private life he enjoyed a reputation for being a model family man.

On June 4 1993, while returning from Branson, Missouri, where he had played a matinée concert in the Jim Stafford Theatre, Twitty collapsed in his tour bus while parked at a truck stop. Crew members found him when they returned to the bus after stopping for food. On June 5 Harold Lloyd Jenkins (a.k.a. Conway Twitty) died of an abdominal aneurysm at Cox Medical Centre South, Springfield, Missouri. He was 59 years old. In tribute, veteran country singer Porter Wagoner described Twitty as 'a legend with a genius for picking his material'. It is a fitting epitaph for an extraordinary artist.

★*The Very Best of Loretta and Conway* (MCA MCABD-31236)

There are 14 duets on this CD and one listen will confirm the wisdom of pairing these two country balladeers.

The opening song is a spirited rendition of 'Louisiana Woman, Mississippi Man'. It starts on a swinging note that will get your toes tapping. Lynn and Twitty keep up the pace throughout and are framed by some lively Cajun/rock fiddling.

The closing song is the Bobby Bare, Boyce Hawkins flag-waver 'God Bless America Again'. The title says it all.

Packaged between is a gentle rendition of stolen love 'From Seven Till Ten'. There's no question what the lovers are up to. 'We'll have to steal all the lovin' we feel/And we're feelin' that feelin' again/We'll never be free/So it's got to be/Lovin' from seven till ten'. Originally released in 1978 it sounds more like a '90s ballad.

Many Lynn/Twitty fans consider 'It's Only Make-Believe' to be their premier duet. Few will argue with the evaluation. The blending of their voices is exceptional. The catch in Twitty's on a phrase like 'my one and only prayer will be some day you'll care for me/But it's only make-believe' is a beautiful counterpoint to Lynn's distinctive style which at times can be shrill. She holds her voice in beautiful control on this song and squeezes out every drop of emotion that she can muster.

★*Silver Anniversary Collection* MCA MCASD-8035

The invitation reads, 'Conway Twitty requests the pleasure of your company at his 25th Anniversary in country music'. All it takes to be part of a magnificent event is to put this CD in your player and sit back to listen to a musical retrospective of one of country music's greatest ambassadors. This CD was mastered on the JVC digital audio mastering system and the sound reproduction is as near perfect as one could demand. 'The Image of Me' was written by Wayne Kempt. It's a torrid crescendo of feeling that assails the emotions.

The throaty 'Hello Darlin'' is a sensual elegy to a lost love. It's a musical prayer for what once was and a tearful plea for a return to better days. The background is worth listening to. It's a benchmark for neophyte arrangers on how to showcase a singer.

Twitty was as versatile in his singing as he was in his career. Just when one settles back, in a thoughtful melancholy frame of mind, he jolts one back to reality. He does it with a piercing, power-packed, number like 'I'm Not Through Loving You Yet'.

One of the best cuts is 'Linda On My Mind'. It's a favourite with grieving men. All they do, as they sing along with Twitty, is change Linda to the name of their lost love.

Van Shelton, Ricky

(born Danville, Virginia, January 12 1952)

For all of his early life Ricky Van Shelton was just plain Ricky Shelton to his family and friends. When he began getting mail for another Ricky Shelton, and the other Ricky Shelton began getting his mail, he added his middle name Van. Not only did he now get his mail, the 'Van' added a touch of class to a man who has become synonymous with class in country music.

Shelton's success is not surprising. It is just what one would expect from a talented individual with an extra portion of drive. What is surprising is the fact that he was once a dedicated rock 'n' roll fan who had no intention or desire of becoming a country singer. It was his brother Ronnie who engineered the change in musical taste. Ronnie had a bluegrass band and invited Ricky to join in. As an added incentive he let him drive his 1964 Ford Fairlane 289. The temptation was too great for a 14-year-old to pass up. It is difficult to say which was the greater thrill, driving the car or realizing that he really liked bluegrass and country music. Once he was bitten by the country music bug he began to listen seriously to classic country artists like the Osborne Brothers and Hank Williams Sr. Before long he was immersed in country.

Proficient on the guitar from early age, Shelton began to perform wherever anyone would stop long enough to listen and that included fish fries, small clubs, living rooms and back yards. Endued with a strong work ethic, Shelton earned a living during the day and devoted his spare time to song writing. A slow rock 'n' roll song titled 'My Conscience is Bothering Me' was his first composition. He was 13 when he wrote it.

Shelton was so consumed with performing and songwriting that there was no time for romance. He still jokes about the fact that his only close companion, during the early years, was his guitar. It was 1980, and he was nearly 30, before he met his future wife, Bettye, and married. More than one supportive wife has been the foundation upon which a country career has been built, and Bettye Shelton was just such a wife. The Sheltons moved to Nashville and Bettye got a job to support both of them while her husband tried to break into show business. Success was not instantaneous and disappointments were many.

Shelton cut a demo tape that he was trying to get heard. Through a stroke of luck, his wife gave it to a woman she worked with. She gave it to her husband, Jerry Thompson, who just happened to be a highly-read columnist for *The Tennessean*. Thompson thought Shelton had promise and badgered his friend Rick Blackburn, who was head of CBS Records, to give it a listen. Blackburn liked what he heard and made a point to hear Shelton perform, in person, at a showcase. Within a couple of weeks Shelton had a recording contract and was in a studio cutting his first album with Blackburn producing.

Wild Eyed Dream took off. One of the major reasons it was a winner was the choice of material recorded. There were songs from some of the best songwriters in the business including Harlan Howard, Buck Owens, Roger Miller and MERLE HAGGARD. One of the songs, 'Crime of Passion', hit the top-10 and Shelton was on his way. The hard work, sacrifices, and Bettye's faith had finally paid off.

Whenever a new, exciting artist gets hot and people begin to talk, the Grand Ole Opry takes notice. To be added to the Opry's roster of stars is one of the highest honours a country performer can receive. To be introduced by Opry icon Roy Acuff was an added memory that Shelton will always cherish. 'I hope I can carry on with what you and the rest of the Opry members have done over the years, 'cause you are country,' said Shelton, in response to Acuff's enthusiastic introduction. The Opry audience agreed with Acuff and, following Shelton's number, they applauded so enthusiastically that he was called back for an encore. Encores at the Opry are a rarity.

Shelton's career took off like the proverbial rocket. Platinum for 'Wild Eyed Dream' was just for openers. The Academy of Country Music named him their 1988 male vocalist. He was *Music City News* star of tomorrow and the Country Music Association honoured him with their distinguished Horizon Award.

Loving Proof was Shelton's second album and it too was a smash success. Eventually it was certified platinum.

The fans liked Shelton for his singing and personality which is warm and outgoing. They voted him both male vocalist and Entertainer of the Year for the 1990 combined TNN and *Music City News* awards show.

Shelton knows where his career strength lies and is not reluctant to give praise where praise is due. 'Without the fans I wouldn't be here,' he says, without apology.

His third hit album, *RSV III*, maintained the astounding pace set by its predecessors. It too went platinum. *Backwoods* was released in 1991 and mirrored the masterful blending of old and new songs with some honky tonk and rockabilly, to give the song mix added spice.

Shelton has a rich country voice and is as equally comfortable with a slow, languid ballad as he is with a rollicking toe-tapper. *Rockin' Years* was a winner because it had DOLLY PARTON joining Shelton in duet. The two mega stars also made a video with the same title. It was the number one video for 1991.

Shelton is musically fulfilled when he is on stage performing. 'I love the music, I love the people. That's when I'm happiest.'

★*Ricky Van Shelton Greatest Hits Plus* (Columbia CK 52753)

Whenever 'plus' is added to any album title one expects the ultimate with that extra touch and this CD is no disappointment.

'Just As I Am' was written by Larry Boone and Paul Nelson with no apology that the title is a direct lift from the old, time-honoured revival hymn that has been used, by countless ministers and evangelists, as a mood-setter for the altar call. 'I was lost but aimlessly searching/Lord knows I was one lonely man/Then you came along/Like that old gospel song/You took me just as I am.'

When Van Shelton went into the studio on May 16 1988 he knew he was in for a great session. Backing him up were Mark O'Connor on fiddle, Eddy Bayers on drums, Steve Gibson on electric guitar, Tom Robb on bass, Mark Casstevens on acoustic guitar, Randy McCormick on piano, Paul Franklin on steel and John Wesley Ryles, Harry Stinson and Dennis Wilson on harmony vocals. 'I've Cried My Last Tear For You' was the result of this spellbinding collaboration. It's classic Van Shelton. Few country singers can bring off a lively fast-paced, hand-clapping number the way Van Shelton does. There are shades of Buck Owens in this one.

Included in the luminescent lineup is 'I'll Leave This World Loving You'.

There is not a weak link in this melodic 14-song chain.

Wariner, Steve

(born Noblesville, Indiana, December 25 1954)

Fast sale starts, which propel the albums and singles of superstars such as Clint Black, GARTH BROOKS, PATTY LOVELESS or PAM TILLIS to the top of the charts, generally begin with high-energy media attention and instant fan demand in record stores. In the case of Steve Wariner it's another story.

This talented artist has been making some of the finest music to come out of Nashville for the past 26 years and virtually hiding his talent under a bushel. Until his latest album, *I Am Ready*, was released to rave reviews, his music had a higher identification quotient than he did. Only the dedicated fans were able to put his face to his music. It is not unusual for a fan attending a concert to nudge someone sitting next to them and whisper, in utter amazement 'I didn't know he did that,' when he starts into one of his songs.

There's no question about Wariner being a certified hit maker. His musical quiver is filled with 14 albums, 30 top-10 hits, including over 10 that reached number one, and a level of radio airplay that is the envy of many stars with much higher profiles. Add to his body of work the fact that he is one of the most accomplished instrumentalists in Nashville. He is such a powerhouse on the guitar that Takamine brought out a limited edition Steve Wariner signature model, the SW341 acoustic.

Whenever a top-10 songwriting list is drawn up, Wariner's name is included. His songwriting skills have been long recognized, and admired, since four of his songs were included on Bob Luman's comeback album. *USA Today* polled country fans and, to Wariner's astonishment, and amusement, he made the top 10 of Nashville's sexiest men. When asked for his reaction to being named on the poll Wariner replied, 'I thought that was the funniest thing! I always tell people I think Boxcar Willie probably came in first.'

In spite of all the applause for his work and admiring glances for his boy-next-door good looks he does not have an Opryland size ego. He is self-effacing, down-to-earth and sincere, genuinely liked by his peers and the industry. Part of the reason why he is not in the superstar class is his distaste for grandiose self-promotion. In trying to explain how he sees himself Wariner said, 'I'm not real flashy, I'm not controversial, I haven't had six wives and I like to do a lot of things. I guess it is hard to put a handle on me.'

Even before he was a teenager Wariner had told his mother and dad that, when he got old enough, he was going to move to Nashville and make records. He first visited Nashville when he was 15 and fulfilled his dream by moving there permanently when he was 17. 'I never thought of doing anything else but sing, play and write,' he recalls. 'In fact I've never done anything else. I've never had another job in my whole life.'

Raised in a musical family, in rural Indiana, Wariner's big country music break came when the late Dottie West spotted him in a Kentucky nightclub and offered him a job with her band. 'My mom wasn't too high on the idea of me going on the road because I had never really been out of a two-state area. To her I was only 17 and I was leaving home.' Dottie assured Wariner's mother that she'd personally keep an eye on him. She would be his road mother. A strong bond grew up between Wariner and Dottie. One of the hardest things he has ever had to do was sing 'Amazing Grace' at Dottie's funeral following her death from an tragic automobile accident.

Wariner toured North America with the Dottie West show and looks back on it as his primary musical education. He left the West organization to play in Bob Luman's band. Another strong bond of respect and friendship was formed, only to be broken by Luman's untimely death from pneumonia, in December 1978. Another friend and mentor came into Wariner's life in the late

'70s, in the person of the legendary guitarist Chet Atkins who was his long-time idol and became his mentor. Atkins was with RCA at the time and signed Wariner to a recording contract. 'The guitar has always been important to me,' says Wariner. 'Singing was an afterthought. My hero was always Chet [Atkins]. At one point in my career I just wanted to play recording sessions.'

A number of fine singles followed, the biggest being 'All Roads Lead To You' in 1981. It was Wariner's first number-one hit. Other 1980 singles that have become his standards include 'Small-Town Girl', 'Kansas City Lights', and 'Lonely Women Make Good Lovers'. He is especially proud of his collaboration with MARK O'CONNOR, VINCE GILL and RICKY SKAGGS in 'Restless' for the *Mark O'Connor & The New Nashville Cats* album which won a Grammy and Country Music Award. 'I have never been obsessed with awards,' says Wariner. 'I've been nominated a number of times and a couple of times I thought I'd win but I didn't. That's why The "Cats" awards are really special.'

Life on the road is never easy for a married man who places great importance on time with his family. Wariner has a well balanced family life and time with his wife Caryn, who is also his business manager, and their young sons Ryan and Ross is of prime importance.

Media interest in Wariner exploded following the release of *I Am Ready*, his first album after he amicably left MCA and signed with Arista Records. The accolades for the hit single 'Leave Him Out Of This', and a remake of the Bill Anderson classic 'Tips Of My Fingers' only added to the momentum.

Wariner has been referred to as 'Nashville's next Vince Gill'. What really is being said is that Steve Wariner is one of the most admired and well respected people in country music. He's a fan favourite who is long overdue for superstardom.

★*I Am Ready* (Arista 1869-2)

It's not uncommon for an artist to enthuse about the latest album and spew forth adjectives like 'great', 'best' or 'tremendous'. It's expected because the only way to sell is by being enthusiastic and 100% positive. When Steve Wariner is quoted as saying, 'I feel the whole package is there on this one. There's a lot more emotion and heart than on any of the other albums,' one tends to believe him because he is an artist of understatement and few can remember him being so rhapsodic.

In 1960 Bill Anderson took his country classic 'Tips of My Fingers', which he wrote, to the top of the charts. Three decades later it is back to chart-topping levels thanks to Wariner's fiery vocal performance.

'Leave Him Out of This' is a haunting rendition of a haunting song. 'We're here in the dark alone/The three of us again/You and me lying here with the memory of him'. Wariner's vocal prowess has never been showcased to better effect than on this song. Vince Gill and Billy Thomas shine on the background vocals. Their voices blend perfectly and add the finishing touches.

Wariner wrote, or co-wrote, five of the ten songs on this CD. The power of his lyrics confirms his reputation as one of the best tunesmiths in Nashville. He co-wrote 'Everything's Gonna be Alright' with Bill LaBounty and all one has to hear is the first line to know that a musical treat is in store: 'Too little money – too many tears'. Eddie Bayers caresses his drums with just the right beat and Reggie Young, on steel guitar, is a joy to hear. *The Denver Post*, a journal not renowned for blatant enthusiasm, wrote the following: 'Steve Wariner is one of the most talented people in country music. His superb vocal and instrumental skills are the envy of his Nashville peers and his albums are always a notch above the standard.'

Williams, Don

(born Floydada, Texas, May 27 1939)

Don Williams has a goal in life and it's the complete opposite to the goal of many aspiring country music stars. 'Greed does strange things to people,' he once told an interviewer. 'I never want to get so filthy rich that I become a hermit who can't go out on the street.' While his worse fears haven't materialized he has become 'filthy' rich in success and in the admiration of his fans and associates.

On the stage Williams is an imposing figure. At 6'1" the man they affectionately call the 'gentle giant', is a refreshing change from some of the publicity-hyped artists who depend upon glitter and glitz to sell their product. There are no pretensions about

Williams. He lets his impressive country music track record stand on its own without the 'puff' that is supplied by slick public relations practitioners.

When Williams was young his mechanic father moved from place to place, wherever the job took him. Williams learned very early what it was like to be nomadic. By the time he was 12 his mother had taught him the guitar and while he was drawn to country music he also enjoyed Elvis Presley, Chuck Berry and the earlier rock artists.

A two year army hitch followed high school graduation. It was during his army service that he met and married his wife Joy. Once discharged, he had to earn a living and, for a while, he worked at a series of odd jobs and in the Texas oil fields. The evenings were devoted to his music. Before long he and his friend, Loften Kline, were singing and playing in the bars and honky tonks. For want of a better name they called themselves the Strangers Two. The name lasted until 1964 when Susan Taylor joined them. They renamed themselves the Pozo Seco Singers. The group began recording and had a 1965 top-10 hit with 'Time'. A few minor successes followed and they progressed from bars and honky tonks to lounges and dance halls which Williams hated. He chafed at the rigid structure of a set show. Having to play in the despised halls, and lounges, was more than he could stomach. The outcome was a strong abhorrence for anything that assaulted his privacy and stripped away his independence.

The Pozo Seco Singers disbanded in 1971. Williams was so disillusioned that he quit performing and opened a furniture store with his father-in-law.

It was a year before the craving for music started to gnaw at his creative soul. Williams struck out for Nashville where he fully intended to devote his energies to songwriting instead of performing.

One way music publishing companies make money is to have artists choose songs from their catalogue to record. They hire knowledgeable people like Williams to bring their songs to the attention of singers and producers.

After a while of pushing the songs of other songwriters, as well as his own, Williams decided it was time to get back into the performing side of country music and start recording again. *Don Williams, Volume One*, with Allen Reynolds producing, was his first album for JMI Records. Two classic country singles came out of the lineup – 'Amanda', by Bob McDill, and his own song, 'The Shelter Of Your Eyes', which hit the charts in 1972. JMI Records folded and a short time later he signed with ABC/DOT Records.

Williams embarked upon an active period of producing his own records. *Don William Volume Three* was released in 1975 and, among others, *Don Williams' Greatest Hits* followed.

During the '70s and early '80s, Williams enjoyed high sales and enthusiastic fan support in North America but it paled in comparison to his popularity in the United Kingdom. His superstar status in Great Britain was partially due to the smash album *You're My Best Friend*. It was 1975 Album of the Year. Williams was honoured and elated to be named 1975 Male Country Singer of the Year and Country Performer of the Year by the Country Music Association of Great Britain. One of Williams' greatest fans is British rock star Eric Clapton. Following his 1975 British triumphs Williams was to later team up with Clapton for a Nashville concert.

The momentum was maintained through 1976 with six albums in the top-10, four of which were in the top-5. The music flowed and hit followed hit. 'Tulsa Time' was written by a member of Williams' backup band, Danny Flowers. It became one of his biggest hits and was named 1979 Single of the Year by the Academy of Country Music.

Williams leads a quiet, disciplined lifestyle. Ranch life and church-going are more alluring for the non-drinking, non-smoking, unassuming singer than the artificiality of show business.

★*Don Williams Greatest Hits* (MCA MCAMD-5944)

The secret to Don Williams' success, and longevity, in a business where only the strong survive, is his ability to stick with a simple, relaxing, repertoire that keeps his fans comfortable. With a deep relaxing baritone he delivers reassuring songs that touch the heart. 'You're My Best Friend' is one of Williams biggest hits. It was written by Waylon Holyfield and it's a vocal love offering to a man's best friend, his wife. 'You're my friend when I'm hungry/ You're my shelter from troubled wind/You're my anchor in life's ocean/But most of all you're my best friend'. Williams has a set backup that was crafted to fit his voice and delivery. It includes brushed drums with a soft walking beat, acoustic guitar, dobro, harmonica and keyboard.

'Come Early Morning', with as fine a harmonica bridge as one could wish for, stands out. So does 'Lord, I Hope This Day Is Good'. Everyone can identify with the message of this song.

Williams' best review came from a fan. 'I've never met him personally but I'm sure he's the kind of man I'd want for a friend.'

Williams, Hank Jr

(Born Randall Hank, Shreveport, Louisiana, May 26 1949)
When Hank Williams Sr died, from an apparent drug overdose on New Year's Day 1953, in the back seat of a Cadillac while driving through West Virginia, he left two legacies that have perpetuated his memory: he died just nine months short of his twenty-ninth birthday and in a six-year compressed career he turned out a body of work that would have been a crowning life-time achievement for others. His music, which revolutionized country music during his brief career, is as fresh today as it was when he first wrote and recorded it. Countless country artists include a Hank Williams' song in their album line-up, knowing that it will be safe and that it will strengthen the album's overall fan appeal.

If Hank Jr's name had been anything but Williams he would have made it as both a country singer and writer because there is little debate that he is one of the most talented country artists in the business. However his name *is* Williams and for many years he lived under the shadow of his father's fame and reputation. It took years of rebellion, hard living and a near fatal accident before he came to grips with his heritage and identity, both professionally and personally.

By the time Hank Jr was born his father, who nicknamed him 'Bocephus', was an established Louisiana Hayride star and a performer with great promise. Ambitious Hank Sr knew that his next major career move had to be the Grand Ole Opry and when Hank Jr was just three months old the family moved to Nashville.

Hank Jr was three when his father, whom he hardly knew and today has difficulty remembering, died.

During his public and high school days in Nashville Hank Jr

proved to be a fine athlete and excelled in football, basketball, boxing and swimming. He also proved that his father's musical genes had been passed down by showing an early flair for music. By the time he entered his teens he was a masterful guitar player with a talent for improvisation.

His mother, Audrey Williams, retained custody of her son after her acrimonious divorce from Hank Sr. She paid the bills with an act called the Caravan of Stars and by the time Hank Jr was 14 he was accompanying his mother when school was out. The experience helped him hone his performing and songwriting skills.

As to be expected, record companies soon began to notice him. They realized that the combination of talent and a trademark name made him a highly marketable commodity. Audrey Williams was very shrewd: she resisted the blandishments of the record companies until she felt the time was right to launch seriously her son's career. In 1964 she and Hank Jr moved to California and an MGM Records contract was signed. The debut album, *Hank Williams, Jr, Sings* was released in May of that year. Fan reaction, which was translated into album sales, exceeded marketing expectations. An album featuring the scion of the great Hank Williams Sr, singing his father's greatest hits, was irresistible.

Before long Hank Jr had chalked up his first single: his father's 'Long Gone Lonesome Blues'. He was just 15 years old.

Next came a sure-fire winner, the album *Your Cheatin' Heart*, which was also released in 1964. The song 'Your Cheatin' Heart' became Hank Jr's theme song and the name of his backup band until he changed it to The Brama Band years later.

His fame and reputation as a recording artist grew and by the end of the 1960s he was on the road performing in more than 200 shows a year. The gruelling pace, for a young man who had not only inherited his father's musical talents but also his weakness for pills and booze, took its toll both physically and emotionally.

During the horrendous period that saw his personal life reduced to a shambles – due to excesses that at one low point drove him to attempt suicide – Hank Jr continued to perform and keep recording an impressive list of albums and singles, including *Ballads of Hills and Plains* in 1965, *My Own Way* in 1967 and *The Best of Hank Williams Jr* also in 1967.

Though Hank Jr was grateful for a top-ten single in 1966 it was somewhat ironic that the song, 'Standing in the Shadows (Of a Very Famous Man)', was both a tribute and a thinly veiled plea to be allowed to get out from under the shadow.

During his illustrious career Hank Jr has been honoured by his peers on numerous occasions. He has received a number of BMI Songwriter Awards, and when he accepted a BMI award at 16 he set a record for being the youngest person to be so honoured.

By the end of the 1960s Hank Jr's fan appeal was so great that on May 4 1969 he and JOHNNY CASH appeared at Detroit's Corbo Hall. The gross box-office take, plus programme and album sales, topped $100,000 – at that time a record for a country music show.

During the early 1970s, when Hank Jr was still in his early twenties, he suffered an identity crisis and seriously began to take stock of his relationship with his father, his generation and his future. In his candid 1979 autobiography *Living Proof* he wrote, 'I'd been singing Daddy's songs almost every night for the past 15 or 16 years and I thought I knew everything there was to know about it. What I'd forgotten was that knowing is not the same as feeling. I knew my father but I had let his soul slip away from me and a lot of other people had found it.'

Determined to modernize his music and break new ground, Hank Jr moved from Nashville to the small community of Cullman, Alabama, where he spent time reflecting and recharging his artistic and emotional batteries. He found a new focus by talking to musicians and studio operators in Muscle Shoals where a mix of country and Southern Rock was being recorded for a new audience.

Hank Williams Jr and Friends was the result, released in 1974. The 'friends' included musical innovators like CHARLIE DANIELS, Toy Caldwell, of the Marshall Tucker Band, and Allman alumnus Chuck Leavell. The album was an enigma. Many country music purists found it difficult to accept Hank Jr in such non-traditional country music company. Today some consider the album to be a classic. Regardless of the qualified response to the album, Hank Jr was convinced that he was on the right musical track. He was looking forward to the new musical roads that he was mapping out for his career – when tragedy struck.

While mountain climbing in the Montana Rockies he was caught in a snowslide that sent him hurtling down 500 feet. 'It was like falling out of a plane,' he recalls. 'I thought: You're dead! You're gonna splatter on the rocks.' He hit the snow in a swan dive and literally split his face in half upon impact. A long convalescence period followed a seven-hour operation and numerous reconstructive surgery sessions.

'It was my wife Becky, friends like Johnny Cash who came to my bedside, and my music that helped pull me through,' he says. Fortunately there was a backlog of songs, which were released while he was incapacitated, keeping his name prominent until he could once again resume his career.

During the period that Hank Jr had been with MGM Records Mike Curb had been president. In 1975 when Curb left MGM to set up his own company, Curb Records, Hank Jr went with him. A number of charted songs were produced, including 'One Night Stands' and 'I Fought the Law'. Another label move came in 1979 when Hank Jr joined a number of Curb alumnae on the Elektra roster.

Family Tradition was his first release under the new contract and it was an album heavily weighted with Hank Jr songs. Many, like 'I Just Ain't Been Able' and 'I've Got Rights', were based upon events in his life and offered yet more insights into what makes this complex man tick.

Title songs often bring rewards, and 'Family Tradition' is a case in point. In 1979 it was nominated for a Grammy for Best Country Male Vocal Performance and brought Hank Jr his first BMI Writer's Award in five years. He previously won in 1974 for 'The Last Love Song'.

In October 1981 Hank Jr reached a career milestone – 'My Rowdy Friends' was a smash single from his *Pressure Is On* album and marked his twenty-fifth top-ten single and sixth number-one hit. Not only does Hank Jr know his way around sparkling lyrics, he also has a unique knack for choosing titles which immediately attract: 'Whisky Bent and Hell Bound', 'A Country Boy Can Survive' and 'Women I've Never Had' are three that stand out. On 'Leave Them Boys Alone' he is joined by the late ERNEST TUBB and WAYLON JENNINGS and sings, 'He's still the most-wanted outlaw in the land.' He is singing about his father. With the reverence of a man who has come to grips with his demons and insecurity, he affirms his own musical independence and self-determination.

Hank Jr is more popular now than ever before. He constantly

fills halls and auditoriums with a wild, kinetic stage show. In the opinion of many he outstrips the 'Killer', Jerry Lee Lewis, for untamed creative excess. Although he is in total control of his life and character weaknesses, there are no reigns placed on his creative talents. He is without question one of country music's major figures.

★*Habits Old and New* (Warner/Curb 278-2)

Habits Old and New from 1980 has to be one of the musical bargains of the season. In the ten-song lineup there are two Hank Williams Sr originals, one by Kris Kristofferson (who has to be one of America's premier songwriters) and seven by Hank Williams Jr. The music is a mix of fundamental rock and pure, unadulterated country in the finest tradition. This sound has made Hank Williams Jr one of the most popular and influential performers on the contemporary music scene.

'Kaw-Liga' needs no introduction. It's a Hank Williams Sr evergreen classic that originally topped the charts in 1953, even though Williams had died on New Year's Day.

Hank Jr pulls out all the stops and gives 'Kaw-Liga' new shadings with his high-powered country-rock version. He is in rare voice and, pushed by the driving beat, he pulsates with souring notes and full-throated growls.

'Here I Am Fallin' Again' is a perfect counterpoint to 'Kaw-Liga'. It's a tender song about falling in love again and Hank Jr strokes the lyrics and melody with a velvet glove that evokes vivid images of love.

'If You Don't Like Hank Williams', is Kristofferson's contribution and a cheeky one it is too. It begins, 'I like Charlie Daniels/And I love big John Cash.' It goes on to list all the country greats from MERLE HAGGARD to WAYLON JENNINGS to Linda Rondstadt to GEORGE JONES, then lashes out with, 'But anyone who don't like Hank Williams can kiss our ass.' Typical irreverent Hank Jr.

For the multitude of Hank Jr fans there is a liberal helping of his songwriting genius with such stellar compositions as 'The Blues Man', 'All In Alabama' and 'The American Way'. He places his indelible musical stamp on each song.

Wright, Michelle

(born, Chatham, Ontario July 1 circa 1957)

When Michelle Wright won the 1993 Canadian Grammy award for Country Female Artist she joined Anne Murray and k.d. lang in the winners' circle and, as one reviewer wrote, she 'added a touch of class to the proceedings'. No eyebrows were raised when Michelle's name was called out. The Grammy is just one of an impressive list of awards this Canadian country singer has garnered in a relatively short career.

Michelle's country heritage is impeccable. She grew up in the small farming community of Merlin, Ontario, just 45 miles from the Canada/U.S. border at Detroit. Her earliest memories are of being on stage with her country performing parents and seeing her father in his cowboy costume. In recalling her early years, and an equally early love for singing and performing, Michelle said, 'My stepfather was a grain farmer so after putting in time on a tractor my brother and I used to perform in the garage. He played the guitar and I played the drums.'

Michelle's career is one of memorable performances and each has special meaning. But nothing will ever top the one she gave with her mother and brother when she was in the 7th grade. She sang 'Satin Sheets' in the school's talent show.

Being so close to Detroit radio stations her musical influences were mostly American, especially country, which she learned to love as a child. Although the Motown rhythm and blues was the 'in' music during her youth it was country which was played in the Wright home, morning, noon and night. The years on stage, with her parents, gave her an early performing confidence that stood out when she began touring and playing clubs right out of high school. Blessed with a unique voice, which at times is low, husky and at times sensual, Michelle was skilled at giving a song that special touch even as a young performer.

By 1988 she had released her first album in Canada and, recognizing her star potential, Arista Records made her the third artist signed when the label opened its country division. 'Success has been an 11-year process in Canada,' says Michelle. 'It took a long time for people to get to know me but that experience really prepared me for the American audience.' One only has to listen to the smoky-voiced singer to know that she is not only in total control during her recording sessions, she deeply identifies with the lyrics and melody.

When asked to explain how she chooses the songs for her albums and concerts Michelle replied, 'The main thing for me is always the song and what it says. I have to believe in the song's message.'

Arista's faith in Michelle's sales potential was well founded when her second album for the label, *Now & Then*, was released on May 22 1992.

By February 1993 it had reached platinum status in Canada and received the 1992 Album of the Year nomination by the Canadian Country Music Association. U.S. sales were impressive and, by mid-March 1993, they hovered around the 300,000 mark.

'Take it Like a Man' was a 1992 smash hit for Michelle. The CCMA honoured it with two prestigious awards – Single of the Year and Video of the Year. It also scooped up the 1992 Country Video Award from Much Music. To cap off a near-perfect 1992 Michelle was named CCMA Female Vocalist of the Year and Country Music Person of the Year.

Michelle brings an emotional commitment to her singing that comes from deep, at times painful, personal experiences. She had to cope with the trauma of her parents' divorce and a serious drinking problem which she openly talks about. 'I hope talking about it will prove to be a positive thing,' says Michelle, who is in her fifth year of sobriety. 'To understand me and the choices in my life, and in my song selection, you would have to know that about me.'

Another star in Michelle's crown of achievements came when she appeared in the bestselling home video *Remembering Patsy*. It was released in March 1993 on the thirtieth anniversary of the legendary country star's tragic death. With deep feeling, and a remarkable empathy, Michelle reads Patsy's personal letters and bridges between Patsy's music, the reminiscences of her family and friends, and the stars who knew her.

The reviews for both *Remembering Patsy* and Michelle's performance were rave. She was the perfect choice for narrator.

Michelle scored again on September 18 1993 when she swept the Canadian Country Music Awards with Single of the Year, Entertainer of the Year, her fourth consecutive Female Vocalist of the Year and shared the Video of the Year award.

★*Now & Then* (Arista 1 8685-2)

This is an album of powerful emotions. 'Take it Like a Man' is Michelle's tough-minded petition for just the right man. 'I keep looking for a friend and a lover/When I find one he ain't the other/ Sometimes I just want to quit'. This song had hit stamped on it the moment Tony Haselden dotted the last 'i' and crossed the last 't'.

Michelle's strong gutsy, no-fooling, delivery makes mincemeat of 'Mr Right' who forgot to mention that he had a wife.

In the idiom of the music business, 'Now & Then' is a ballad that will blow you away. *Cashbox* (May 30, 1992) singled out the title cut, 'He Would Be 16' and 'Don't Start With Me' as the three strongest on the CD. One can't argue with the selection. However, 'Now and Then' is a standout. Michelle's full-throated voice matches beautifully with the delicate piano stylings of Steve Nathan.

Any woman who has ever given up a child for adoption will identify with 'He Would Be 16'. The first time Michelle performed it on stage she cried her eyes out. It's a moving song of regret.

Michelle Wright is a talent whose time has come.

Wynette, Tammy

(born Virginia Wynette Pugh, near Tupelo, Mississippi, May 5 1942)

Tammy Wynette is a multi-talented singer, guitarist, accordionist, pianist, and songwriter who rose from a humble tar-paper shack to international acclaim. She is a country artist with spectacular appeal and an ability to reach the very soul of those who listen to her. Her albums and CDs are an integral part of any country music collection. One French entertainment critic dubbed Wynette 'the Edith Piaf of country America'. In 1976 she was named Number One Female Vocalist of Great Britain.

There is nothing subtle about Tammy Wynette. She has a husky, alto voice that drips with choking emotion; she reaches deep down for every drop of pathos and wrings it dry. 'D-I-V-O-R-C-E' and her signature song, 'Stand By Your Man', are classic examples of the Wynette style.

The feeling and emotion that Wynette puts into her songs

come from personal experience, much of it bitter and painful. Married at 17 and divorced a few years later, with three small mouths to feed, she knows what it is like to live on the cutting edge of despair. Her major strength, in addition to her unquestioned musical abilities, has been her Gibraltar-like determination. Anyone who has butted heads with Tammy Wynette will attest that she is one determined woman. When she sets her sights on a goal she lets nothing stand in her way.

Before she became the protégé of Epic Records' Billy Sherrill, many doors were closed in her face. Like any profit-driven business the Nashville record industry can be cruel and insensitive. Sherrill's faith paid off when she turned a Johnny Paycheck song 'Apartment #9' into a major 1966 top single. It got her career off the ground and soaring. She followed 'Apartment #9' with an even bigger hit 'Your Good Girl's Gonna Go Bad'. By 1969 she was dueting with the legendary GEORGE JONES as both singer and wife. Their voices blended perfectly. Jones has similar tonal qualities. He can match her, note for note, when it comes to tugging at the heartstrings.

The marriage was a star-crossed version of the songs that they sang. Unlike some who keep their problems behind closed doors, Wynette and Jones placed their joys and sorrows centre stage. Duets like 'Take Me', 'Golden Ring' and 'We're Gonna Hold On', gave their fans vocal, intimate glimpses into their private lives. They divorced in 1979.

Wynette gave marriage another chance with country music producer, arranger and writer George Richey who is now her manager. Wynette's autobiography *Stand By Your Man* was turned into a high-rated TV movie. The honesty of the book and movie further cemented the loyalty of her fans who constantly pack out her North American and overseas concerts. They identify closely with the songs of this country music giant and always give her the standing ovation that she so richly deserves.

Wynette's fans, to say nothing of the recording industry, were genuinely excited when it was announced that she was teaming up with LORETTA LYNN and DOLLY PARTON for a collaborative album due out sometime in 1993.

★*The First Lady of Country Music Tammy Wynette Anniversary: Twenty Years of Hits* (Epic EGK 40625)

Epic Records' Billy Sherrill shudders at the thought of how close he came not only to missing Wynette but loosing 'Apartment #9', her breakthrough hit. The disillusioned and dejected Wynette was preparing to check out of her hotel and leave Nashville for good when Sherrill tracked her down and got her into a studio. Wynette's emotionally choked alto voice is just perfect for this tear-jerking song. Following a mournful steel guitar intro she jumps into a song of heartbreak with a style and verve that has become her hallmark.

'D-I-V-O-R-C-E' was the 1968 Single of the Year. It's another sad story about a mother and father who spell out divorce so their four-year-old little boy won't know that this is the day it becomes final.

No Wynette collection would be complete without 'Stand By Your Man', her biggest hit. Recorded in 1968, it became the biggest-selling single ever released by a woman. 'Sometimes it's hard to be a woman', is the opening line and Wynette sends shivers down the back when she rips into 'Stand by your man/ Give him two arms to cling to/And something warm to come to'. The title of this CD is without doubt the longest one in any catalogue but this 20 song collection makes it worth every letter.

Yearwood, Trisha

(born Monticello, Georgia, September 19 1964)
Trisha Yearwood exploded on the music scene in 1991 with her first single 'She's in Love With The Boy'. The song spent two weeks at *Billboard*'s number 1 spot and three more impressive singles followed. Yearwood's album *Trisha Yearwood* was released in July 1991 to rave reviews. More than 500,000 copies were sold within three months and it has gone platinum. The Yearwood debut was one of strongest for any woman in country music history. That's high praise when you consider the talented women who have burst on the scene going all the way back to Kitty Wells, PATSY CLINE and LORETTA LYNN.

Yearwood grew up in the small, sleepy town of Monticello, in north Georgia, about an hour's drive from Atlanta. Her father was a bank executive and, following his banking career, became city manager of Monticello. Her mother still teaches school. For as long as Yearwood can remember she loved to sing. When she was five or six a neighbour gave her some old Elvis records. 'I played them and sang along with Elvis,' she recalls. 'I was a six year old in love with Elvis. I also sang along with all the artists on my parents' country music collection. Those singalong sessions were the joy of my young life.

'Linda Ronstadt's music intoxicated me. She was an early, and profound, influence on me because of the strength and emotional resonance of her voice.'

As Yearwood grew up, and lost her infatuation for Elvis, her musical horizons expanded. She began to absorb all musical genres from southern rock to country. Shortly after enrolling at the University of Georgia, Yearwood convinced her parents that her interests and future lay in country music. With their approval, and support, she transferred to Nashville's Belmont University and signed up for music business. While juggling lectures and studies she got a job in the publicity department at MTM Records and following graduation she became their full-time receptionist. 'It was a great job,' she recalls. 'In addition to meeting many important people in the country music industry it sharpened my knowledge of the industry.'

Yearwood's trek to stardom mirrored the route followed by HOLLY DUNN, Janie Fricke and many others who started out singing on demo sessions, then background vocals on master sessions. Before too long she had built up a sufficient reputation to be noticed and MCA signed her to a contract.

Yearwood was clearly focused on where she wanted her music to take her and where she wanted to take her music. 'I know when a song means something to me and that's the first thing. I also knew, from what I grew up on [Linda Ronstadt and the Eagles], that I wanted my music to be country.' It was during this professional growing period that she met Chris Latham who worked for EMI Music. They fell in love and married.

There were many hard business lessons she had to learn. One focused upon gender. Yearwood was told, in no uncertain terms, not to set her career sights too high. Few woman recording artists equal the sales of their male counterparts. Demographics confirm that it is women who buy most records and the records they buy are not those of the same gender. But history has proved that the one way to get Trisha Yearwood motivated is to tell her 'it can't be done'.

'I really warmed to the way REBA McENTIRE deliberately chose songs that represented a woman's point of view. I was determined that, if I had a chance in this business, I'd do the same,' said Yearwood. She proved it was possible with 'That's What I Like About A Man'. It's a song written for a man who lists the attributes he likes in a woman. Yearwood gives it a gutsy spin and reverses the stereotypes.

With her career skyrocketing, Yearwood had to take a firm hold on both her private life and career. Touring has probably been the most common reason for marriage breakdowns in the music industry. Yearwood was not immune. Citing touring and long absences as one of the major reasons for their problems Yearwood and her husband split in 1991. She also got herself a new manager, Ken Krasgen. He's regarded as one of the best in the business. In addition to Yearwood, he manages Kenny Rogers and TRAVIS TRITT. With her personal life stabilized and her career firmly in control Yearwood is well on the way to achieving her goals.

★*Trisha Yearwood* (MCA MCAD-10297)

It was good marketing sense to make Yearwood's debut single hit 'She's In Love With The Boy' the lead-off song on this CD. There is a distinct edge to her voice and it is this, no doubt, that caught the ear of radio programme directors.

On 'We Never Had A Broken Heart', the edge is gone and one gets a beautifully moving love story. GARTH BROOKS is featured on harmony and they combine for a gentle blending of voices. It's hard to lose with a song that has these opening lines. 'Don't be afraid to hold me tight/You know I won't break in two/What we're doing here tonight sure beats what we're going through'. On a scale of one to ten, 'We Never Had A Broken Heart' is a nine-and-a-half. Come to think of it, this CD is a nine plus.

Yoakam, Dwight

(born Pikeville, Kentucky, October 23 1956)
When Dwight Yoakam was told that, while he certainly was talented, he was 'too country' for Nashville he couldn't believe his ears. Yoakam had always thought that he was just about as pure country as one could get. He still shakes his head in bewilderment when he thinks about Nashville's initial evaluation of him and his talent.

Yoakam's birthplace, Pikeville, is a small town in Pike Floyd Hollow, in the hills of Kentucky. It's just a short hike to Butcher Hollow, LORETTA LYNN's birthplace. He was just a baby when his parents moved to Columbus, Ohio, where his father found work at a service station. It was there that he first heard the word 'hillbilly'. Because his mother and father had heavy hill-country accents, and used rural expressions that some found laughable, they were ridiculed. Yoakam has a long memory. He'll never forget 'hillbilly'.

A skilled songwriter, Yoakam penned his first song when he was only eight and has not stopped writing to this very day. Many of his songs form the foundation for his albums and concerts. Three years after graduating from high school, and learning his craft by performing in and around the Ohio Valley, he landed in Nashville. He was going to set the mecca of country music on its ear – but it didn't happen the way he had planned. Deciding that Nashville was not for him or, probably nearer to the truth, he was not for Nashville, he moved on to Los Angeles. He rented a one-room apartment with sparse furnishings and began another phase of his climb to the top. By day he drove an airport freight bus and by night sang in the suburban Los Angeles honky tonks that catered to the working class. He became popular with the fans who liked their country music hard and raw. For fours years his life was a cycle of working, eating, sleeping and singing.

Those four years paid off when he met Pete Anderson who was passionate about Yoakam's style of music. With Anderson's encouragement, Yoakam became more determined than ever not to compromise just to please people. Anderson eventually became Yoakam's producer. His producing genius was a major factor for the success of Yoakam's first two albums for Reprise Records. They topped 1.5 million in combined sales, in just two years.

For some time Nashville's fortunes had been on the downturn. Rumours of its demise were rampant. *Time* magazine did an in-depth feature on the plummeting sales figures for country music and *The New York Times* declared, on its front page, that the 'Nashville sound' was terminal, if not already dead. Thanks to the new breed of singers, such as Yoakam, RANDY TRAVIS, the JUDDS and CLINT BLACK the predictions were premature. They, and others who came along at that difficult time, infused new life and excitement into the staggering industry. Country music recovered and is now a stronger force, and more vibrant than ever before, not only in North America but around the world.

Yoakam is not just a certified country star he is a highly respected songwriter with a string of hits to his credit. He has collaborated with such hit-writers as Roger Miller and, as he says with tongue firmly planted in cheek, 'a Greek named Kostas who lives in Montana and writes hillbilly music'. One achievement that Yoakam looks back upon, with significant pride, was being able to pull singer Buck Owens back out of musical retirement. Owens remembers the day vividly when Yoakam turned up at his Bakersfield, California, office totally unannounced. Yoakam was performing at a fair and invited Owens to join him on stage that night for old times' sake. He figured that once Owens heard the applause he'd be hooked and come back to the fans who felt he had retired much too soon. It worked. The performing fires were rekindled. The next hurdle was to get Owens back into a recording studio. It was a hurdle that Owens readily jumped at. The two men recorded a duet 'Streets of Bakersfield', plus two more albums for Capitol Records. They were enthusiastically welcomed by the fans. Buck Owens was back in harness thanks to the persistence of his greatest fan, Dwight Yoakam.

Vanity Fair wrote, 'Yoakam strides the divide between rock's lust and country's lament. He's kept his music pure, which is something everyone can understand. But, just as importantly, he's always kept his eye on the horizon.'

★*If There Was A Way* (Reprise 9 26344-2)

Produced and arranged by Pete Anderson, this album has 14 songs and Yoakam either wrote or co-wrote 10 of them.

'I Don't Need It Done' is a must for any Jerry Lee Lewis fan who enjoys spirited vocal interpretation backed by some marvellous keyboard work. It would be difficult to find anything to match it short of a Lewis concert or album. Yoakam's brilliant blending of raw honky tonk with a touch of rock 'n' roll makes this number shine. Adding to the lustre are Skip Edwards' flying fingers on the keyboard. It is one of the few songs not written by Yoakam. It was penned by John Sieger.

Yoakam co-wrote 'It Only Hurts When I Cry' with the late, lamented Roger Miller of 'King of the Road' fame. The lyrics are as brilliant as the musical arrangement, which is lively and finger-snapping. The melody is one that you will remember and find yourself singing. 'The only time I feel the pain/Is in the sunshine and the rain/And I don't feel no hurt at all/Unless you count when the teardrops fall'.

Ask Yoakam about the current state of country music and through his satisfied grin he'll tell you, 'I think a lot of people really like country music if the truth be known.' Truth be told, the reason why people like country music and new fans are finding it in droves is because of artists like Dwight Yoakam and CDs that are as pleasing as *If There Was A Way*.

INDEX

INDEX

BIBLIOGRAPHY

Barnes, Harper, *Standing On a Volcano: The Life and Times of David Rowland Francis* (St. Louis: Missouri Historical Society Press, 2001).

Fox, Timothy J., "St. Louis Hills," *Gateway Heritage* 22:2, 2001.

Minutes of the St. Louis Hills Neighborhood Association.

News of St. Louis Hills, November 1935; June 1936; September 1936; November 1936; April 1937; July 1937; September 1937; December 1937; May 1938; October 1938; February 1939; April 1939.

Norbury Wayman, *History of St. Louis Neighborhoods: Southwest* (St. Louis Community Development Agency, 1978).

Primm, James Neal, *Lion of the Valley: St. Louis, Missouri, 1764– 1980* (St. Louis: Missouri Historical Society Press, 1998).

St. Louis Post-Dispatch, 24 January 1963; 14 May 1981; 5 February 1984; 2 October 1984.

St. Louis Globe-Democrat, 24 January 1963.